Also by Christopher S. Wren

The Cat Who Covered the World
The Adventures of Henrietta and her Foreign Correspondent

Hacks

The End of the Line
The Failure of Communism in the Soviet Union and China

Winners Got Scars Too
The Life and Legends of Johnny Cash

Christopher S. Wren

Walking
to
Vermont

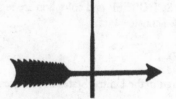

From Times Square

into the Green Mountains—

a homeward adventure

Simon & Schuster

New York London

Toronto Sydney

SIMON & SCHUSTER
Rockefeller Center
1230 Avenue of the Americas
New York, NY 10020

Designed by

Manufactured in the United States of America

10 9 8 7 6 5 4 3 2 1

Library of Congress Cataloging-in-Publication Data

ISBN-13: 978-1-4165-4012-0
ISBN-10:   1-4165-4012-1

For information regarding special discounts for bulk purchases,
please contact Simon & Schuster Special Sales at 1-800-456-6798
or business@simonandschuster.com

For Ginny Wren Moore

My very first travel companion

Contents

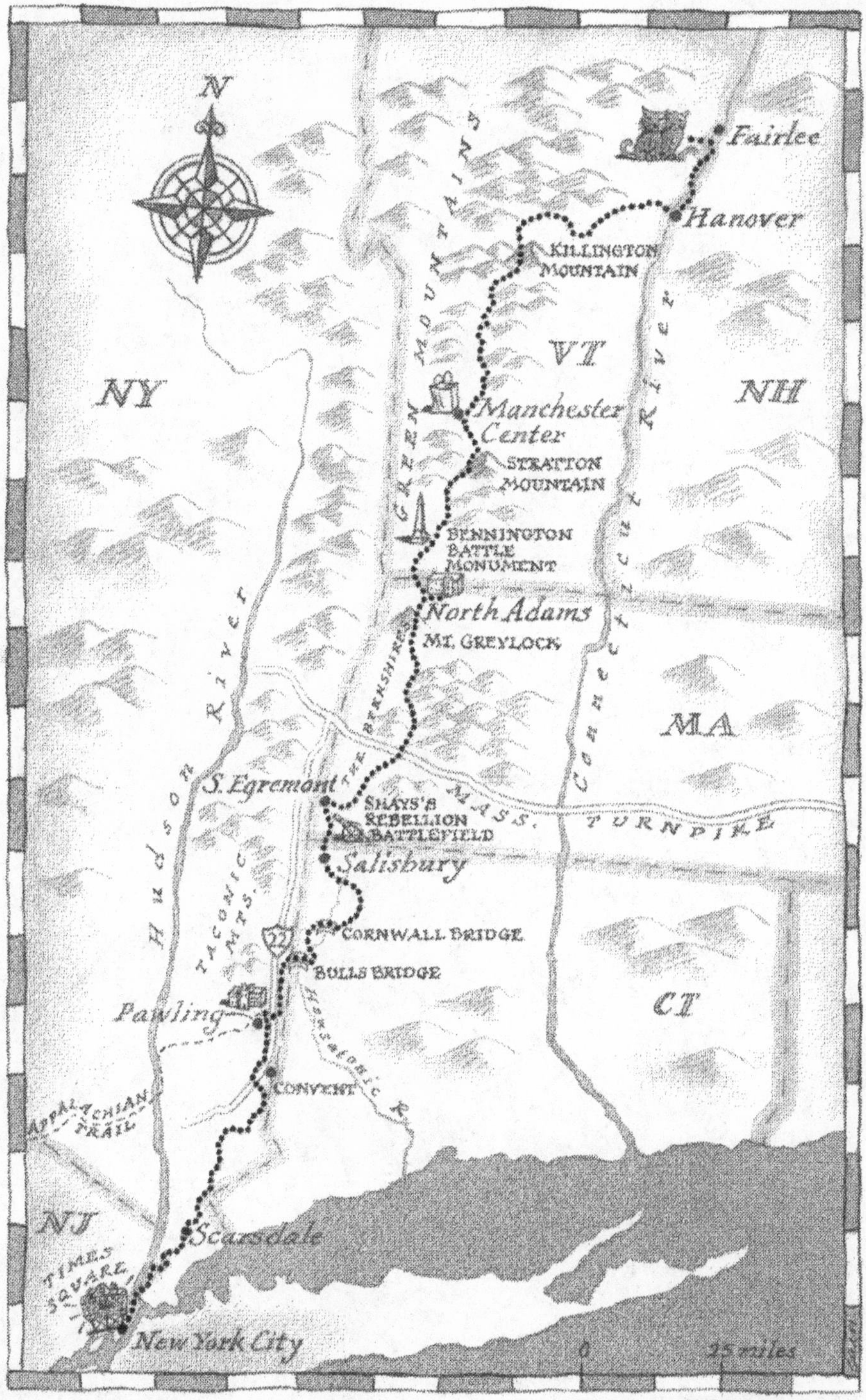
N
Fairlee
Hanover
KILLINGTON
MOUNTAIN
GREEN MOUNTAINS
VT
NH
NY
Manchester
Center
STRATTON
MOUNTAIN
BENNINGTON
BATTLE
MONUMENT
North Adams
MT. GREYLOCK
THE BERKSHIRES
CONNECTICUT RIVER
MA
Hudson River
S. Egremont
SHAYS'S
REBELLION
BATTLEFIELD
MASS. TURNPIKE
Salisbury
TACONIC MTS.
22
CORNWALL BRIDGE
BULLS BRIDGE
Housatonic R.
Pawling
CT
CONVENT
APPALACHIAN TRAIL
NJ
Scarsdale
TIMES SQUARE
New York City
0
25 miles

New York

One of the pleasantest things in the world is going a journey; but I like to go by myself. I can enjoy society in a room but outdoors nature is enough company for me. I am then never less alone than alone.

William Hazlitt

One

IT WAS not yet noon and hotter than a July bride in a feather bed when I trudged a half-dozen miles down the wooded northeastern flank of Mount Greylock, which is, at 3,491 feet, about as high as you can go in the state of Massachusetts. The descent, steep and muddy, made my footing precarious under the weight of a pack that felt stuffed with rocks. By the time I emerged from the spruce woods onto Phelps Avenue, a street of tidy wooden houses on the southern fringe of North Adams, I was hurting as hard as I was sweating.

Before I got bitten, I had planned to follow the white blazes marking the Appalachian Trail north across a green footbridge over some railroad tracks and the Hoosic River. Instead, I turned east on Main Street and caught a ride to the regional hospital on the other side of town.

Within minutes, I found myself stretched out on a white-sheeted bed in the hospital's emergency ward, feeling the soothing chill of saline solution dripping antibiotics into my vein through a long needle taped to the top of my hand.

It was not where I expected to be.

I had been walking into retirement, from Times Square in the heart of New York City to central Vermont and a house bought eighteen years earlier while I was working in China. My wife and I talked of retiring someday to Vermont, of blending into its crisp mornings and mellow afternoons and worrying no more about fighting Sunday night traffic back to New York City.

Someday had finally arrived.

Now, a few miles short of the Vermont border, I was stopped by a suspected case of Lyme disease. The ugly red inflammation streaking across my right arm, the consequence of an apparent encounter with a hungry tick, only confirmed the ineffectuality of my wanderings over the previous three weeks.

It didn't help that I had passed a restless night on top of Mount Greylock, poring over a worn copy of the *Appalachian Trail Guide,* which among its earnest descriptions of trailheads, shelters, switchbacks, and sources of drinkable water found room for dire warnings about snake bites, lightning strikes, and maladies like Lyme disease and a pernicious newcomer called hantavirus ("The virus travels from an infected rodent through its evaporating urine, droppings and saliva into the air.").

My guidebook went on to catalogue some effects of Lyme disease for the hiker foolish enough to contract it: "Severe fatigue, dizziness, shortness of breath, cardiac irregularities, memory and concentration problems, facial paralysis, meningitis, shooting pains in the arms and legs, symptoms resembling multiple sclerosis, brain tumors, stroke, alcoholism, depression, Alzheimer's disease and anorexia nervosa."

I am not a hypochondriac, but none of these sounded conducive to a serene and healthy retirement. The *Appalachian Trail Guide* left me to infer that the safest place was on a living room couch in front of the television set.

"It may be necessary," my guidebook nagged, "to contact a university medical center or other research center if you suspect you have been bitten by an infected tick."

Since my travel preparations hadn't included compiling a list of medical research centers, I headed for the nearest hospital.

"Age?" The admissions lady ran through her repertoire of questions.

"Sixty-five," I replied, and for the first time believed it. It's been said that inside every older person is a younger one wondering what the hell happened. It was dawning upon me that when Elvis Presley was my age, he had been dead for twenty-three years and Schubert for thirty-four.

I pulled from my pack a crisp Medicare card. The hospital admissions lady made a copy and handed the red-white-and-blue card back.

I looked like a vagrant, but my motley appearance raised no alarms among the nurses. They hooked me to an intravenous drip and, glancing over my unkempt appearance and muddy boots, were solicitous enough to ask if I wanted something to eat. I allowed as how I was hungry. Walking for three weeks had given me a ravenous appetite that even a nasty infection could not diminish.

For the first time, hospital food—the plat du jour was a turkey sandwich accompanied by a Coke—tasted scrumptious. By the time I polished off the strawberry Jell-O, all but licking the little plastic cup clean, one of the nurses marveled, "We've never had a patient in emergency who cleaned his plate."

CALL MY walk, interrupted, a rite of passage. After forty years as a working journalist, I had collided with the life change that is the stuff of which dreams and nightmares are fashioned. Once the fizz is gone from the goodbye champagne, how do you enter this next stage of your life with any semblance of style or self-respect? You can press ahead, or you can cling to the past while time keeps stomping on your fingers.

As a scared young paratrooper, I had it screamed over and over at me by foul-mouthed instructors that an exit from an aircraft in flight had to be vigorous to clear the propeller blast. Otherwise, the jumper risked being slammed back into the metal fuselage by the screaming wind with such hurricane force as to leave him unconscious—or dead.

My career at the *New York Times*, which took me to a half-dozen news bureaus in Moscow, Cairo, Beijing, Ottawa, Johannesburg, and the United Nations, was winding down after nearly three decades as a reporter, foreign correspondent, and editor. It was time to collect what I had paid into Social Security and claim the perquisites with which America honors its senior citizens—train and movie discounts and dinner bargains at hours early enough to get you home in bed before sundown.

The prospect left me restless and a little apprehensive. I no longer needed to chase deadline news, but there had to be better times ahead than falling back on golf and gated retirement communities. T. S. Eliot's observation that old men ought to be explorers was finally making sense.

As for exploring retirement at a brisk walk, the notion may have been planted by *The Elements of Style,* the gem of a stylebook compiled by William Strunk Jr. and E. B. White, which serious writers, and even newspaper reporters, rely upon to resolve questions of grammar. I had been sitting at my cluttered desk in the *Times* newsroom a year earlier, consulting the rules about restrictive and nonrestrictive clauses, when Strunk and White caught my eye with an example they cited for enclosing parenthetic expressions between commas:

"The best way to see a country, unless you are pressed for time, is to travel on foot."

I don't know whether Strunk and White reached their conclusion after setting out on foot themselves, I hope with a picnic lunch, to prove their theorem, which grappled with the eternal problem of when to bracket a phrase between a pair of commas. They did concede that "if the interruption to the flow of the sentence is but slight, the writer may safely omit the commas."

I grew less interested in the commas than in their advice. Were Strunk and White inviting the reader with a wink to interrupt the flow of an uneventful life by taking a hike? They did not write that the best way to see a country was from the window of an air-conditioned Elderhostel tour bus.

And since Strunk and White had brought it up, there was a country that I was curious to see on foot.

Journalism is a great way to perpetuate the curiosity you developed as a child. I had climbed the Great Wall of China, ridden on horseback past the Great Pyramids of Giza, waded through snow-drifts to view St. Basil's Cathedral in Moscow's Red Square, and gaped at the filigreed interiors of Samarkand's gilded domes on the Silk Road of Central Asia.

I had talked my way through encounters with guerrillas and their AK-47s in Lebanon and Somalia, met drug-thugs in Colombia and Burma. I roamed the backcountry of Tibet and Yemen, as close as you can get to the dark side of the moon without actually leaving earth. I interviewed presidents and prime ministers, and saints and scoundrels, on four continents. And at the risk of sounding immodest, I contrived to do it all on an expense account.

After seventeen years abroad as a foreign correspondent, it was time to fill in some blank spaces at home. I must have traveled through more than seventy countries, if you include all fifteen republics of the shattered Soviet Union, but had taken for granted the stretch of New England that separated our Manhattan apartment from the Vermont house where I wanted to retire. We usually drove there at night, more preoccupied with headlights of on-coming traffic than the darkened scenery. What I knew about the countryside amounted to fuel pumps, fast food restaurants, and takeaway coffee.

THE E-MAIL careening around the online listserv of the Dartmouth Class of 1957 swapped tips about retirement, beginning with how to plug in to Social Security and Medicare. I learned that I qualified for medical care at Veterans Administration hospitals if I could find my military discharge papers. There were tips about cheap flights for seniors and more than I cared to know about aching joints and balky prostates.

Some of the soundest advice was posted by my classmate Joel Mitchell. "As you are now in the house for the first time rather than the office, don't ever get into the habit of watching afternoon soaps," Joel wrote. "Always keep the TV off, unless you're watching the market channels.

"Lunch dates are important," he added. Gets you out of the house. Keeps the mind stimulated. It can be lunch with just about anyone (well almost).

"And get out of your chair, and go outside often," Joel concluded. "Walk, ride a bike, golf or whatever."

I posted my own e-mail explaining that I planned to walk into retirement to Vermont, and soliciting suggestions about bed-and-breakfast places, campgrounds, or backyards to pitch my tent.

"I also welcome any '57 who wants to hike a mile or two or three with me," I added, "though I'm doing this alone and don't plan to linger anywhere longer than overnight."

I made clear there was no hidden agenda, such as extorting money from friends for a worthy cause according to the miles covered.

"I'm not marching on behalf of anything, just celebrating my new freedom," I wrote. "Let me know if you want to come along for an hour or two, bearing in mind that my whereabouts will depend on how well my knees and ankles hold out under the weight of a forty-five-pound pack."

Several classmates, Joel among them, e-mailed back promises to join me for a day when I hit Massachusetts. I also heard from Harry, who had graduated from Dartmouth a year before me.

"Big mistake," he warned.

Harry had done marathons and other vigorous activities, he wrote, "but if 1) you think that the total distance will be as you estimate, you are way off, it will be much more, as you can't walk a straight line on your intended track, and 2) if you indeed will carry a forty-five-pound pack, you will wear out your no-longer-youthful body early on.

"Don't let your ego get in the way of making you feel that you are less than a man if you don't make this odyssey by foot. Rather you could make a slow trip by pickup truck, or an old VW bus with your wife, and really enjoy your passage into retirement, instead of beating yourself up while trying to prove that 'I know that I can do it, dammit!' No one will care about a change in plans; in fact most will admire that you chose a wiser approach.

"Just a suggestion," Harry concluded, "from one who doesn't have to prove as much as he used to think he had to."

Harry was probably right. I wanted to prove that retirement did not mean retiring my dreams.

The truth was that my walk to Vermont was about more than just walking to Vermont. I had reached the age when regrets set in. My own were blissfully few, involving mostly sins of omission rather than commission. We are likelier to rue what we failed to do than what we did.

If I didn't walk from Times Square to Vermont now, when would I get around to doing it? "Live the life you've imagined," exhorted Henry David Thoreau, the nineteenth-century contrarian whose account of life alone in the woods, *Walden*, I admired, even if I did discard it in his native Massachusetts.

I decided not to take a companion, though my twin sister, Ginny, volunteered. Since we were kids, Ginny has had an enthusiasm for what she calls "fun things," like bounding up the mountains of Wyoming on a month-long outdoor leadership course prior to retirement from her own career as a special education teacher in Lake Forest, Illinois. My son, Chris, also spoke wistfully of joining me, but his workload as a new lawyer in New York would not spare him time off.

I thanked Chris as well as his Aunt Ginny, but it seemed important to walk this one alone. I had taken chances for a living; why stop just because I hit the milestone of sixty-five years? I had survived in less hospitable neighborhoods than I expected to visit on this trip.

But I would not be rushed into retirement. There should be time to saunter on unpaved roads. For as Thoreau pointed out in his essay on walking in 1862, "The saunterer, in the good sense, is no more vagrant than the meandering river, which is all the while sedulously seeking the shortest course to the sea."

In journeying to Vermont on my terms, I could picture myself, having cooked a simple but satisfying supper, lounging beside a small river, reading *Walden* by the flicker of an evening campfire, falling asleep under a canopy of bright stars.

Well, as a Russian proverb reminds us, "If you want to make God laugh, tell him your plans."

Still, I was not to be disappointed by the people I encountered in the five states through which I walked, and sometimes limped. Yes, there were mean-spirited locals who pointed speeding vehicles at me, or balked at letting me use a toilet without buying something, or wished I would go away before they dialed 911.

But there were others. A nun at a convent in New York shared old folk songs while she fed me supper. In Connecticut, a shopkeeper had me watch her cash register while she rummaged in the basement for the raisins I wanted. A woman I didn't know in Massachusetts baked me chocolate chip cookies; another stranger let me sleep in his yard and invited me for ice cream on his porch. In Vermont, trail angels left cold drinks and fresh fruit by the wayside. In New Hampshire, a store manager whipped up a frosty milkshake on a hot day and refused to take my money.

I also failed to anticipate the extent to which my experiences as a foreign correspondent would resonate on this journey, evoking memories of memories as I trudged northward at the rate of something over four thousand paces per hour. For better or worse, reminiscences constitute the only acquisitions in this life that remain uniquely our own.

BUT FIRST I had to walk out of New York City and through its dense suburbs. Once in the country, I could pitch my tent in the woods or spread out my poncho at a lean-to. But this did not solve the immediate problem of where to sleep before I got there.

I surfed the Internet for cheap hotels within a day's walk from our apartment on Manhattan's Upper West Side, without much success. The amenities at one motel just beyond the city limits, I was told, included complimentary condoms in a bowl on the registration counter. (The management's gesture said a lot about the clientele.)

Online evaluations of another hotel across the city line were no more encouraging. One former guest complained that "1) the bathroom had black mildew in the corners and on the wallpaper, 2) the security chain was broken, and 3) when I checked out they tried to charge me $99 per night instead of the $89 on the confirmation." That did not sound restful either.

I gave up and turned to other logistical problems. I arranged to have my final *Times* paychecks, plus eight weeks of unused vacation and accrued compensatory time, deposited in my bank account, along with my pension checks. I compiled a list of bills for my wife, Jaqueline, to pay in my absence.

My RETIREMENT started in Midtown Manhattan, with a farewell lunch in one of those discordant Asian restaurants where the overpriced drinks wear pastel paper umbrellas and the waitresses—servers—eventually slink over in black leotards and introduce themselves with names like Sonya.

My boss, Jerry Gray, anxious that I be nutritionally fortified for my walk, had layered the round table with multiple orders of sweet-and-sour ribs, egg rolls, butterfly shrimp, fried wonton, and other artery-cloggers in preparation for the really high-cholesterol stuff to come. Forget those tales about how journalists drink and pay more attention to how we eat.

Jerry complicated my retirement. He was that virtue in journalism, a demanding editor who was also a reporter's best friend. It's much easier to start off your career with a nice boss and bid farewell to a bastard. Everyone complains at the *New York Times* about being overworked and underappreciated, but it can be a lot of fun and is seldom dull. There were only a few people I wouldn't miss, like the editor who ordered me back from vacation on grounds that too much news was happening, then disappeared to the seashore with her family.

But I would miss the *New York Times*, which is why I needed quite literally to walk away from it. I didn't want to sit around my apartment wondering what the next day's front page would look like and whether my byline could have been on it.

Other colleagues from the continuous news desk at the *Times* joined me around Jerry's groaning table. They were friends too, because not a snicker passed at the notion of my wandering like Ulysses—a graying, slightly arthritic, nearsighted Ulysses—to a destination that normally took a good five hours to drive to, pushing the speed limit.

"Where are you starting your walk?" asked Jerry as he reached across to shovel more dim sum onto my plate.

The truth is that I hadn't decided. "Right here," I boasted, then corrected myself.

"From the newsroom," I said, since the restaurant was five blocks from the *Times,* and I wasn't sure we'd find our way back if Jerry carried through on his threat to order yet another liquid round of paper umbrellas.

AN ATTEMPT to clean out my desk upon returning to the newsroom was scuttled by the appearance of bottles of chilled champagne and some chocolate truffle cakes, which attracted more well-wishers.

Joyce Wadler, the most endearing *Times* reporter of my acquaintance, came by to confer a big hug. "Be sure to take your laptop on your walk," she said, like a mother reminding her child not to forget his mittens.

Though Joyce was born in the Catskills, within sight of trees, her roots are transplanted deep enough in New York City to make Woody Allen look like a hayseed. To forgo a computer was incomprehensible to Joyce.

"Laptop?" I told her. "I don't need no stinking laptop."

"You could sit down at the end of each day, and write up what you've seen and done," Joyce said.

"Plugging in to what?" I interjected. "Woods don't have electrical outlets . . ."

". . . and file it," Joyce said.

". . . or telephone jacks."

"The *Times* might even print it," Joyce persisted.

"My laptop weighs six pounds," I said.

"You could buy a smaller one," Joyce said.

"I'll have a tent in my pack," I explained. "Sleeping bag. Stove. Food."

"You've got to write it down or you'll forget it. What if you decide to do an article?"

"I'll take a notebook," I promised. "Maybe even a tape recorder."

The party picked up with fresh well-wishers and clicks of more plastic glasses. I became giddy with champagne and bloated with truffle cake. At the end of it all, I went home, leaving the accumulation of stuff on my desk for another time.

On the first day of my retirement, I sneaked back to the *Times* with a daypack, into which I stuffed as much as I could. What was left overflowed several wastebaskets. My telephone rang. It was a flack pitching a potential story. I interrupted his oozing description of its page-one possibilities.

"I've just retired," I said. "I don't work here—"

"Lotsaluckgoodbye," he said, and hung up before I could finish. If I didn't work at the *Times* anymore, I was no longer worth his time. I should have been offended, but I felt relieved.

I cast a last staffer's look around the newsroom before heading for the elevators. When I had arrived at the *Times* more than twenty-eight years earlier, pop-up typewriters were bolted to the rows of battered desks. Copy boys and girls, as we called them then, bustled about conveying our freshly typed pages to the copy desk, where editors marked up the stories with pencils before they were passed upstairs to be set in hot metal type. The *Times* in those days looked like what Hollywood expected a newspaper to be, except for the mousetraps underfoot.

I looked up. When had they painted the newsroom ceiling and ducts a designer eggshell white? I always remembered them as gunmetal gray.

Now the carpeted newsroom resembled an insurance claims office with quiet computers in small cubicles, where news stories flew away electronically to be paginated and printed on presses relocated to cheaper real estate in the borough of Queens or New Jersey. Copy boys and girls had given way to administrative clerks and news assistants. Editors no longer yelled, not deliberately, and cub reporters now were called interns. Even the bottles of Scotch that veteran reporters squirreled away in the bottom desk drawer for deadline courage had been replaced by plastic liters of designer water. When I got hired, *Times* reporters and editors shifted after deadline to Gough's, a seedy bar across the street, to hash over the handling of the day's news. Now they headed for their health clubs to unwind on the squash court or treadmill.

The mysteries of the *Times* lingered. How could a daily newspaper stuffed with more words than a Russian novel be created from a dead start every morning? And why did computerized news-gathering generate more paper than back when the news copy physically passed from hand to hand? I had had trouble finding enough empty wastebaskets to deposit the accumulation of notebooks and other clutter on my desk.

It was late afternoon when I walked out of the *Times* building, just in time to hit theater matinee gridlock at Times Square and the first drops of a thunderstorm. I sidestepped a man hawking a pamphlet with "251 sex positions for $5." (A dozen positions seem adequate for propagating the human race.) I shook my head and the vendor pitched to a more curious cluster of teenagers from the suburbs.

Walking west, I ducked into a doorway and pulled an umbrella from my backpack. Then I splashed up Eighth Avenue to Columbus Circle, one foot slipping into the gutter, a little like Gene Kelly in *Singin' in the Rain,* and turned up Broadway on the first mile of my journey.

The crowds thinned out as I continued north. I cut across the plaza of Lincoln Center, the arts complex where we would no longer renew our concert subscription to the New York Philharmonic. I moved westward with the traffic lights toward Riverside Park and the Hudson River.

BY THE END of the second mile, I regretted not putting myself into better shape. I could offer a number of excuses, most of them having to do with indolence. I had tried climbing eight flights of stairs from the newsroom to the *Times* cafeteria, which left me panting too hard to want lunch. I experimented with push-ups, but lost count. Sometimes I walked home from work, as I was doing now, but only in daylight and fair weather, if it wasn't too cold or hot and I wasn't late for dinner.

I had given up jogging because of a pain shooting into my right ankle, which I blamed on a recurrent sprain. It was not enough to discourage me from starting out, but could hobble my progress to Vermont without proper diagnosis and treatment.

My doctor referred me to an orthopedic surgeon, who sent me off for X rays before sitting down to discuss my complaint. He studied the large negatives delivered to him, and traced with his pen some grayish patches along the ankle joint.

"Osteoarthritis," he announced.

"What can we do about it?" I asked, afraid of where his diagnosis was heading. "I'm going to hike to Vermont."

The surgeon smiled and set aside the X rays. "Let's be precise about this," he said. "You're driving to Vermont, then you're going hiking."

"No," I said. "I'm walking to Vermont. From here. Hiking will be just part of it." I didn't bring up my bad knee, a testimony to arthroscopic surgery.

After more pondering of the X rays, he peered at me over the rims of his spectacles.

"Do you have heavy boots?" he asked. "Your ankle will need the support of a wide sole so it won't buckle. As for something anti-inflammatory, I'll prescribe Vioxx, that's rofecoxib, easier on the stomach."

We agreed upon a plastic brace that inflated with air, to cushion my ankle on rough terrain. I packed the brace for my journey and never got around to using it.

THE RAIN had let up by the time I reached 90th Street and our apartment, where my wife, Jaqueline, who was into clay pot cooking, had prepared a lamb casserole for dinner.

She had moved eight times with our children while I was a foreign correspondent. After we came home from overseas and again settled down on Manhattan's Upper West Side, I was offered a diplomatic beat in the Washington bureau. Jaqueline put her small foot down. So we struck an agreement to move no more until I retired, and that would be to Vermont.

Jaqueline had let me charge off to cover a half-dozen wars without fussing about my safety. But we both accepted I was slowing down, as I discovered a half-dozen years earlier during the war in

Bosnia, when I attempted to vault out of an armored personnel carrier manned by Pakistani peacekeepers, who were snacking on hardboiled eggs at the time, and got briefly stuck in range of a Serbian machine gun nest.

On my sixty-fifth birthday, I assured her that I still had the body of a sixty-four-year-old. But Jaqueline insisted that if I was walking to Vermont, I must take my cell phone for emergencies. In return, she would rendezvous with me a couple of times for resupply.

My son, Chris, who had worked as a law enforcement ranger for the National Park Service before becoming a lawyer, brought by some useful gear: an orange plastic whistle to toot for help if I plunged into some ravine and lay injured and invisible to other hikers. A snug watch cap to pull over my ears if it turned cold. A ceramic filter pump to purify water and a couple of wide-mouth drinking bottles. Between New York and Vermont, Chris said, unless the water came from a faucet I was not to drink it, unless I filtered it through a ceramic pump or added some iodine pills.

Chris offered his mammoth green backpack festooned with attachments and gadgets, including a coil of nylon parachute cord. I told him I would stick to my battered blue Lowe pack.

"I say, beware of all enterprises that require new clothes," Thoreau counseled in *Walden*.

Jaqueline pointed out that camping gear had become lighter and much improved technologically. "You've had that pack for twenty years," she said. "Even the straps are falling apart."

"Only eighteen years. Nothing that a roll of duct tape can't fix."

I did accept the nylon cord, which my son said should be used to hoist my bag of food on a limb high enough that bears couldn't reach it.

"I've got to worry about hungry bears?"

"Just two kinds to watch for, Dad," Chris said. "Black bears and grizzlies. Grizzlies are much more dangerous. I recommend carrying pepper spray and some little bells.

"Tie the little bells on your pack so the bear can hear you coming and run away," he said.

"What if it refuses to run?"

"Then zap the bear with pepper spray."

"So the less dangerous bear is black, and the meaner one is grizzlier?"

"Not that simple, Dad. Look at their scat to check their eating habits. Black bear droppings have berries and little twigs."

"What about grizzlies?"

"Grizzly droppings have little bells and smell like pepper spray. I don't know if you want this."

My son handed me a palm-size blue plastic canister containing enough pepper spray to repel the advances of any critter on two or four feet. At the end of his ranger days out in California, Chris used pepper spray to break up a gang fight and cart the instigator off to jail. He saved paperwork on that arrest by not drawing his service revolver, which would have made him late for starting law school in Vermont.

"Um, Dad," my son, now the lawyer, advised, "pepper spray is illegal in New York City. Don't get caught with it when you walk out of here."

THOUGH I had planned an early departure for Vermont, I didn't sally forth until nearly ten A.M. It seemed politic to perform my usual chores of making the bed and cleaning up the breakfast dishes before disappearing on my wife.

"Have a wonderful day," called out Maurice, our doorman.

"I plan to," I told him. I habitually turned left to take the subway to work. This time I turned right across Riverside Drive and toward the Hudson River.

In Riverside Park, several park officials clustered around what remained of an old tree, discussing how to dispose of its last prominent limb, which winds had torn off in yesterday's storm. It made more sense to chop down the tree and cart it away, but the limb had also drawn civic-minded kibitzers who rally in opposition to any diminution of their greenery.

The promenade in Riverside Park was busy with joggers, cyclists, and nannies pushing baby carriages. A woman wearing an orange tank top was trying to walk her dachshund, but the dog stubbornly refused to budge when most other dogs weren't wearing leashes.

Inbound commuter traffic shwooshed overhead as I passed through a pedestrian tunnel under the West Side Highway and emerged at the Hudson River. The sky was clear, but for fleecy pillows of clouds hovering over the George Washington Bridge to the north.

New York reinvents itself so continually that the squawk and screech of traffic on asphalt made it hard to imagine what Manhattan looked like when the original inhabitants had to walk and wooded glens abounded among the outcroppings of schist. Under Dutch colonial rule, the best transportation was on the Hudson River with its sailing ships, rafts, and canoes. Fertile beds of oysters nourished the early Indian inhabitants, at least until they bargained away their island for sixty guilders'—twenty-four dollars—worth of baubles and other trinkets. New York City's official seal includes a beaver, denoting its origins as a trading post for furs and other natural wealth.

New Yorkers didn't cut their politicians much slack in those days either. Consider New York's first elected governor, Jacob Leisler. An ambitious German immigrant, Leisler was not quite twenty when he arrived in 1660 as a mercenary for the Dutch West Indies Company. This was a few years before the British grabbed New Amsterdam and renamed it New York.

Leisler gave up soldier's wages to get rich in the fur and tobacco trade and accumulated half of Manhattan. Enticed into politics, he organized the first free elections for mayor and city council, and was elected governor. But his enlightened notions of democracy annoyed the establishment, who contrived treason charges against Leisler that sent him to the city gallows in 1691. The deposed governor was hanged, then beheaded with an axe before an eager crowd. Today, wayward politicians get indicted.

I was less preoccupied with Leisler's ignominious demise than with finding a place to pee on my walk off his property. New York City boasts more of almost anything you can conceive, from art galleries to zoos, but not public toilets, of which it may have the world's fewest per capita. Given this dire shortage, my route required some planning. A close encounter with prostate cancer in the past had not left me with an iron bladder.

On my city map, I had selected a succession of potential bio-breaks, beginning with a few public lavatories in Riverside Park, which were usually kept locked to keep out heroin junkies, cocaine crackheads, and law-abiding taxpayers. Further north were fast food restaurants along Broadway, the mammoth Presbyterian Hospital on 168th Street, and a bus terminal at the New York end of the George Washington Bridge at 178th Street. Such stops would become easier once I crossed into the Bronx and entered Van Cortlandt Park.

I started north through Riverside Park, keeping the shining Hudson on my left. A tennis instructor was teaching a class of children. Oblivious to a parked police car, a homeless wretch in soiled clothes rummaged through trash baskets, looking for recyclable cans to cash in.

This park had nearly as many signs as trees. "Leash Dogs." "No Barbecuing." "No Loud Radios." "Put Waste in the Trash." Smaller print advised, "Violations are punishable by a fine," which seemed a letdown in our zero-tolerance era.

There were more signs: "No Scooters in Playground." "No Adults Except in the Company of a Child." "No Dogs Allowed." Negative signs have become so unbiquitous in New York City that no one notices them anymore.

Near a lamppost sign, "No Dogs Off Leash at Any Time," a stout man held a red leash and called plaintively for a German shepherd with other plans. A middle-aged woman mouthed a "good morning" as she strolled past me. Her miniature collie, trailing a blue leash, trotted a half-dozen paces behind.

The city fathers have cranked up the volume by replacing some generic "No Parking" signs with the warning, "Don't Even Think About Parking Here," which raises First Amendment issues of free thought. The Orwellian threat failed to alarm the American Civil Liberties Union or spook motorists, but variants might have worked in the city parks: "Dogs Found Unleashed Will Be Donated to Korean Restaurants." "Light a Barbecue Grill Here and We'll Make You Sit on It." "Children Who Deface Playgrounds Subject to Confiscation."

Some metal grates along the leafy esplanade of plane trees turned out to be air ducts for a railway tunnel used to shuttle trains in and out of New York. I arrived at the public tennis courts, with a sign warning, "You Must Wear Appropriate Attire." I climbed a steep path back to Riverside Drive, emerging from the foliage across from the bell tower of Riverside Church.

At the curb, I stumbled upon a rare sight in New York City: a legal vacant parking spot, so spacious that a driving school dropout could occupy it without having to slam the next vehicle onto the sidewalk, as had happened with our car. And street cleaning regulations did not require it to be vacated for three days.

It was the kind of discovery that prompts New Yorkers to stop and think where they parked their own car and whether there might be time for a fast shuttle. I was walking to Vermont and I stopped instinctively.

I passed Grant's Tomb, the largest and possibly best known mausoleum in the country. Its imposing white granite facade had finally been cleaned of accumulated soot and graffiti. I barely knew the neighborhood, though I lived there for a year as a graduate student at Columbia University. I walked on through dainty Sakura Park, which commemorates a gift from Japan to New York City of two thousand cherry trees nearly a century ago. Two flights of stone stairs took me down to Claremont Avenue.

I passed the Ethiopian Tigri Drop-In Center, and directly across La Salle Street, Praise the Lord Dental. Either could have inspired a feature article about homesick Ethiopian immigrants or evangelical orthodontists. I reminded myself that I no longer wrote for a newspaper.

I turned north along Broadway, New York City's most celebrated avenue, past the Obaa Koryoe West African restaurant, a Mexican restaurant, a Chinese eat-in-take-out parlor, and a laundromat named Bubbles.

My plan was to follow Broadway through Harlem, Washington Heights, and Inwood, and cross the bridge into the Bronx and Van Cortlandt Park. If I moved along, I could reach my mother-in-law's house in Scarsdale before dark. It was a good twenty miles from our apartment, but in summer the sun wouldn't set before nine P.M.

In the carts outside the El Mundo department store in Harlem, sandals were selling for two dollars a pair, shirts for three dollars, and sneakers were five. I was sorry there wasn't room in my pack. Block by block, Spanish gradually took over Broadway, the butcher shops were called carnicerías and the small groceries became bodegas selling cerveza rather than beer. A bilingual sign on a red-brick building proclaimed the Meeting with God Church, or La Iglesia el Encuentro con Dios.

Salsa music thumped from boomboxes on sidewalk tables displaying Hispanic tapes and compact discs. The staccato of Spanish spoken around me was occasionally drowned out by sirens of passing police cars, ambulances, and fire trucks. Competing aromas of pizza, fried chicken, and burritos wafted from the doorways of cafés, mingling with the fragrance of a vendor's burning incense. I felt like a foreign correspondent again.

People I encountered later on my journey expressed surprise that I crossed Harlem on foot. "Wasn't it dangerous?" one asked.

"Not unless you jaywalk," I said. Walking was more perilous in New York's posh suburbs, I explained, where you had to dodge sport utility vehicles jockeyed by expensively coiffed ladies running late for a tennis lesson.

My white face attracted no particular attention. I stopped for directions at a flea market and drew more smiles than stares. I considered making a detour to Sylvia's, a restaurant on Lenox Avenue where I used to eat while working stories as a reporter. But feasting on Sylvia's fried chicken, candied sweet potatoes, and cream pies would diminish my chances of making it to Scarsdale.

Finding a lavatory in New York City wasn't so hard after all. Our family doctors were affiliated with Presbyterian, so I talked my way past the hospital security desk by dropping their names. I later stopped at the municipal bus station on 178th Street, following an unwritten rule of foreign correspondence: "Whenever you pass a bathroom, use it."

(All but one of the other rules I learned as a foreign correspondent bore some relevance to my walk to Vermont: Always eat breakfast. Don't travel with anything you can't carry at a dead run for a half-mile. When you get into a place, start thinking about how to get out. Don't stand behind a teenager fiddling with a rocket-propelled grenade—the last rule no longer applied.)

The red-brick monolith housing the 34th Precinct of the New York City Police Department looked more like Lenin's tomb. Several dozen private cars were parked in a ragged row perpendicular to Broadway, half on the sidewalk under a sign that read "No Standing." They all but obscured the fire hydrant. A New York City cop gets few perks, but improvisational parking is one of them.

I came upon Fort Tryon Park, once dominated by Revolutionary War battlements and now home to the formal gardens and medieval art of the Cloisters. There wasn't time to view the Unicorn Tapestries, but I sat down on a bench to remove my boots and massage my feet.

I stopped at a Citibank branch near 180th Street for another hundred dollars. The screen on the ATM reported my balance as zero.

I scrolled back through the latest transactions. The *Times* had neglected to deposit any paychecks for the past two weeks. My pension and two months' worth of vacation and comptime had yet to kick in. I debated catching the subway back to the office. No, a phone call would clear up the confusion.

The first Irish bar appeared as I resumed my walk up Broadway, past Inwood Hill. Here at the northern end of Manhattan was Baker Field, the football stadium where Columbia plays the rest of the Ivy League and traditionally loses.

Beyond the metal link fence to my left loomed the Allen Pavilion, a branch of Presbyterian Hospital where I was operated on for prostate cancer eight years earlier. I rode the subway at dawn to this hospital, to be anesthetized and split open while my cancerous prostate was carved out and the surgeon determined that the cancer had not spread.

I now reached the age when my father died from pancreatic cancer. It had so consumed his body that the surgeon could do no more than stitch him back up. As he lay dying in the Los Angeles hospital where I had been born, he whispered through a fog of painkillers that he craved ginger ale. Would I bring him some?

The chart at the foot of his bed stated that my father was not allowed liquids. He promised not to drink the ginger ale, merely to slosh it around his parched mouth to take away the choking dryness. So I smuggled in a six-pack of cold ginger ale.

True to his word, my father held each sip in his mouth for a few seconds, then spit it into a basin that I cradled under his chin. His head fell back on his pillow and his eyes closed thankfully. He lived another two days.

It took time to accept his death and longer to pay off the medical bills. Now I was walking away from my own cancer, as though my father and I were conspiring anew, and he had willed me to escape what he could not. I turned my back on the Allen Pavilion and crossed the bridge into the Bronx.

I felt like walking forever.

THREE AND a half centuries ago, a Dutch carpenter named Frederick Philipse arrived from the West Indies and walked through these parts seeking his fortune. Philipse secured it, as Jacob Leisler had, in what was to become a quintessential New York City obsession: real estate. By the time Philipse died in 1702, he was said to own ninety thousand acres of what is now Westchester County, extending as far north as Tarrytown, and a large chunk of the Bronx, beginning with Spuyten Duyvil, now an enclave of Riverdale. That was more land than you could cross on foot in a day.

I mention Philipse and Leisler, and more to come, like Caleb Heathcote in Scarsdale, because I was looking for ghosts along the way. I don't believe in actual ghosts, not of the chain-rattling sort in which Europe claims to abound. But it was hardly a stretch to imagine what our immigrant ancestors had to say about the forgotten battlefields and the ruins of farms, mills, and taverns absorbed by the woodland through which I passed. Fading tombstones testify to the kind of people who preceded us, and so do old stone walls, and, back in Manhattan, what little remains of Fort Tryon.

I entered the Bronx onto Philipse's turf, past Spuyten Duyvil and up Broadway to 240th Street, where I paused at a McDonald's. After consuming a Big Mac, fries, and a Coke, I refilled my water bottle in the men's room and walked into Van Cortlandt Park.

Van Cortlandt Park takes its name from another dynasty of Dutch colonialists who collected property. The park belongs to New York City, but pockets look so untamed that I lost my bearings for the first time on my journey. Thickening clouds obscured the sun, making it impossible to judge which direction I was moving. I had postponed packing a compass, assuming with a New Yorker's arrogance that that it was impossible to get lost in the Bronx.

I worked my way along jogging paths, around a small lake, and past a tightly fenced golf course, only to be hemmed in by the Henry Hudson Parkway. It cuts through the northern edge of the park, winding from Manhattan through the Bronx and into Westchester County. There was no way to sprint across and survive an unrelenting whiz of traffic from both directions. I had to retreat back into the park, where I finally found an inconspicuous underpass that took me under the highway.

If I was lost, there were ominous clues that others were not —soiled socks and discarded scarves, an orphaned shoe, torn plastic bags blown against bushes, scorched twigs gathered into the ashes of ineffectual campfires, liquor and beer bottles, spent condoms, a few crack cocaine vials, and messy human turds. It has become harder to get mugged in broad daylight in New York City, but this dismal expanse of vegetation seemed an excellent venue to find myself surrounded by shadows emerging from the undergrowth, calling with menacing politeness, "Hey man, got a match?"

I grew anxious to leave the tangled thicket, but its feral trails promised to lead nowhere. I stopped and listened for some audible clue to civilization, a technique that I came to employ increasingly on my travels. I heard traffic.

More by luck than by navigational skills, I broke free of the woods and into a quiet side street of modest homes, startling a man pruning his miniature lawn.

"Which way is McLean Avenue?" I asked, selecting a street that my map showed as dipping toward the northern rim of Van Cortlandt Park.

The homeowner jumped, as though I had sidled up behind him and asked for the time of day while wearing a wristwatch.

"Where did you come from?" he asked. "The park?"

"I was walking and got lost."

Concluding that I was not a burglar, the man pointed down the street. I had arrived in Yonkers, the first city in Westchester County, and once a commercial village set in the middle of Frederick Philipse's land grab.

My thoughts kept returning to my empty bank account as I followed McLean Avenue past grander houses. At Hillview Avenue, I sat down on the curb to dial the *New York Times* on my cell phone. After some confusion, I was told that there was no record of my wages being deposited for the last couple of weeks.

I resolved not to break off my walk now that I had put New York City behind me. I took a long pull on my water bottle and worked my way around the wooded slopes of Hillview Reservoir. At this pace, I might reach Scarsdale by dark.

My resolve melted later when I crossed the Saw Mill River Parkway and saw the northern terminal of New York City's No. 2 subway line back in the Bronx. Walking to Vermont or not, I had to do something about the missing bank deposits before the checks I had written began bouncing. I bought a subway token and caught the next train south.

Just forty minutes later, I was back in the *New York Times* building on 43rd Street. Fortunately the security guard recognized me and did not ask for my blue-and-white *Times* ID card, which I was no longer carrying.

"We know that you didn't get paid," I was assured at the news administration office on the fourth floor. "We're still trying to find out why."

I lobbied my cause as forcefully as I could. I could take the subway back to the end of the line and resume my walk into Westchester's suburbs. But it was past six P.M., with rush hour in full force. There was no way to reach Scarsdale before dark.

I telephoned the nearest overnight accommodations.

"Is there any of your excellent lamb stew left?" I asked.

"In the refrigerator," Jaqueline said. "Why? Where are you?"

"Back at the *Times*. Put the lamb back in the oven, and I'll explain over dinner."

"What happened to your walk?"

"Unavoidable detour. The ATM says we're broke."

MOST PROBLEMS you encounter are neither permanent nor personal, and are best remedied after a good night's sleep. I had learned that as a foreign correspondent.

During my first trip to Beirut more than three decades earlier, I approached the Popular Front for the Liberation of Palestine, one of the nastier Marxist guerrilla factions, and asked to visit one of their camps. A week later, I was driven with Tom Koeniges, a photographer I worked with for *Look* magazine, to a base in the parched hills along Jordan's border with Lebanon. The militant Palestinian commander exploded.

"America is our enemy because you support Zionist aggression," he snapped through an interpreter. "You don't belong here, but you come anyway."

"However," he added after some thought, "my brother studies engineering at the University of Texas."

The commander ushered us into his tent. We quarreled for most of the night over endless cups of hot tea and flat loaves of Arab bread. The next morning, he introduced us to his heavily armed Palestinian fighters. They invited us to go along on their next raid into Israel. We declined. When we departed the next evening, the commander kissed me farewell on both cheeks. He still hated America, he said, but not Tom and me. And his brother was happy in Texas.

Later, I ran into the fixer who had set up my visit and asked what had happened to my guerrilla host and his band. "They were killed when they tried to cross the river," he said.

In 1979, when the *Times* dispatched me to Iran to cover the embassy hostage crisis, ordinary Iranians explained to me that their professed hostility toward the United States wasn't about me. One afternoon, I followed the crowd to a mass rally in downtown Tehran. I bought a paper bag of hot popcorn from a street vendor, which I nibbled as the orator denounced my motherland as the Great Satan.

A Revolutionary Guardsman stepped forth to frog-march me off for questioning. The Iranians around me blocked his passage, berating him for violating their traditional hospitality to strangers. Even though I was American, they argued, I had done nothing wrong. The Guardsman returned my popcorn and apologized. My neighbors smiled warmly and resumed chanting, "Death to America!"

Two

"LIFE IS a performance that, for most of us, is all too rarely broken by applause," my daughter, Celia, observed once. "You're out of the spotlight—or even worse, you're in it—or you're waiting in the wings, or botching your big scene, or playing a bit part in a scheme whose magnitude dwarfs your own. And even when you've pulled off your own personal coup de théâtre, you can be left with the nagging suspicion that people are admiring a character—a shell of personality that doesn't fully coincide with the real, inner you."

Celia, a journalist herself, wrote that in a drama column for *Commonweal*, a lay Catholic magazine covering religion, politics, and culture. I saved it not just to show who the real writer is in our family, but also because her observation applies to most of our lives. I had taken my own one-man show on the road, literally fresh from Broadway, without knowing how it would play on tour or whether it would be forced to close before the end of its scheduled run.

The performing arts get defined so promiscuously these days that I regretted not having applied to the National Endowment for the Arts to subsidize my own performance piece, titled "Awfully Long Walk to Vermont by the Aging Artist Formerly Known as a *New York Times* Byline." Having read about a performance artist acclaimed for wearing a diving mask and flippers on the New York subway, which is no stranger to bizarre costumes, I should have demanded the same respect for my scam. Was I not also flouting middle-class conventionality by hoofing my way offstage into retirement, when current wisdom had it that I should be riding a golf cart? Was not my solitary walk as deserving of derisive outrage from spectators, who were unlikely to notice me otherwise? I could have been a contender for some big bucks from the NEA had I brazenly announced that I would be dipping my boots each morning in buffalo dung.

The swiftness with which my subway train had swept me back to Times Square from the outermost Bronx on the previous afternoon underscored just how little distance I had covered walking out of New York City. Still, succumbing to a fine meal and a comfortable bed—my own—I slept well enough.

Before setting off again the next morning, I went to the bank to deposit a four-figure check from our home equity line of credit, to ensure our solvency during my walk. Having increased our mortgage indebtedness by another few thousand dollars, I descended into the IRT subway station on West 86th Street and caught the express train to the end of the line in the Bronx, where I had broken off my walk the day before. Starting over from scratch made no sense, and neither did leaving my spouse with an overdrawn bank account, which constituted a justifiable emergency.

Resuming my journey where it had broken off didn't violate the rules, because I set no ground rules beyond physically walking every inch of the way to Vermont without getting run over or caught breaking the law. I had lost some time, but not much. Other setbacks would lie ahead, but as long as I kept moving, Vermont was attainable.

Across the subway car from me sat an elderly couple, foreign-born, like many other New Yorkers. Shabby and frightened, they clung to each other. At the next to last stop, they shuffled together toward the door, but it slammed in their faces before they could exit. They sat down again, as though this affront had happened before.

I returned to my copy of *Walden*. "The mass of men lead lives of quiet desperation," Henry said.

At the last stop, I paused at the door to hold it for the old couple, but they sat fast in their seats, determined to give their stop another try after the subway train was cleaned and headed south.

I left the terminal, making sure to descend the same stairway I had ascended the day before. As White Plains Road left the Bronx for Westchester, it metamorphosed into Vaccarella Boulevard in Mount Vernon, through a gritty neighborhood of auto repair shops, gas stations, shuttered bars, and no-name warehouses. I turned north on West Lincoln Avenue, which led me into a more familiar mix of small stores and old brick apartment buildings.

"What are you doing here?" a woman shouted.

I saw the smiling face of Robin Summers, one of my colleagues when I worked editing business stories at the *Times*.

"Walking to Vermont. What are you doing here?"

"I live here." Robin implicitly reminded me that we weren't so far from the office. She introduced me to the wife of her church pastor.

"I just retired from the *Times*," I explained. "That's why I'm walking to Vermont."

"Well," said Robin, as though it finally made sense, "we're going to pray for you."

"We all stand in the need of prayer," I agreed, and we hugged goodbye.

* * *

I FELT giddy, as though something wonderfully subversive had been achieved by leaving New York City on foot, and in broad daylight, for wherever fancy took me. In the Soviet Union and China, and some other lands where I have worked, strolling out of a city could land you in jail. You needed the bureaucracy's explicit permission to come and go as a foreigner, even if you traveled by road. Only spies would want to wander unsupervised.

I remembered driving with my wife and two young children from Moscow on a glorious autumn day. We had gotten government authorization to spend the weekend in Yaroslavl, a river town on the upper Volga. I proposed eating our picnic lunch in the next grassy pasture. No sooner had we spread our blanket and Jaqueline distributed the sandwiches than a police car squealed to a stop and a policeman jumped out.

"Nelzya!" he shouted. Not allowed!

He scrutinized our passports with a sour face. Foreigners were not permitted to stop on the Yaroslavl Road, he said. We must drive straight to our destination.

I promised to as soon as our children finished their sandwiches. "Nelzya!" the policeman yelled again, amazed at my obtuseness. Not allowed! He hinted at possible arrests. I could picture seven-year-old Celia and four-year-old Chris being marched off to the gulag in manacles for eating cheese sandwiches in a Russian meadow in violation of state security.

We grabbed our sandwiches and rushed back to our car. The police tailed us to ensure that we wouldn't attempt another stealth picnic. But why, our children wanted to know.

"Because we're not in America," Jaqueline explained.

In China, we experienced a similar disconnect with the translator I inherited at the *Times* bureau, a man named Wu, during a sixty-mile drive from Beijing to Tianjin. At the outskirts of each city, I had to stop at a police checkpoint to have our passports and car license registered.

"Is this how your checkpoints for foreigners work in America?" Wu asked Jaqueline.

"We don't have them," she replied.

A country without checkpoints? Wu huffed his skepticism and sulked.

MY WALK continued north along Gramatan Avenue in Westchester County, over the Cross County Parkway and past Hunt Woods Park. As I approached Bronxville, the homes grew bigger and more elaborate.

It was soon time to find a lavatory, but the shop signs in Bronxville read "Customers Only." I was ready for lunch anyway. I ducked into a busy sandwich shop, ordered a melted-cheese-something wrapped in a flour tortilla and an iced tea, and lunged for a newly vacated table.

"Is this seat taken?" inquired a pleasantly graying woman. I waved her into the other chair. My companion, Irish-American by the sensible look of her, introduced herself as Mary.

I explained that I was walking to my mother-in-law's house in Scarsdale, the next gilded suburb. Walking to Vermont sounded too bizarre for Bronxville.

I asked whether Mary lived in Bronxville. Her son still did, she said, but soaring property prices and rentals had driven out almost everyone else she had grown up with. They relocated to less pricey communities, like New Rochelle or Mount Vernon.

"The original residents can't afford to live here anymore." Mary sighed as she stirred some milk into her coffee. "People who work here can't either. Even their homes disappear. They get bought up and leveled and the new houses get bigger. Some are enormous, though the land they sit on is the same."

I finished my sandwich and iced tea and said goodbye to Mary. I was eligible for admission to the basement rest room after paying my bill of more than nine dollars. The old-timers, it appeared, couldn't afford to use the toilets of Bronxville either.

Dodging a convoy of large sport utility vehicles driven by high-toned ladies wearing sunglasses over their hair and with cell phones glued to their ears, I avoided the perilous zebra-stripe crossing and jaywalked obliquely across to Baskin-Robbins. The secret of jaywalking, as any New Yorker knows, is to keep another pedestrian between you and oncoming traffic.

I bought a chocolate chip ice cream cone, which began melting into my palm after it was exposed to the midsummer sunlight.

My planned route followed the Bronx River Parkway, the country's first landscaped highway when it was opened in 1924. Having driven the parkway countless times, I recalled a footpath along the river. But the Metro North railway tracks blocked my passage. In frustration, I turned back to White Plains Road, a busy thoroughfare filled with trucks belching exhaust.

A swatch of green on my map promised a clearer shot at the Bronx River. This turned out to be a golf course, gated and fenced in so tightly as to make trespassing impossible. Following the chain link fence, I found the train tracks again, and the riverside footpath.

Maps are only as good as those who can read them. During the American Revolution, the British admiralty in London, seeing the Bronx River on a map, ordered the British navy in New York to sail up it from New York City. This pleasant but insubstantial stream could not accommodate even a dory. The river, as I walked along it, looked knee-deep, and narrow enough in places to jump from one bank to the other.

Thanks to human enterprise, the bucolic little Bronx River was left to deteriorate into a cesspool by the early twentieth century, in good part from spillage at a sewage plant built upstream in White Plains, the county seat. "From White Plains to the Bronx, the stream became an open sewer, and when it reached the old milldams near its mouth it turned picturesque lakes into veritable settling basins that polluted the breeze," a local historian, Harry Hansen, wrote in a book published by Scarsdale's Town Club.

A reclamation project revived the Bronx River by 1915. But subsequent neglect turned the river back into a repository for worn tires, hubcaps, oil cans, beer bottles, and rusting junk until a fresh cleanup campaign a few years ago. A shame, because this sylvan stretch along the Bronx River was the loveliest I had traveled so far.

My arrival in Scarsdale coincided with the rush hour discharge of a trainload of commuters evacuated from the front-line trenches of the unending battle for profit in New York City. The weary warriors surged upstairs from the platform, clutching briefcases, umbrellas, and folded copies of the newspaper for which I had toiled until a few days ago. I had become a conscientious objector in their Great Commuting War, but they paid me no mind, jostling past like an army in demoralized retreat, barking into cell phones at spouses in tennis whites who sat double-parked somewhere within the gridlock of luxury vans and SUVs. The warriors had put in their hard day's work. Well, I had put in a hard day's walk.

These harried commuters had no time to discover the incongruous serenity on the other side of the tracks. Beyond the southbound train platform and parking meters lay a millpond dating from colonial times. A half-dozen ducks paddled in the placid water just upstream from the spillway over the rocks. A glade provided the shade of Norway spruce and maple, mulberry and

American elms. There were a couple of green benches to sit on. Through the riverside scrim of trees flashed occasional cars passing on the Bronx River Parkway.

This was the site of Samuel Crawford's mill, where early farmers brought their harvested corn and wheat to be milled and their trees to be cut into wagon axles. Crawford was killed in a clash with British troops, the first Scarsdale resident to die in the American Revolution. His mill burned down in 1863, though the spillway of a subsequent milldam remains.

Scarsdale, where Jaqueline was raised and her mother still lives, is nationally synonymous with suburban affluence. A century ago, before the advent of fast trains and automobiles, the suburbs did not exist as we know them. Scarsdale's recorded history extends back to the seventeenth century, though you wouldn't infer it from the constant facelifts given to the houses I passed.

Scarsdale was named by Caleb Heathcote for his home area in Darbyshire, England. Heathcote had been dumped by his pretty fiancée, who married his brother Gilbert. Caleb emigrated to New York in 1692, where he consoled himself with—what else?—the acquisition of real estate, including the manor of Scarsdale, which the Crown granted him in 1701. A decade later, Heathcote became mayor of New York City (and his brother Gilbert became mayor of London). Caleb Heathcote took office in time for a slave rebellion in 1712, which was crushed by burning some of the slaves alive.

There are slaves too in Scarsdale's colonial closet. The early gentlefolk, pious Christians and faithful subjects of the king, held slaves, two dozen as late as the 1820 census. (New York State did not legally end slavery until 1827, a half-century after Vermont.) Scarsdale now hires its domestic workers from New York City and White Plains and has grown more liberal as its population has become more Jewish.

I stopped at the Scarsdale post office to buy stamps for the postcards I hoped to send along the way. To avoid rush hour traffic, I took the back way to my mother-in-law, Frances Braxton, who has lived in the same house off Heathcote Road for nearly sixty years. It lies just over a mile from the train station, via Fox Meadow Road and Wayside Lane. Many of Scarsdale's streets sound redolent of Merrie Olde England, with Wayside, Rectory, Horseguard, and Tory lanes, and Stonehouse and Paddington roads.

To my left were the athletic track and tennis courts of Scarsdale High School, where my wife was a student body leader and, though her teeth grate when I mention it, a cheerleader. The walk to my mother-in-law's house nearly ended prematurely when a black minivan brushed me back as it raced into a precious parking slot near the tennis courts. The driver was too preoccupied with her children and cell phone to notice me.

I turned onto the Post Road toward White Plains, passing Wayside Cottage, Scarsdale's oldest remaining structure. The tidy cottage dates back to sometime between 1717 and 1729. It was first a farmhouse and later an inn for drovers heading to New York City who kept their livestock in the pasture where the tennis courts now stand. British troops occupied the house during the American Revolution, scarring the old front door with their sabers and bayonets. Now Wayside Cottage survives under the protection of the Junior League of Scarsdale.

Behind every successful man, they say, stands a surprised mother-in-law. Mine, still vigorous in her nineties, hugged me when I showed up safely at her kitchen door to spend the night.

"Would you like something to eat?" she asked, which is no small question, coming from the world's finest cook of homemade tomato soup.

"If you don't mind," I told her, "I'll start with a hot bath."

* * *

FEW COMPETITORS for space evoke as much derision from American motorists as does the solitary walker. Joggers they can understand and sometimes tolerate. Cyclists they merely loathe. But to a driver behind the wheel, a stranger walking for hours along the same road with a pack on his back is presumed to be homeless, newly released on parole, too lazy to hitchhike, or otherwise unstable.

This contempt is relatively recent, because walking doesn't sound so bizarre in the context of, well, the history of mankind. My ancestors walked. So did yours, for that matter, before the advent of the horse-drawn carriage, the steam engine, the automobile, the really gross sport utility vehicle, and the executive jet aircraft.

The Bible is resplendent with people walking in the course of prophesying, leading forth from bondage or smiting their foes. And smiters and smitees both walked if riding in a chariot was above their pay grade. Moses hoofed it from Egypt nearly to the Promised Land. Jesus walked to heal the lepers and feed the five thousand, and befriended two strangers on a day's walk from Jerusalem to Emmaus. The Popemobile was not to be invented for another two thousand years.

Saint Paul practically loped around the ancient Mediterranean, inspiring him to write, "Let us also lay aside every weight and the sin that clings so closely, and let us run with perseverance the race that is set before us."

"Therefore lift your drooping hands and strengthen your weak knees," Paul exhorted the Hebrews in one of his epistles, "so that what is lame may not be put out of joint, but rather be healed." If that's not advice from a serious walker, I don't know what is.

America was founded and made independent by Americans who walked, unless they could afford the luxury of a horse, which most could not. "I have learned that the swiftest traveller is he who goes afoot," Thoreau wrote in *Walden*, and worked out the math to show that walking could be more cost-effective than waiting for a train, a conclusion shared today by commuters on the Long Island Rail Road. Thoreau's observation qualified him to be a travel companion. His *Walden* was the only book I had packed.

When my great-grandfather Frederick Sale went off to fight the Confederate "rascals," as he called them, he and the other bluecoats in the 125th Illinois Volunteer Infantry marched all over Kentucky and grew weary of it, judging by his letters home.

"We have taken the back track towards Louisville and have marched three of the hardest days we have marched in the whole of our journey," he wrote his young wife, Maria, from Lebanon, Kentucky, in October 1862, after getting shot at in the Battle of Perryville. "We have no idea why we have turned back or what we are after, or where we are going. Our officers go on the principle that our business is to know nothing, but mind them. We have a most inhuman lot of officers ever put over men. Men gave out on the road, lay down sick, but were punched up with bayonets and made to travel and several of these same men died that night."

Not until well into the twentieth century did Americans claim a patriotic right to drive gas-guzzlers to neighborhood block parties and the corner store. This preceded a recent finding by the Centers for Disease Control that three out of five adult Americans are seriously overweight.

There were even precedents for journalists who walked in the days before expense accounts let us hail taxis. Look no further than Edward Payson Weston. Born in 1839, he worked as a reporter on the *New York Herald* before becoming, in his words, a "propagandist for pedestrianism." It took ten days and ten hours for Weston to walk from Boston to Washington, where he shook the hand of the newly inaugurated president, Abraham Lincoln.

Propelling himself at the pace of a twelve-minute mile, Weston later walked from Portland, Maine, to Chicago in twenty-six days, from San Francisco to Los Angeles in less than ten days, and, at the age of sixty-seven, from Philadelphia to New York City in just under twenty-four hours. At seventy-one, he walked from Los Angeles to New York in eighty-eight days, averaging forty-one miles a day.

Competing against European race-walkers in London in 1879, Weston covered five hundred fifty miles of laps in five days and eighteen hours. A *New York Times* correspondent marveled that "the pedestrian and his wonderful achievement are the all-absorbing topics of conversation, and he is the hero of the hour."

"A large number of Americans were present," my old newspaper reported, "and their shouts of encouragement and the many bouquets and baskets of beautiful flowers showered upon their plucky countryman seemed to imbue him with new life; and with a smiling face he reeled off the laps as though he were walking for the fun of the thing." In fact, Weston was rewarded with a trophy belt and a victory purse of twenty-five hundred dollars.

I learned of Weston and his fast-paced life partly from a *Smithsonian* magazine article by Edward Lamb, another serious walker who met Weston as a boy. My college roommate, Wally Ackley, passed along the July 1979 article to motivate my journey to Vermont.

Alas, Weston, nicknamed the Old Pedestrian by his fellow Americans, met a pedestrian's fate with which New Yorkers could only sympathize. In phenomenal health at the age of eighty-eight, he was striding to church on a Sunday morning in New York City in 1927 when a speeding taxi sideswiped him. Confined to a wheelchair, his legs now useless, Weston died two years later.

Perhaps the biggest difference between Edward Payson Weston and me was that the Old Pedestrian started out in better shape.

* * *

NAVIGATING the shoals of New York City's cluttered suburbs was proving trickier than I had expected. I needed a canny guide who knew the geographical and social terrain of Westchester as instinctively as a Cajun alligator hunter understands the depths and currents of the Louisiana bayou that spawned him.

Fortunately, I had engaged the services of such a guide, who was also an intrepid walker.

Bill Borders was born in St. Louis, Missouri, and went to Yale. But early in his *New York Times* career, he covered Westchester County before moving overseas to other exotic beats in West Africa, India, and Britain. Bill was more sedentary now as a senior editor at the *Times*, but his appetite for adventure was unsated. As for his walking skills, several years earlier Bill had tramped a hundred miles to Lakeville, Connecticut. When I told Bill about my walk to Vermont, he volunteered to accompany me for a day. We agreed that his skills in reading suburban spoor would be put to best use in Westchester County.

We met early the next morning at the Scarsdale train station and set out together in an annoying drizzle along the old Post Road, which has been around since 1717. We stopped at a gas station to buy some sodas, and continued into White Plains.

Bill was a fount of walking wisdom. He suggested that we avoid highways identified by numerals and look for roads retaining their old names, a sign that they get less motor traffic.

I had never hiked through shopping malls before, but our course took us between the Galleria Mall and the Westchester Mall, across Westchester Avenue. We walked under the overpass of the Cross Westchester Expressway, heading past some dreary apartment complexes into the city park at Silver Lake, known in colonial times as Horton's Mill Pond. Walking into the park was easy enough, but the continuous chain-link fence made it impossible to find our way out without leaving the way we came. We curved back around the lakeshore and into Harrison, a township depicted on my map of Westchester County as a few serpentine roads winding through open countryside.

Here was fought the Battle of Merritt Hill, a modest Yankee victory in the American Revolution that none of us might have known about but for a small roadside marker. On October 28, 1776, a patriot named Lieutenant Fenno fired his cannonball at a score of British lancers as they approached Hatfield Hill on their way to Connecticut. This caused the horse soldiers to retreat in some disorder back to White Plains, where a larger battle was unfolding between American militiamen and British troops who had marched up the same road that Bill and I followed from Scarsdale.

More recently, the builders had been busy with their bulldozers. We soon found ourselves stymied in a cluster of new mansions squeezed together on skimpy lots.

"So where are we?" I asked.

Bill studied the map carefully. He squinted up into the leaden sky where the sun should have been. He smiled reassuringly.

"Gosh, I don't have the slightest idea."

"I thought you knew Westchester like the back of your hand."

Bill supposed that Westchester County had been rearranged while he was off reporting from India. We checked the map and compass again, but together they couldn't tell us where we were.

We were lost in a thicket of million-dollar homes, none of which were recognizable even as a street address. Vast tracts of luxury housing had sprouted across the blank spaces on my map of Westchester like toadstools in the wake of a spring rain. There seemed little alternative but to retire to the nearest tavern, if we could find one, frittering away the remains of the day in retracing our errant steps.

We looked up to see a young deer, standing so still that I mistook it for a lawn ornament. The animal shared our confusion at being so relentlessly hemmed in.

As we approached, the frightened fawn bolted off down a narrow driveway between two houses. We followed it into a patch of woods along a rough trail that led downhill to Stonewall Circle, a new neighborhood of even grander homes.

The drizzle had let up by the time we worked our way down to Old Orchard Street, which no longer had orchards, and to Route 22, a busy highway that runs up the eastern edge of New York State. In 1907, a driver in White Plains had been sent to jail for ten days and fined a hundred dollars for speeding at nearly thirty miles an hour.

Notwithstanding the corollary to Bill's cardinal rule of suburban walking—that the odds of pedestrian survival diminish when the road taken is designated by a number rather than a name—we had no choice but to employ Route 22 to cross the coves and inlets of the Kensico reservoir system, squeezing between the girders of the bridges to arrive at our next checkpoint, the town of Armonk.

We stopped in Armonk for lunch at the first restaurant we found. Its theme involved car racing and there was some kind of vehicle hanging overhead. Bill ordered a Cobb salad; I ate some chicken salad rolled up in a flour tortilla.

We walked out of Armonk along the wooded High Street to a now defunct mill once owned by Thomas Wright, where a sign marked another overlooked event in American history. Bill and I found ourselves standing on the spot where the captured British spy Major John Andre, the liaison for Benedict Arnold's treason plot, was delivered by highwaymen to American revolutionary forces. The major was hanged elsewhere.

On the downhill stretch to Armonk Road and the next village, Mount Kisco, I developed the first serious blister, caused by cotton socks chafing on my boots. Bill courteously waited as I padded my burning heel with some moleskin, too little and too late.

At Mount Kisco's southern outskirts, we stumbled upon an

oasis in the form of a Ben & Jerry's ice cream kiosk, where I paid off Bill with a large ice cream cone.

We parted at the railway station in Mount Kisco, where Bill caught the train back to New York City. Unlike me, he had to work the next morning. I promptly missed Bill's jovial company, which had made the time pass quickly. We had covered a good seventeen miles on foot, sharing gossip about our days in the field as foreign correspondents.

Tired though I was, there remained another half-dozen miles to walk to the next town, Katonah, where my wife's nephew, Hunt, and his wife, Molly, had invited me to spend the night.

Downtown Mount Kisco looked all but deserted on the Fourth of July. The large parking lots surrounding the Metro North train station, normally filled to capacity, were nearly empty. A score of Mexican laborers loitered along the streets, trying to enjoy a day off without spending money on it. They were the first of many Latin American migrants I would meet on my walk northward. We seemed to be the only pedestrians in Westchester County.

The last few miles stretched forever, past used car lots along Bedford Road and finally across railroad tracks and the Saw Mill River Parkway. At Cherry Street, I climbed a modest hill into Katonah and Terrace Heights. My navigation skills, getting better, delivered me into the backyard of Hunt and Molly's small but charming house. They had almost finished renovating it with friends.

Hunt, fresh out of law school, was cramming for his New York state bar exam. Molly, slender and dark-eyed, looked even more exhausted. She had been up nights caring for their baby, Marshall, who eschewed the conventionalities of normal bedtime and promised to become the life of every party as he grew older.

The village of Katonah had been relocated in 1898 to make way for a large reservoir. Hunt took me to see a house down the street that had been pulled several miles on wooden rails greased with yellow laundry soap, using a capstan powered by horses.

For supper, Hunt thawed some chili and poured it over the hot dogs he had heated. After a day of walking, it tasted delicious. Hunt cracked open some beers, which tasted even better. I slept well on the pull-out sofa, waking briefly to hear Molly pacing the floor overhead with her lively son.

LEAVING Hunt's house after nine A.M., I walked down into Katonah, along the village green, and turned east on Jay Street, across the railroad tracks of the commuter train. Most of the commuters had already caught their trains to New York City, and the parking lot was jammed with cars.

Crossing over the busy six lanes of Route 684, I saw, to my right, a meandering stream that was Broad Brook. Sunlight played on the tall grass along the lush green banks, evoking a nineteenth-century pastoral painting, with a twenty-first century urban soundtrack. Most of Westchester County once looked like this, primally green and sweet after the night rain. The sun came out in full force, promising another hot day and warning me to smear on sunscreen. According to the map, my journey to the next destination, a convent outside Brewster, did not look as arduous as the walk from Scarsdale, but maps can be wrong.

I crossed an asphalt road and stepped into the shady seclusion of dense woods that ended abruptly at a shining expanse of lake. This was the Cross River Reservoir, part of the New Croton Aqueduct.

The dam, according to the sign on top, was built between June 1905 and November 1907, when George B. McClellan was mayor of New York City. It contained a reservoir more than three miles long with a capacity of over ten million gallons of water, none too much for the kitchen sinks, bathtubs, and toilets of New York City and its suburbs. The watershed covered twenty-eight and a half square miles. The sign did not mention the thousands of Italian immigrants who performed the backbreaking labor while incurring the prejudice of the Anglo locals.

At the center of the reservoir were two small islets and a solitary fisherman in his boat. The only sound was the swish of bright water gliding over the spillway. Watching the liquid curtain fall to the scoured bed of rock below made me sleepy, but there was no time for a nap, with fifteen miles to walk to the convent just beyond Brewster in time for supper with the nuns.

Holly Road wound past lovely old clapboard houses on estates with names like Apple Farm, but updated with electric wire fences installed behind restored stone walls. Some of the driveways had been blacktopped off the dirt main road, when it should have been the other way around. I passed Ramsey Hunt, an Audubon wildlife sanctuary, and moved back onto paved Grant Road.

Throughout the suburbs, thoroughfares like this had been widened substantially from the original cart-and-carriage roads to accommodate automobiles, leaving no sidewalks or shoulders to protect a pedestrian. Walking facing traffic, I was compelled to spring from one side of the road to the other to avoid oncoming motorists, who saluted me with honks of irritation. This made for slow, sometimes perilous progress, though I fared better than the raccoon and woodchuck I saw, both of them recently squished into bloody pelts by passing radials. There was consolation in knowing that when failing sight, hearing, and coordination left me too infirm to dodge this kind of traffic on foot, some states would still let me drive through it.

I consulted my map and decided to try the next dirt road that promised to head vaguely north. This became Turkey Hill Road, though it did not, as the name promised, take me into hillbilly country past shanties with junk cars in the front yard. In Westchester County, Turkey Hill Road meant stately homes with sophisticated alarm systems, set well back on elegant horse farms. The fields to my right were bordered by wooden fences. To my left rose an eminence too indecisive to be called a hill.

A middle-aged horsewoman wearing black boots and a riding helmet over enhanced blond hair paused astride her horse to watch me pass the borders of her mega-acre property. I started to wave and then thought better of it. This was not a road that invited happy wanderers, the mode of transport being more Thoroughbred horse or equally pricey Mercedes SUV. I expected the horsewoman to pull a cell phone from her jodhpurs and alert the police to a suspicious stranger who might be casing her exclusive neighborhood for a burglary.

In my haste to move out of sight, I missed a subtle right turn onto Quaker Road that would have curved into North Salem, the village where I expected to eat lunch. Looking for an asphalt road that would confirm my whereabouts on the map, I came upon a woman in a red shirt tending her vegetable garden. My attempt to ask directions was interrupted by a loud ring. The woman turned her back to me and answered the cell phone tucked into her ample jeans.

I moved on, but her cell phone reminded me that this was a good time to dial up the *Times* again. "Any word on my missing paychecks?" I asked.

"We're still looking into it," I was assured. "We did confirm you were never paid."

"Then you'll deposit the checks?"

"As soon as we find out what happened. Can you call back later?"

"How soon later?" I asked. It was a conversation that I would repeat over the next couple of weeks.

"Maybe a few days?"

I switched off the phone and stuck it back into my pack. My map indicated that I had drifted more than a mile off course, which meant walking at least another half-hour to put myself where I needed to be. Even a slight divergence from my intended route increased the distance to be covered.

I WONDERED where I had seen mansions more grandiose than these estates I was passing in New York's suburbs. And that evoked memories of a cocaine trafficker's mansion in Cali, the Colombian city that was home to a notorious drug cartel.

I was in South America tracking the financial and human cost of cocaine as it moves from the Andean highlands, where the raw coca leaf grows, and ends up in the arms and noses of New Yorkers.

In Colombia, "contratraficantes," as anti-narcotics police commandos are called, took me out into the jungle of San José del Guaviare Province.

"Do you like to see a cocina?" shouted their commander, Lieutenant Colonel Leonardo Gallego, over the racket of the Huey's helicopter rotors. He used the Spanish slang, meaning kitchen, for a drug-processing lab.

"Yes," I hollered back. I leaned forward in my bucket seat, watching the coca fields a few hundred feet below us, and pulled out my notebook in anticipation of a better view.

"Okay!" Gallego's handsome face broke out in a grin. "I'm gonna show you a cocina." He spoke through his headset to the helicopter pilot, who swooped toward a shed roofed with corrugated metal.

"Here's a cocina!" Gallego raised the M-16 assault rifle from his lap and squeezed off an automatic burst. As if on cue, the door gunner beside him laid down more devastating fire with his M-60 machine gun. The stench of cordite from spent cartridges brought back the smell of every war I had covered.

The helicopter plopped in a clearing two hundred yards short of the shed. The commandos jumped out, pulling me along with them. They fired from the hip as we charged forward. I hadn't expected to go on a live raid, but looking at the jungle around us, I wasn't about to be left behind. Narco-guerrillas of the Revolutionary Armed Forces of Colombia, a Marxist insurgency known as FARC, were active in the region.

Running was hard through the tangle of knee-high coca bushes and into ankle-deep mud around the shed. The processing lab consisted of wooden pens lined with plastic sheeting and stuffed with more than a ton of wet coca leaves, waiting to be doused with gasoline, kerosene, sulfuric acid, concrete powder, and other disgusting stuff used to leach the leaves of psychoactive alkaloids into paste the color of dirty snow.

The workers fled when the shooting started, but the commandos captured a shirtless young man in a straw hat. The police promised to let him go if he talked, so he did. Then Gallego asked if I had questions. There followed a cooperative interview with Restrepo, as the prisoner called himself.

Restrepo said he was twenty-five years old, earned ten to fifteen dollars a day for processing coca leaves, and hadn't been paid for three months. "I don't know who owns the patch and I don't ask," he said. "When I did ask, they said, 'Just keep working.'" He missed his wife and kids, he said, and wanted to go home to his village, five hundred miles to the north.

Gallego said we must leave before guerrillas showed up. The commandos sawed apart the processing pens with a chain saw, dumped chemicals, and, finding the coca stash too wet to ignite, blew it up with demolition cord. We took another route to the helicopter to avoid ambush. Restrepo watched us take off without emotion.

"He said he had a family, so we couldn't leave his wife and children alone," Gallego explained on the flight back to Bogotá. It was Restrepo's employers who belonged in jail, the commander said, instead of in their big mansions.

"I'd love to see one of their homes," I said.

"You like to see a drug boss's home?" Gallego grinned again. "Okay!"

And that is how I found myself with Gallego's colleague, Lieutenant Colonel Ramiro Villalobos, banging on the door of a two-story mansion that rose like a fortress in a lush upscale neighborhood of Cali. Villalobos headed the police search team there, though he looked more like a professor. We were joined by a pretty prosecutor, armed with a search warrant in one slender hand and a revolver in the other. More plainclothes cops and a platoon of soldiers with a machine gun deployed around us.

The owner, a notorious cocaine trafficker, had left for his ranch in the countryside, the maid contended. His mansion had marble floors, crystal chandeliers, gilded and tasseled furniture, even a bowling alley. The enormous veranda had fountains and a pool. Built into the concrete exterior was a bunker with firing slits covering the street.

"This house cost fifteen million dollars," one of the cops told me.

For all its gaudy narco-deco adornments—the owner deserved prosecution on grounds of taste—the mansion was stripped of personality. Photographs had been removed from their silver frames; the vast walk-in closets held barely a change of clothes.

The police searchers hit one more house, a lawyer's, in search of documents, before Villalobos drove me downtown in his van with tinted windows. He dropped me off at the entrance to a shopping mall in Cali that looked right out of Beverly Hills.

"You will find your hotel at the other end," the colonel said. "I think you understand why we don't take you."

Now I was walking out of Westchester County and still over-hearing Spanish, spoken this time by a crew of sweating workers laying a drainage pipe. I stopped to ask directions, but the workers averted my gaze. Obviously, they didn't live here either. A young woman who did sped past in her open Mercedes convert-ible.

It was an epiphany to find battalions of Central Americans per-forming the stoop labor that Yankee farmers once took pride in re-serving for themselves. But then Yankee farmers could no longer afford to live here in homes that sold for well into seven figures. Mexicans, Salvadorans, and Guatemalans were now digging the ditches, tending the shrubbery, and planting and mowing the fields, in the spirit of hard work that had built America. The white suburbs of Westchester County ran on brown wheels.

One of the old tombstones I passed in Salem Center marked the grave of James Crane, who was born in 1795 and died on May 20, 1865. What would old man Crane have made of these changes? In his seventieth year, he was still adjusting to the absence of the local farm boys who had volunteered to fight for the Union.

More by luck than diligence, I reached the village outskirts of North Salem. I considered picking up a sandwich and cold soda at the next grocery store. Then again, I deserved to pass a pleasant hour at some trendy little inn where I could sit outside under an umbrella on the patio, while the staff tended to my bottomless glass of iced tea, topping each refill with another slice of lemon and sprig of mint.

But there was no longer any inn or a grocery store, never mind a sandwich. I could not find one useful thing to buy in the venerable village of North Salem. What I took at a distance for a store was at closer range an old union hall that had been converted into a commercial art gallery. Further ahead rose a spire, a sure sign of the village community. But the old church under the spire was now privately owned and garishly painted in alternate panels of red and green. A couple of motorcycles were parked out front. Across the street was another profaned church with a rocking chair on the porch and a pot of freshly cut flowers by the door.

On the northern fringe of this Potemkin shell of a village, I finally spied what looked like an inn. But it served French country cuisine at New York City prices, and it was temporarily closed to customers. In the gravel parking lot, a delivery van was unloading wholesale produce that menus describe as garden-fresh.

Slouching northward on Peace Lake Road, I passed an adopt-a-highway sign informing me that this stretch of trash-strewn road was being kept tidy by the Westchester County Bowhunters Association. It had been a long time since bowhunting season. The road soon opened up to broad fields on either side.

I was famished to the point of hallucinating about the chow back at the New York Times cafeteria. And I was parched. All the water I had drunk reappeared as sweat on my soggy T-shirt. But I found no nourishment till I reached an intersection outside North Salem that offered a saddlery, a gardening shop, a gas station, and a delicatessen. These were the new merchants of North Salem. Down the road a pizzeria beckoned, but I craved something cold and wet.

I went into the nondescript delicatessen, where I ordered an egg salad sandwich and a couple of pint bottles of iced tea. A pair of sullen young men behind the counter acted annoyed to have a customer intrude upon the argument they were having. The sandwich, once I cajoled them into assembling it, tasted pretty good. The bottled iced tea, I fetched from the stand-up refrigerator.

The management did not invite me to linger, so I licked my fingers of egg salad and resumed walking north. This seemed a good time to take a swim in Peach Lake, which shimmered invitingly in its girdle of weekend cottages. There was a prominent sign ahead that I expected to point to a public beach.

"Private," the sign warned. "No Trespassing, No Soliciting, Violators Will Be Prosecuted." In other words, no swim. I moved on, past a small golf course occupying what had once been prime pasture.

At length, I saw ahead the divided lanes of Interstate 84. A concrete underpass offered cooling relief from the heat. I could hear the traffic droning overhead. When I drive to Vermont from New York City, I hit this spot in an hour and a half. On foot, it had taken me nearly five days.

The convent lay a few more miles due north, beyond another large body of water called East Branch Reservoir. I tried to cut through the woods and follow the shoreline, but the reservoir was fenced off. Even if I got in, I wasn't sure where I could get out. My resolve to do nothing illegal on my walk seemed naive.

I had walked off my map of Westchester County and into Putnam County, named for General Israel Putnam, commander of the American forces in the Hudson Highlands during the Revolutionary War. A search of my pack failed to find the Putnam County map I purchased in New York City. This left me with the options of turning either east or west around the reservoir. Eastward would take me into Connecticut. Westward would take me to Route 22, a main road with more possibilities.

I walked west until I reached Route 22 at a complex spaghetti junction that also merged Interstate 84 as well as 684. In the tangle of concrete highways, I could only find one on-ramp that would lead me uphill onto Route 22. I would have to share the ramp with a stream of accelerating cars.

There was another problem. A traffic accident had tied up the road at the entrance to the ramp. A police car, blue lights flashing from its roof, arrived to join a patrol car from the county sheriff's department. A tow truck arrived.

The police officers were questioning a distraught woman whose gray sedan sat disabled in the middle of the road. Another blue car was parked on the shoulder. If I hung about, the police might ask whether I had seen the accident and what I was doing there anyway. I tried to cut into a thicket of sumac trees and other weeds, to emerge at the other side of Route 22. But the trails into the thicket conspired to bring me back to where I started.

I followed the roadway beyond the overpass until I found the first commercial business, an automobile dealership. I went inside to ask for directions to northbound Route 22. The receptionist looked out the window and said something about not having heard me drive up.

"Take the second light on the left," the receptionist said. And her directions were excellent for a motorist but led back to precisely where I started. Fortunately, both patrol cars were leaving. The tow truck had dragged away the damaged car.

No sooner were the cops out of sight than I bolted up the entrance ramp to Route 22, or more precisely into the cover of a line of trees. A rotting log blocked my way, forcing me back to the asphalt shoulder. By now, it was rush hour, and this was not a thoroughfare that attracted walkers, even in the quiet hours. I tried to look inconspicuous, hugging the fence as I walked along the road with my pack, trying not to inhale the passing exhaust. I had given up looking for water, having long ago emptied the liter bottle that I filled up in Hunt's kitchen.

Eventually, I turned right onto Milltown Road, taking a shortcut through the parking lot of an office complex. From there I followed the directions provided to me by Sister Penelope Mary when I telephoned the Convent of the Holy Community and asked to stay overnight at its St. Cuthbert's retreat center.

"Will you arrive by car or train?" she had asked. The convent supported itself by holding retreats, but for faith-based groups, not for a lone secular traveler.

"I'm walking from New York City," I told her, and added before she might hang up, "You could call it a spiritual journey into retirement."

There was but a brief pause on the other end of the line. "Careful of the traffic," Sister Penelope Mary advised. "It's a narrow road and they drive very fast."

The Milltown Road took me past an old cemetery to Federal Hill Road, with winding stone walls and overhanging maples. By the time I crossed the Croton River over a modest bridge, I had grown adept at hugging the road's shoulders to avoid presenting a stationary target for oncoming traffic. I passed two fine houses, whose electronic gates and high fences erected behind low stone walls told me this couldn't be the convent. St. Cuthbert's was more modest, set in a cluster of quite ordinary buildings between a primary school and a soccer field. The three nuns in residence wore sky-blue habits and darker wimples; they were Episcopalians, preparing the retreat center for a weekend visit by Zen Buddhists. The nuns seemed puzzled to see me. I reminded them that I had telephoned to reserve a bed.

Sister Penelope Mary, tall and slender, waved off my apologies about arriving late. The traffic, I explained, was terrible.

"We're about to go in for vespers," she said. "Would you join us? Perhaps you would rather wash up and meet us afterward. Supper will be family-style."

Sweat had stuck my soiled T-shirt to my skin. My face was streaked with a mask of sunblock cream and road dust. I looked disgustingly unkempt for vespers. But after a day of noise and frustration, the prospect of serenity appealed more than a hot bath.

I followed Sister Penelope Mary into a small chapel set apart from the school auditorium. The other nuns, Sister Dominica and Sister Emmanuel, had opened their prayerbooks. Sister Penelope Mary sat me alongside her, facing the other nuns. She handed me a loose-leaf notebook with pages of prayers and responses highlighted with a felt-tipped pen. The nuns lit the candles.

After the introductory prayers, we launched into an antiphonal recitation of Psalm 106, one of the less lyrical psalms of David:

"They intermingled with the heathen and learned their pagan ways, so that they worshiped their idols, which became a snare to them." I wondered whether David was predicting the coming of sport utility vehicles.

"They sacrificed their sons and daughters to evil spirits." Could "evil spirits," I wondered, be construed as the exhaust I had been breathing along Route 22?

Sisters Dominica and Emmanuel across the small aisle took up a verse. At first I joined in, until Sister Penelope Mary nudged me and whispered, "We're on the same side."

Thereafter, I followed her clear voice, struggling with the cadence at first, interrupting the silent beats that denoted pauses in the verses.

I felt on more solid ground once the worshippers turned to praying for the doctors, nurses, and paramedics at the Putnam County Hospital, where a fourth nun lay hospitalized after recently fracturing her shoulder and suffering a heart attack.

I kept losing my place in the prayerbook as the nuns flipped with practiced familiarity from one page to another, seldom in sequence. By the time I got the hang of it, vespers were over. I felt refreshed. The noise and traffic seemed a world away.

After the benediction, the candles were extinguished, the prayerbooks put aside until the next morning. I followed the trio out into the evening. Clouds had obscured the setting sun. It definitely looked like rain.

Supper family-style at the convent meant raiding the big refrigerator. The nineteenth-century order that these nuns served evidently did not produce hearty eaters. Yet there was enough lettuce, cheese, bread, and potato salad to make a fine sandwich or two. So I ate two.

Our table talk was sparse and a little strained until I mentioned my interest in folk music.

Sister Penelope Mary appraised me through her rimless spectacles.

"Do you know a little brown dog?" I thought I heard her say. The turn in conversation puzzled me.

"The song," she explained. "'Little Brown Dog.'" And seated at the kitchen table, she sang a verse, unaccompanied, in a crystal soprano.

"Once I had a little dog, his color it was brown . . ."

It evoked a song that I associated with Peter, Paul and Mary, until Sister Penelope Mary gently corrected me. Yes, they had recorded a version, she said, but the original song was passed down by an old man in Virginia who never got credit.

Before long, we were sharing snatches of folk songs learned years ago. Sister Penelope Mary sang "Lowlands of Holland," which I knew as "Golden Vanity." We compared our different versions of "Man of Constant Sorrow" and "The House Carpenter."

I had been a folkie in the 60s, I told her, and kept a couple of guitars and a five-string banjo at home. Sister Penelope Mary also played guitar, it turned out, but hers was at her order's headquarters in New York City.

When we paused from singing in the convent kitchen, Sister let slip that she had recently returned from a vacation spent with her own sister, at the Newport Folk Festival.

"Willie was there," she confided.

Surely this cloistered nun didn't mean Willie Nelson, the Texas singer and pothead who nearly went to jail for falling behind on his income tax. He was a favorite of mine.

That's right, Sister Mary Penelope confirmed, she heard Willie Nelson. She had lived in a convent for forty-two years and had been consecrated as a nun for forty of them. But sitting in the convent kitchen, we found common ground as Willie Nelson fans as well as Episcopalians, which goes to show how God moves in mysterious ways, sometimes to the rhythm of pedal steel guitars.

We summoned up a few more folk songs before Sister abruptly rose. "I'm sure you're tired and want to go to bed," she said. She walked me outside, passing some newly primed boards prepared for icons she painted in her spare time. I had noticed some lovely icons on the convent walls.

The first decisive drops of an imminent rainstorm threatened to still the chorus of crickets as I crossed the road to St. Adrian's House, a men's residence that I had to myself for the night.

A small sign on the kitchen wall under a straw likeness of the Virgin Mary cautioned me, "In quietness are all things answered, and is every problem quietly resolved."

My room was small and comfortable. I enjoyed a hot bath and slipped into the snug bed. I awoke after midnight to the pleasant sound of rain tapping on the window and as soon fell asleep again.

THE RAIN overnight had cooled the hot weather, making walking more pleasant. I changed my bed with clean sheets, reciting a prayer that the nuns had left for me.

"Oh Lord, guide my hands as I make this bed ready for another's rest," it began, and concluded, "Help me perform this act with care and love, and may the one who follows me here be refreshed in body, mind, and spirit." I haven't been so motivated to make a bed properly since I was in the army.

I ventured into the kitchen to find something for breakfast. The nuns had invited me to take what I needed from the refrigerator. I cooked some oatmeal, toast, and tea. My traveling T-shirt, still sweaty from the previous day's walk, I draped outside my pack to dry.

I was washing up my dishes when out of the drain of the stainless steel sink crawled one of the most garishly repulsive bugs I had ever seen, even in Africa. My first instinct was to squash it. But I was preparing to depart, so why not leave its demise to the next guests?

No, you would hardly entrust a contract killing to a bunch of Zen Buddhists. And gentle nuns were hardly more formidable if there was extermination to be done.

I turned on the hot water full force and blasted the interloping insect down the drain.

Sister Penelope Mary was busy with other tasks, so I said farewell to Sister Emmanuel. She came outside and, shading her eyes, peered up toward the sun.

"God has watered my flowers," Sister declared. "Now I don't have to do it."

I HAD to walk back to the Milltown Road before turning north. A blanket of puffy new clouds was already obscuring the sun. Wind stirred the leaves of the trees along the road. I tried to tune in the morning news on my pocket radio, but all I could get was a radio evangelist rattling on about Saint Paul's instructions to "redeem your time" by making the most of each opportunity.

I was passing a field of blue wildflowers when a green van

pulled up alongside. The driver asked whether I knew of a private golf course, and acted disappointed and a bit surprised when I didn't. He had taken me for a local because I was on foot. The road had a thirty-five-mile speed limit, which didn't deter the drivers who hurtled past. The only other sounds were the chirp of cicadas and the wind rustling through the leaves and the screech of crows. Then a man in a red T-shirt began attacking leaves in his front yard with a leaf-blower. I stepped around a dead rabbit, run over by a car and evidently eviscerated by a dog.

Walking through New York's suburbs and exurbs, I endured the noisy derision of every dog I passed, from snotty little barking handbags to junkyard mastiffs who threatened to tear my arm off once they snapped the restraining chain. I pretended to ignore the yapping. My pepper spray stayed in the bottom of the pack, but I took to loading one pocket with stones to use if I was attacked.

I learned to read each neighborhood I sauntered through. The modest dimensions of the houses suggested that blue-collar folks lived here. A schoolbus stop sign confirmed there were children. One house had an old-fashioned swing, fashioned from a rubber tire, hanging from a tree in the front yard. It would have taken a father to install the swing. Some blue boxes mounted alongside the mailboxes showed who read which newspapers.

Development was encroaching on this quiet street. Ahead, a sign advertised "Luxury custom colonials on exclusive settings. Will build to suit." The houses erected so far looked only slightly smaller than Gibraltar. Big bucks would be made from people who yearned to buy a chunk of country and were in the process of destroying it.

Further ahead, a maroon sign gilded with gold paint announced a new development for Salmon Daily Brook Farm, though nary a brook nor farm nor salmon were in sight.

A road sign abruptly announced that I was now in Connecticut, where I did not expect to arrive for another few days. I had been traveling at right angles to where I needed to go. After an hour, I had walked too far.

I retraced my steps to Sherwood Hill Road, which was not visible at the uppermost corner of my Westchester County map, sat down on my pack and watched the license plates of passing cars for some clue to the direction back to New York. Two cars with New York plates emerged from Sherwood Hill Road, and a third New York car entered it. So I walked down Sherwood Hill, which was steep enough to leave me praying that I hadn't made a mistake. I had developed a second blister, this time along my right big toe, and sat on someone's driveway to cushion the blister with a moleskin patch and a fresh sock.

I emerged at Green Chimneys School and Farm Center, and guessed at which road to take, checking the compass to confirm a northerly direction.

At the next junction, I asked directions of a resident who had gotten out of her car to check her mailbox. The sudden appearance of a solitary walker startled her. She jumped back into the car, locked the door, and sped up the driveway to her house.

It was noon when Route 22 appeared. I stopped at a diner for spinach pie and iced tea, then continued north along the highway, following a line of pizza crusts thrown from passing cars.

I entered Dutchess County, named for a bygone Dutchess of York who predated Sarah Ferguson. Here my wife, who was meeting me in Pawling with the rest of my camping gear, drove past in our green Volvo without noticing me.

In 1766, struggling tenant farmers in Dutchess County rebelled against the wealthy landowners because of high rents. When the Revolutionary War broke out a decade later, the landowners remained loyal to the Crown, so the tenant farmers and laborers joined the patriots, driving out their economic oppressors. Across from the Pawling golf course stands the two-story white clapboard house of John Kane, a prosperous eighteenth-century Tory landowner whose house was commandeered to serve as George Washington's headquarters in the autumn of 1778.

Pawling, but a few miles from the Appalachian Trail, attracts hikers who detour into town to stock up on groceries, get their stoves or boots repaired, and find a good hamburger. In the summer, thru-hikers are permitted to camp overnight in the town park. I was initially dubious about taking the Appalachian Trail, which followed a more circuitous route to Vermont than paved roads. But the prospect of meeting more drivers like those I had encountered planted doubts that I would fare better than the roadside wildlife reduced to successive mounds of defunct fur on the asphalt.

I also wanted to pass through Pawling to revisit a preparatory school called Trinity-Pawling, where I had spent four years as an athletically challenged, nearsighted adolescent a half century ago.

Pawling looked prettier than I remembered, with trendier stores, no more movie theater, and McKinney and Doyle's Fine Foods Cafe. I was reunited with Jaqueline at Sharadu, a bed-and-breakfast place on the second floor of an old house downtown. My wife feels strongly about not sleeping overnight in public parks. The proprietress wasn't home, but she had posted a note of welcome, confiding where she hid the key. She signed herself "Mother."

Before going to dine at McKinney and Doyle's across the railway tracks, we did meet Mother, a free-spirited woman. Mother took her "nom d'hôtel," she explained, out of maternal solicitude for the young hikers who accounted for much of her business. "They've all been marvelous, without exception. Considerate and honest. I haven't had a single case of stealing over all these years." Mother paused. "Well, once."

I pressed her for the details, Yes, Mother conceded, there had been a thief. She hastened to add that we had no cause for worry. "He wasn't a hiker," she said. "He arrived on a motorcycle. He looked like one of those Hell's Angels.

"He said he didn't have any money, so I let him stay overnight for free," Mother complained. "He snuck out early the next morning—with one of my pillows!"

If the outlaw biker absconded with only her pillow, I thought, Mother got off lightly.

I WALKED through four geographical zones of attitude on my way to Vermont: Go away. Don't bother me. Hello. And: How can I help you?

I had left the frown-and-sneer zones in New York City and Westchester and Putnam counties, but I didn't encounter unsolicited smiles until I reached Dutchess County and Pawling, where a local approached me in the laundromat to help me sort out the washers and dryers. "You get a lot more time with that dryer over there," advised the woman, who was doing laundry herself.

Waiting for my own clothes to dry, Jaqueline and I sat on a bench outside the corner bakery, drinking coffee from Styrofoam cups and eating apple turnovers warm from the oven. It was time to acquaint Jaqueline with my old school, whose adherence to the traditions of jackets and ties, daily chapel, and sit-down dinners might seem archaic to someone unfamiliar with the erosion of good manners in public education, where almost any undisciplined behavior short of homicide or grand theft auto gets grudgingly tolerated as a sop to self-esteem.

After breakfast, I gave Jaqueline directions for driving to Trinity-Pawling, less than two miles away. I wanted to retrace an old route through the town cemetery that I took as a student returning from the Saturday night movies downtown.

While I was at T-P, the cemetery was declared off-limits by the headmaster, who feared that we might sneak in there to smoke, drink beer, and cavort with high school hussies on the gravestones. I was clueless about how to organize these infractions. But I walked through the cemetery anyway on Saturday nights to raise suspicions among my classmates that I had some hanky-panky cooking on the side. The only brush with lust that I recall at T-P came during a formidably chaperoned tea dance with Emma Willard School, when I met a fifteen-year-old with a cute ponytail and fast mouth named Jane Fonda. This happened years too soon to do me any good.

More than twenty years later, I interviewed Fonda when she came to Moscow to star in a forgettable movie titled *The Blue Bird* and inveigh against the Vietnam War. I reminded her of our brief encounter. Fonda, who clearly had no memory of me, played her part like the gifted actress she was.

"So," she asked with a dazzling smile, "how've you been all these years?"

JANE FONDA notwithstanding, I never enjoyed looking back, though that was what I found myself doing today. Keep your eyes on the rearview mirror, and you will miss the hairpin turns ahead.

On the other hand, the singer Dolly Parton, who has the best yodel in country music, once said of her own rural roots, "Sometimes to know how far you've traveled, you've got to go back where you began."

My walk through the cemetery was an acquaintance with local history. Here lay the wife of John Cook, Lydia Dodge, born August 30, 1817, and died November 29, 1876. Her eroded headstone featured a hand holding six flowers, one of which had been dropped. A berry bush obscured the epitaph, but I inferred that one of her six children had died in infancy. She was surrounded in her grave by other Cooks and Dodges.

I crossed a small brook. Another monument, eight feet tall, featured an anchor and the name of Rear Admiral John Worden, a Civil War naval hero who lived from 1818 to 1897. Further on, a stone dog sat vigil over the polished headstones of three generations of the DiLaurentis family who died since I left T-P.

Beyond the cemetery were the athletic grounds of Trinity-Pawling. A middle-aged man in a gray T-shirt was jogging with his dog around the very track where I once came in twelfth in an interscholastic track meet (my quarter-mile event had only twelve runners).

The brick school buildings lay imposingly atop a hill across Route 22, the highway I had lately walked. In my day, we had to sprint across the road to and from football or track practice. Thankfully, some parents bought the school a pedestrian overpass in 1991.

T-P was small enough in size to let even the likes of me play varsity football and run track. Its teachers, seizing me by the metaphorical scruff of the neck, had inspired and nagged me into earning grades that got me accepted at Dartmouth and Princeton. It was an easy choice when Dartmouth offered a full scholarship and Princeton didn't.

My last visit to T-P came on a balmy spring evening when I was invited to embroider my exploits as a foreign correspondent for some students seated in the school chapel. Following my inspirational musings, the audience bolted to join their more fortunate friends playing softball on the grass outside. I was left chatting with William Taylor, T-P's assistant headmaster at the time, who asked, a trifle hesitantly, "Would you remember someone named Nancy Edmonds?"

I recalled a lively blue-eyed blonde who had been my date at Dartmouth Winter Carnival when we were college freshmen. Buried somewhere under the layers of clutter in my Vermont basement was a Mount Holyoke beer mug she had given me.

"I sure do," I blurted. "Nancy was really cute."

The assistant headmaster interjected politely, "She's my mother-in-law."

Today, I was showing up at T-P unannounced, wearing hiking boots rather than a Timesman's blazer and tie. But the students were on summer vacation, and so were most of the faculty. The son-in-law of my pretty Winter Carnival date had left to become headmaster at another school in Tennessee.

I led Jaqueline down the hallway of the administration building in search of my name inscribed on a laquered wall plaque, academic excellence at T-P having been calibrated more casually in those days. The gilt letters spelling my name seemed to have shrunk since I first admired them.

We wandered about the campus until someone called out, "Do you need help?" She was Nicolle McDougal and taught swimming. Her husband, Jim, taught history. When I explained my T-P connection, she offered to show us the new environmental learning center, constructed on a large pond. "I played hockey here," I bragged, though the pond triggered more conflicted memories.

I began my editorship of the school newspaper by scolding my fellow students as an immature, selfish lot who goofed around too much and ought to grow up and study harder to avoid being unemployable after they graduated, if they weren't expelled first. After my editorial hit the mailboxes, I was dragged from my room. Dozens of hands vied to haul me to the pond and swing me over its chilly water preparatory to the final heave. The alarmed headmaster arrived in time to prevent my dunking. I learned the downside of community journalism early.

Visits to old haunts trigger unpredictable memories. These did not trip me up until I peered through the big doors into the school dining room and, to one side, the kitchen where I worked. Everybody was assigned a chore, some grubbier than others. I washed dishes. For those who don't know better, washing dishes as a scholarship kid sounds right out of Dickens's *Oliver Twist*. But far from having my self-esteem bruised, I felt lucky. When the kids on full tuition had to don the required jacket and tie for dinner, I got to wear a T-shirt and jeans and eat early in the kitchen, where the cooks spoiled us with choice cuts of meat and slabs of warm pie. My crewmates were jocks on athletic scholarship, the strapping sort whom I was thrilled to hang out with. We bonded over trays stacked with food-specked dishes that emerged spotless through the scalding steam at the far side of the stainless steel dishwashing juggernaut.

Or does the mind similarly steam-clean our memories to make them more palatable for the soul? It didn't matter, because I left Trinity-Pawling on this summer day fighting back nostalgia. This world has enough Ivy Leaguers, Phi Beta Kappas among them, but how many of us were taught to wash dishes too, and can recall the joy of doing it well?

Jaqueline drove away to check us into a new motel nearer the Appalachian Trail, while I continued north on foot. Walking along Route 22 became easier as the shoulders widened, though the cars moved just as fast, which is to say well over the posted speed limit.

INVARIABLY someone, upon learning that I had been a foreign correspondent, would inquire, "Wasn't that dangerous?"

"Depends," I usually replied, referring not to the wars but to the traffic, in which you were statistically likelier to lose your nerve, if not your life. Traffic on New York's backroads, I had to concede, was somewhat less lethal.

Cairo's chaotic streets remained hopelessly snarled. I found it faster to walk home three miles than attempt to drive across the Nile from the *Times* bureau. The traffic was even more insane in Bangkok and in Tehran, where pedestrian sidewalks were used as on- and off-ramps.

But for real demolition-derby driving, nothing compared with Libya's capital, Tripoli. Smash-ups were so routine that when I visited Tripoli, government ministries imported their cars, mostly Fiats from Italy, in volume and lined them up in rows. When one car was crashed, it was towed off to the lengthening rank of wrecks. If the driver survived, another was selected from the dwindling row of new vehicles for him to demolish.

One night, some of us visiting journalists were rushed by bus to meet Muammar Qaddafi, the fruitcake running Libya. Our cortege, accelerating through the usual red lights, totaled the sedan of a driver foolhardly enough to be venturing through a green light, which in Tripoli can be more hazardous than stopping at a red one. Our police escorts yanked the dazed driver from his crumpled heap and arrested him, waving us on to our audience. The priority treatment given our inept driver let us arrive in sufficient time to wait only two more hours for Qaddafi to receive us sometime after midnight.

I wish Qaddafi had been as much fun as his *Green Book,* a self-published compendium of nonsense such as: "Democratically, a natural person should not be permitted to own any means of publication or information. However, he has the natural right to express himself by any means, even if it is in an irrational manner to prove his madness."

During my visit, Qaddafi only turned entertaining when a European reporter blurted: "Are you crazy?"

Qaddafi giggled back in English, "If you say it."

Foreign correspondents cover wars too. But more often, we had to doorstep diplomatic talks where the press was made to stand around outside, wondering where the nearest toilet was, until a spokesman popped out to announce, "The talks will continue in a frank and businesslike atmosphere." In other words, they can't agree, so come back tomorrow.

I suppose the scariest moment in my career happened in the city of Tabriz in northern Iran, during factional fighting between the armed followers of rival Shiite ayatollahs. The rebels had kidnapped four Revolutionary Guardsmen from the government and were holding them in a heavily fortified building downtown. I wanted to interview the rebel chief, on the misassumption that an enemy of America's enemy, meaning the Islamic government, just might be America's friend. My Azeri interpreter, who arranged the interview, corrected my flawed logic after we got inside the chief's fortress.

"He hates Americans," she confided.

My blood chilled a few degrees. "Then why did they let me in?"

"I told them you were Swedish," she whispered, with a conspiratorial wink.

The rebel chief was a mountain of a man, and born to bellow. He had jammed a .45-caliber pistol into his ample waistband. I noticed that its hammer was cocked back in a gesture of bravado, putting the pistol at risk of firing whenever he leaned forward. As he harangued me, folds of body fat enveloped his pistol. And if it did go off, his bodyguards were bound to charge into the room, find the smoking gun and their leader emasculated in mid-diatribe, and grab the imposter Swede with a United States passport. I wrapped up that interview and got out of there.

As they say in our business, it's not the bullet with your name on it that you need to worry about, but the one that comes addressed "To whom it may concern."

I nearly missed the Appalachian Trail sign, which pointed vaguely toward an unremarkable track heading into a meadow. It didn't look like the celebrated footpath I had expected until a trio of hikers emerged with big packs. They were gaunt and dirty.

I crossed the road to talk to them. "What's the trail like?" I asked. "I'm hiking it tomorrow."

The hikers grunted weariness. "Lots of blow-downs," one said, alluding to fallen trees and limbs obstructing the trail. The hikers were more preoccupied with fistfuls of boiled hot dogs they had bought from a fast food trailer parked at the trailhead and were now wolfing down. The vendor had positioned himself to waylay an undiscriminating clientele.

In a few days, I would look like that.

Connecticut

They walked the roads

Mimicking what they heard, as children mimic;

They understood that wisdom comes of beggary.

William Butler Yeats, "The Seven Sages"

Three

THE SOFT drizzle threatened to become hard rain and my wife's patience was wearing thin while I dithered over what to put in my pack. I sifted through piles of camping gear, clothing, and food that I had indiscriminately tossed into the back of our station wagon a couple of weeks earlier.

Jaqueline had kept her promise to deliver my tent, stove, and sleeping bag on the first weekend after I cleared New York City. The resupply mission had expanded to two romantic nights together. Now Sunday was slipping away, and the family's sole remaining wage-earner had to return to New York and resume working at her school by eight A.M. Monday. It was time to start walking again from where I left off, a few miles north of Pawling. Instead, I was paralyzed by indecision over parkas, sweaters, cookwear, sleeping bags of various weights, and metal gadgetry. Retirement should mean liberation from workaday decisions. Yet here I stood with drizzle rolling down my nose and neck, getting spattered with muddy water by passing cars, as I engaged in Hamlet-like procrastination over what to take or not to take.

I was as deliberately selective as someone dipping into a box of Belgian chocolates. Should I take a spare can opener or rely on the balky tool on my red Swiss Army knife, which tended to stick from years' accumulation of gunk? I put the knife in my pocket and tossed the can opener into my pack.

Would I use my poncho as well as my rain jacket? I was wearing the jacket, but the poncho could come in handy as a ground cloth under my tent. I took both.

Did I need the complete cooking kit, which included a pot, pan, skillet, plate, bowl, cup, and enough utensils to feed an infantry platoon? They went along too; I wouldn't have to wash up after each meal.

What about my black sweater versus the fleece pullover? I shoved both into the pack, just in case. It could turn cold in the mountains, if I got that far.

Should I take my old metal whistle in case my son's orange plastic whistle failed? I did, giving me the option of calling for help in two-part harmony.

Headlamp or flashlight? Well, neither weighed that much. What if one got lost or malfunctioned? Double-A or triple-A batteries for my lamps and tiny tape recorder? I threw an extra fistful of batteries into my pack. I added what was left of my roll of duct tape, which I had applied liberally to the pack's frayed shoulder straps.

How many days of food? Two water bottles or three? One loaf of bread or two? Rice or noodles? Powdered lemonade with or without sugar? The difference in lemonades amounted to a couple of ounces. Liquid detergent or an old-fashioned bar of soap?

I also took a stiff broad-brimmed hat that snagged on every passing branch, stiff canvas trousers that soaked up rainwater faster than a sponge, and several clean shirts with collars to wear off the trail. Jaqueline argued that I should carry something decent to wear if the mayors and lairds I passed invited me to dinner. I argued that where I was walking, people called it supper, not dinner. But the weight added up.

Every traveler undergoes this exasperating anguish. But what I selected would have to travel on my back for a month or more, not in some overhead luggage compartment.

The most painful decision involved a stack of books I had brought to read in the long summer twilights on the trail. In the end, I limited myself to the copy of *Walden*. Thoreau would hardly have approved of the rest of what I was carrying, which could be generically described as "stuff."

"Our life is frittered away by detail," Henry whispered from the pages of my paperback. "An honest man has hardly need to count more than his ten fingers, or in extreme cases he may add his ten toes and lump the rest."

Reloading my pack took more than an hour. Every decision made sense. Taken together, they violated the first rule of going light: pack no more than half of what you lay out. I had toted a lot less traveling through distant backwaters as a foreign correspondent.

At last, Jaqueline drove off in the direction of New York City, having consented to meet me in Manchester, Vermont, a village that, I reminded her, was known as much for its bargain shopping outlets as for its gracious country inns and equally expensive restaurants.

Swinging the pack against my thigh and onto my shoulder, I walked across the highway as jauntily as I could, into a pasture whose white blazes introduced me to the Appalachian Trail.

I considered walking a few miles further up Route 22, then turning right to the Connecticut state line and hiking up Hoyt Road to the first shelter on the Appalachian Trail. But this would have taken me past the Wingdale state psychiatric hospital, whose grim brick buildings, now shuttered, resembled an old-fashioned penitentiary. And I hadn't seen anyone else hiking up the busy highway, at least not with a pack as big as mine. I didn't want to be mistaken for an inmate who had escaped with his mattress on his back.

So I backtracked a few miles to pick up the Appalachian Trail sooner. With my wife having departed at fifty miles an hour, I was in no mood to hang around highways.

Nearly three centuries earlier, New York and Connecticut had quarreled over this nondescript border strip, for reasons unexplained by the marker I passed on Route 22. The dispute was settled in 1731 by creating a tract called the Oblong, fifty-one miles long and two miles wide, which Connecticut later gave up.

It took me not quite ten minutes to lose my bearings, which was no modest achievement. The Appalachian Trail may well be the most famous footpath in the United States, though not here, where the trail kept petering out until it was indistinguishable from the cowpaths intersecting the mown pastures. I plunked my pack in the middle of the field and sallied forth in several directions, without success.

I checked the map again. The trail seemed to meander across the wooded ridge to my left, into a nature preserve set aside by the town of Pawling. I scrambled across a muddy ravine and bushwhacked up to the high ground on the other bank through undergrowth that left my trousers soggy with fresh rainfall. A half-hour out, and I needed a hot bath.

By luck, I found some trees emblazoned with the white blazes of the Appalachian Trail. The trail itself was poorly marked and cluttered by fallen limbs and other deadfall as it wound through the nature preserve. The local hiking club had been preoccupied with something other than trail maintenance. Lesser paths, identified by competing blazes in reds, yellows, and greens, intersected with my route, adding to the confusion. They seemed to lead seductively downhill to Quaker Lake, a local holiday spot.

I was being passed in both directions by brawny Sunday hikers flexing powerful quadriceps, and those were just the women. I forged ahead on the white trail at a retiree's pace, trying not to lose altitude as it led me up and down to the wrought iron gates of an eerily abandoned graveyard, identified by a metal sign as "Gates of Heaven." The graves, not to mention heaven itself, had vanished under a profusion of weeds.

Here I encountered a local man who claimed to know the area well. Andy led me to the Wiley shelter at the head of Hoyt Road, which hugged the state line between New York and Connecticut.

"There's a lot of old magazines that you can read if you want to stay for a day or two," said Andy, who sounded excited by the prospect. The collection was as large as he promised, but sitting around reading month-old soiled magazines at a shelter that looked bug-ridden and a little spooky was not what I had in mind. I decided to push on for three or four more miles, to the next shelter, in Connecticut. From the top of the one hill, I called Jaqueline on my cell phone, to make sure she had returned home. The trail led downhill a thousand feet or so to Ten Mile River shelter.

The three-sided lean-to was built of logs, with a slanted roof jutting out over the open fourth side. Inside was a flat platform broad enough to sleep a half-dozen hikers. It was typical of shelters on the Appalachian Trail. Some were more elaborate, with open windows and a picnic table or campfire pit outside, but the design had changed little since Abe Lincoln, who spent his early childhood in a similarly rude dwelling on the Kentucky frontier and ended up in the White House.

But Abe's lean-to did not have its wooden beams festooned with nylon cords ending in metal cans and jar tops. Their purpose became apparent from the bags of food hanging from the contraptions, which looked like wind chimes for the deaf. They were meant to keep the food supply at a tantalizing distance from mice and insects, leaving these crawlers free to snack on the faces and hands of sleeping guests.

The lean-to was already occupied by some young hikers who

were cooking their respective suppers on tiny camp stoves. They paid scant attention to my arrival. One benefit of turning sixty-five is that the young tend not to see you. Senior invisibility has its advantages, especially when you begin taking notes about what others are saying.

Here in the woods, it was hard not to eavesdrop on conversations that would be lost in the babble of a city street. The words emanated from the lean-to like whispers in the ear, though the punctuation didn't.

"I was, LIKE, really psyched by the killer stove this dude was using. Made it himself, you know? LIKE, it was way so cool and I was, LIKE—hello?—why didn't I think of denatured alcohol, LIKE it was so totally rad?" one hiker said.

"Wicked awesome," another hiker seemed to agree. "Cut the straps off his pack, LIKE, down to sixteen pounds basic, you know? It just totally blew me away, man. And, LIKE, he's doing twenty-five a day over killer puds and hasn't zeroed since Springer. That's so gnarly, man, LIKE cool."

I once fancied myself fluent in Russian and got along well enough in Chinese. I knew how to speak loudly and point in French and Spanish. But the dialect spoken at the Ten Mile River shelter was like—hello?—going so totally over my head, dude. Compared to this, *Finnegan's Wake* seemed a model of clarity.

Still, the tenor of the hikers' conversation did acquaint me with the nature of permissible social discourse on the Appalachian Trail, which falls into three broadly defined categories:

> Stoves.
> Comparative weights of packs.
> Miles covered daily.

Traveling the trail was for these kids a way of breaking away from their families and reinventing themselves, with a new identity forged under whatever trail name they chose. A clinical psychiatrist would tell me, for one hundred and seventy-five dollars an hour, that my annoyance manifested subconscious envy at not having done the same when I was young.

Describing my companions simply as thru-hikers seemed inadequate because it revealed nothing about their lifestyle. I preferred to call them, and myself, trail travelers.

Billowing gray clouds swallowed up a glimpse of sunset and threatened more rain, so I continued downhill to the tenting area before darkness. I pitched my one-man tent under a spreading fir tree near Ten Mile River, which merged with the Housatonic River some twenty yards away. After a week spent walking, this was my first night outdoors, and without a fire. Campfires were prohibited on the Appalachian Trail in Connecticut and, as it turned out, in many other states.

The river flowing over the rocks sounded muffled and tranquil. But the night was muggy and the prospect of rain led me to drape my poncho over the tent, making the interior hot and claustrophobic. Six hours of hiking with a heavy pack had exhausted me, yet I could not fall asleep.

My red Ensolite sleeping pad was supposed to inflate itself when I turned the valve, but it didn't offer much cushioning until I puffed into it for a minute or so. The pad barely stretched from head to waist, insulating my torso from the damp ground, but not doing much for my legs.

The sleeping bag, once I zipped myself into it, was too hot. I tried spreading it over me like a blanket, with a foot sticking out for temperature control. I plumped my fleece jacket and sweater together into a pillow. Inside the tent, it was becoming as humid as a sauna. I kicked off the sleeping bag.

Sleep comes reluctantly on the first night or two outdoors, when the hard ground takes some getting used to and the silence of the woods amplifies the faintest buzzing of a mosquito. It is all part of becoming accustomed to the rhythm of the trail.

Fireflies were dancing in the dark when I crawled outside and pulled off the poncho to let the tent breathe properly. Sometime after midnight, I swallowed half a tranquilizer. The rain I had braced for never came.

I AWOKE a little before five A.M. to the sounds of birdsong and rushing water. Sunlight spilled over my tent and set the interior aglow. I didn't feel up to the chore of finding my stove, so for breakfast I hacked some chunks of bread from my loaf, slathered them with peanut butter, and washed them down with powdered lemonade. Cooking could be postponed till dinner. The reality was that pieces of my stove had been swallowed up by other stuff that was spilling from my pack.

Before setting out, I went to the pump to fill three water bottles. I originally planned to take two, then threw in a third just in case. The downside is that three liters of water add another six and a half pounds to your pack weight.

At the pump, a fortyish hiker introduced herself as Jules. Her clipped Germanic accent made her sound like one of the jolly nuns in a touring cast of *The Sound of Music*. I looked puzzled about the gender confusion until she explained that Jules was her trail name.

"What is your trail name?" Jules pressed.

"I don't have one," I told her.

Jules frowned. "Everyone must have a trail name," she said, bringing a Teutonic logic to what was supposed to be an anarchic activity, namely walking around outdoors.

"I guess I don't," I confessed.

Jules snorted at this breach of trail etiquette. "If you don't have a trail name," she warned, "the other hikers are going to give you one." She implied that any trail name you chose for yourself would be less embarrassing than what others devised.

I didn't relish being called the Old Retired Guy Back There or worse, to my face or behind my back. A trail name, Jules explained patiently, could be whatever you wanted, so long as it wasn't your real name, though it should reveal something about you and be catchy, like the inane label of a punk rock band.

"What if I choose a trail name and then decide I don't like it?" I asked.

"You could change it," she supposed. But her tone made clear that this fickleness was considered poor form because it confused fellow hikers when you signed the trail registers.

Her meticulous explanation made her seem loopier than she was. Jules seemed to know what she was doing in the woods. Her space-age tent, which she had yet to strike, looked as spacious as the Astrodome.

"Mine weighs two and a half pounds," she boasted. Her tent was sewn from parachute silk. "How much does your tent weigh?" she asked.

"More," I told her. Mine was closer to four pounds and much smaller.

An alias did made sense on the trail, when you are eating and sleeping and excreting and sneezing in intimate proximity to others whom you might not want to appear on your doorstep later to borrow money or take up living space on your floor. Nor might they relish your looking them up when they were back in their workaday world, clean-shaven with matching socks.

Donning my pack, I crossed Ten Mile River over a small bridge. There was ample time to ponder a trail name while I walked among the hills and dells of Connecticut. In the course of my journey to Vermont, I acquired and discarded many sobriquets. I started out as Chris's Dad, the name I answered to when my son

was a teenager. But other hikers looked around for Chris and inquired where my son was.

By the time I hit Massachusetts I was reborn as Super Tortoise,
conveying a peverse pride in my comparatively slow pace. This
got abbreviated to Tortoise in casual conversation, as in, "How
many miles did you do today, Tortoise?" I was inviting insults.

Before I reached Vermont, I changed my trail alias to Hack,
which is British slang for a foreign correspondent (and the title of
a novel I wrote once). But Hack came across like a persistent
cough if I was short of breath when I introduced myself. I invariably had to spell it, which ruins the fun of a trail name.

I slogged across New England scattering more aliases behind
me than a master forger of bad checks. My trail name ultimately
metamorphosed into Jaywalker, which summed up what I had
been doing since I left Times Square. Though most of the thru-
hikers I met would not recognize me as Jaywalker, the reinvention
of identity was familiar enough to many others who traveled the
trail for any distance.

I passed Bull's Bridge, a covered bridge across the Housatonic
River that gained renown as the spot where George Washington's
horse fell into the water back in 1777. The father of our country
spent five hundred dollars, big bucks for a fledgling nation that
tottered on the brink of bankruptcy, to get his horse pulled out.
How did Washington list the retrieval of his horse for the Conti-
nental Congress on his expense account—as transportation or
entertainment?

Nowadays, tourists are more likely to get wet when they are
brushed back against the timbers by vehicles competing to drive
through the single-lane covered bridge from opposite directions.

I was tempted to follow the road along the Housatonic because
the morning was turning hot, but stayed on the Appalachian Trail
as it veered up Schaghticoke Mountain. The mountain's name in

Mohegan meant "the place where the river divides," referring to the juncture of the Housatonic and Ten Mile rivers. The Schaghticoke Indian reservation lies just below the mountain, and though the trail passed through it, I never saw any Indians.

Only fifty-two miles, hardly two percent of the Appalachian Trail, wind through Connecticut, but they seemed to go on forever. It didn't help that I was loaded down like a Himalayan yak. As I walked, mostly up and down, my mind became preoccupied with what I could jettison, or at least mail home from the post office in Kent, the next town upriver.

"Simplicity, simplicity, simplicity!" Thoreau kept reminding me, but I only came up with more reasons for keeping everything I had stuffed into my pack. My *Walden* weighed barely eight ounces, though as I was to learn the hard way, eight ounces here, another eight ounces there add up to a backbreaker. It fortified my resolve to empty my closets in New York City and Vermont of their accumulated clutter, assuming I would see those places again.

The temperature was pushing into the nineties. I sweated profusely as the trail meandered up and along the mountain ridge. My three bottles of water were quickly consumed. When I stopped to drain the last drops, I paid little attention to the rewarding views of the Housatonic River Valley. I assumed that I had left New York behind, but my compass showed the trail swinging westward, indicating that I was wandering back into New York State.

Who decided that such trails should wend back and forth over every unnecessary hill devoid of a view? These pointless ups-and-downs, or puds as some hikers called them, could only have been designed by a committee. I suspect that the local Appalachian Trail Club chapter in each state was determined not to have its section derided as the easiest in the 2,168-mile trail system. You could easily imagine Connecticut's discussion:

"It's easy to let the trail follow this brook down to the river so hikers could swim in the waterfall and fill their bottles, but gosh darn it, we would be considered wimps by New Hampshire and Maine."

"You're right, so why don't we double the trail back over the high ridge to the stretch where the bears carried off that small child last year? Then add a new switchback past the rattlesnake den and down over the cliff into the poison ivy?"

When the Appalachian Trail was assembled, my guidebook reports, some planners wanted it to follow the east bank of the Hudson River in New York over to Massachusetts, snubbing Connecticut. In 1932, the trail was built along the relatively flat east bank of the Housatonic but more recently moved back to the mountains west of the river, where I was hiking.

There actually exists a jumble of boulders called Rattlesnake Den through which the trail passed about five miles into my day's walk. And timber rattlers do sun themselves on such rocks, even in Connecticut. My trekking poles, which I had bought on a whim to cushion the shock to my arthritic ankle on the continuous uphills and downhills, helped me balance my way through the obstacles. Hikers used to rely on a stout wooden staff, but the collapsible poles are lighter and superior to a hunk of wood.

I was overtaken by an affable youth. He wore his hair in dreadlocks and carried a small knapsack from which a thin blanket dangled by a string. As I walked on, he would be sitting by the trailside to let me overtake him and then pass again, which I found not a little weird.

Lone Wolf said he was from Roanoke, Virginia. He said that he planned to enlist in the navy in the fall, earn a high school equivalency diploma, and then join the marines, which wouldn't take him without a high school education.

Lone Wolf had joined the Appalachian Trail at Harpers Ferry,

West Virginia, he said, and kept intending to head for some beach and find a job. He might just hitchhike to the Connecticut coast tomorrow, he told me. Or he might keep walking to New Hampshire or even Maine.

I encouraged him to pass. My pack, my reluctance to break for lunch, and the oppressive heat had slowed me to a crawl. A file of fresh-faced teenage campers flashing the smiles of expensive orthodontics approached with elegant new packs. One little debutante-to-be called to her friend, "You smell like a monkey's ass." Their conversation deteriorated as the kids, who smelled more of money than monkeys, slogged past me.

I had covered barely eight miles so far that day, which doesn't sound like much because it was mostly up and down. But I decided to overnight at the next lean-to, tucked into a shady hollow of Mount Algo. I found Lone Wolf reclining on his thin blanket inside the shelter, cupping his hands around a lit candle. It occurred to me that if he lacked the most basic camping equipment, he might be short on other necessities.

Lone Wolf looked longingly at the freeze-dried dinner packet of beef teriyaki and rice that I pulled from my pack.

"Have you eaten?" I asked. He shook his head.

"Do you have anything to eat?" I asked, instinctively knowing what his answer would be. Again, he shook his head.

So I fired up my gas stove for the first time, boiled up my beef teriyaki and rice, which the label specified was ample for two hikers, and shared it with Lone Wolf. I don't know which hikers the manufacturers had in mind, because our glop stretched nowhere near as far as the package label promised. I was hungry when I finished, so it was not hard to imagine that Lone Wolf was too.

We divided one of my few granola bars for dessert.

I tried calling Jaqueline but the cell phone didn't work in the hollow. I hoped Lone Wolf wouldn't be offended, but told him the shelter was his, that I was putting up my tent fifty yards away to sleep without bugs.

I pitched the tent under a bower of fir trees, this time somewhat more proficiently. The evening was so quiet that in the distance I could hear the sound of a jetliner passing high overhead, possibly after taking off from one of the New York airports, just a couple of minutes' flying time away.

I wondered whether I had properly turned off the gas canister on my new hiking stove.

In Bosnia, I had seen the damage that cooking gas can cause when some British army peacekeepers took me through a village emptied by ethnic warfare in northwestern Bosnia. "Can you guess what happened here?" the lieutenant colonel asked.

No one was in the streets, but the village did not look ravaged by the kind of damage that I had seen earlier down in Mostar, a lovely old town that had been all but gutted by three-sided warfare among Serbs, Croats, and Muslims. Here no bullet marks pitted the walls, such as you find after a battle. The solid stone houses were intact, though almost all lacked roofs and doors. And the empty windows were ringed with soot, like mascara clumsily applied by a drunken old woman.

Armed militiamen came to the village one night and drove its families out in the street, the colonel explained. The raiders lit a candle in the attic of each home. Then they turned on the canisters of butane gas used to fuel the stove in every kitchen, and collected outside with their helpless prisoners to enjoy the fireworks.

The escaping gas wafted into the attic until it was ignited by the flickering candle, blowing apart the interior of each house. I was told that some militiamen laughed and wagered over which home would explode next. The familes were forced to watch everything they owned consumed by flames.

The axiom of small ethnic wars, I learned in Bosnia, is not just that your tribe must triumph, but that the other tribe must be ground into abject submission, as painfully as possible.

"The Serbs did this to the Muslims?" I asked the colonel.

He shook his head. "Here the Muslims did it to the Croatians. The village was Croat."

"It doesn't make sense," I said.

"It doesn't," the British officer agreed, "and they did it anyway."

A HANDFUL of other hikers had pulled into the Mount Algo campsite during the night, including a pair of scruffy middle-aged guys who wore their stubble as if they were born with it. They introduced themselves as Old Rabbit and Doctor Bob.

Unwilling again to cook breakfast, I hiked down to the next asphalt road, and crossed the Housatonic into the quaint little town of Kent. I stopped at Stroubel's, a bakery, and bought a scrambled-egg burrito fresh from the microwave oven, a raspberry croissant, and two cold bottles of iced tea. I sat outside under an umbrella. At the next table, a scrawny young hiker in a grimy tank top that looked about to rot off was writing postcards. When he had finished, he asked me to watch his pack while he went down to the post office.

A middle-aged tourist in an expensive golf shirt, his blond wife, and their two bored-looking children strolled in. They took another table outside the bakery, near a local man wearing a yellow-and-green Lions International cap. The old Lion, who nursed a paper cup of coffee, pointed out to the family a small bird scavenging for crumbs under their table. They stared at the old guy as though he were something to be scraped off their shoes. Concluding he was not worth their time, they pretended that he wasn't there.

Rebuffed, the old Lion turned to me for conversation.

"So where you headed?" he asked.

"Vermont," I said.

"Say, isn't that something?" he said by way of introducing his own tale. He had returned from a Lions convention in Indiana, he said, where a fellow Lion had bicycled all the way from Oregon, pulling a small trailer, and, wouldn't you know, he parked it right next to one of those fancy big rigs that must have cost a hundred thousand bucks?

"Isn't that something?" he said again, marveling at the egalitarianism of a Lions convention. Maybe that's what I needed, he said. I think he meant the bicycle trailer, not the hundred-thousand-dollar mobile home.

"That's something," I agreed. I wanted to ask how the cyclist and his trailer avoided getting flattened by traffic between Oregon and Indiana. But the old Lion moved on to a more immediate subject, the weather.

"They say it's going to get hotter," he reported.

The grimy young hiker returned and agreed to mind my pack while I went into the grocery store next door. I needed more fiber in my diet, but couldn't find any raisins on the shelves.

"I'll check downstairs in the basement," volunteered the storekeeper, and left me to watch her cash register. After a few minutes, she returned bearing a box of raisins.

Outside, the aging Lion was telling the young hiker about the Oregon cyclist who pedaled his trailer to the Lions convention in Indiana, and maybe the young hiker needed a trailer like that. The young hiker tightened the straps on his pack and hit the street.

I waved farewell to them both, shouldered my own pack, and trudged to the post office. I planned to mail all kinds of superfluous gear home, which finally came down to a fleece jacket. That was until the postal clerk took me into his confidence. "The radio said there's a fast-moving cold front moving in overnight."

Who would you tr
International? In the
small lock and chain
pack. Nobody woul
weightlifter.

In a corner of th
"Hikers," overflo
others. These be
Appalachian Trai
Lone Wolf, took
and found several it...
carry them. In the end, I left the hikers ...
solved anew to start clearing out my own closets.

I walked back across the Housatonic and found a shortcut to
the trail behind an athletic field at the Kent School. The trail went
straight up, past fat rocks upon which successive prep school
classes had painted their graduation years, until I located the
white blazes of the Appalachian Trail. Here the walking, under
hemlocks and leafier hardwoods, became easier.

Near the top of Caleb's Peak, I encountered Old Rabbit and
Doctor Bob, dozing shirtless on a couple of rock outcroppings on
their lunch break. Below us, the white church steeples poked up
through the canopy of trees along the Housatonic. It looked a lot
cooler down along the river than up here, at an altitude of 1,160
feet.

I walked on and into a sudden thunderstorm with a violent
pelting rain. For a while I took cover under some maples, until
the storm let up enough for me to begin descending a series of
big boulders that amounted to a staircase. To my left were more
vertical rock slabs, perfectly angled for rock climbing. They were
called St. John's Ledges, after not the evangelist but a local landowner of colonial times.

A heavyset man in an Adirondacks cap was cursing his way

ghtning," he complained. He said he had
n overhanging ledge, which was not the saf-
ount Greylock up in Massachusetts, lightning
hin ten feet. "[Expletive] near killed me," he an-
ow it's happening again, [expletive]. Hear it?"
dered why he bothered to keep hiking. As Mark Twain
d out in one of his letters, "Thunder is impressive, but it is
tning that does the work."

At last I descended to the Housatonic—its name means "land
beyond the mountains"—where I was rewarded by a lovely walk
five miles upstream along its grassy bank. The river trail was said
to be the longest flat stretch on the Appalachian Trail between
Maine and Georgia. Despite the recent rain, I was sweaty and
ready for a swim.

I dropped down the bank to the river's edge, and, seeing no one
about, stripped off my clothes. I piled them neatly on the grass,
hid my wallet inside one boot, and dived in. The water was bracing, though hardly deep enough to float a canoe. I lounged on a
submerged stone, revived emotionally as well as physically.

"Get out of there, you're breaking the law!" came a shout. I
splashed my way to my clothes, looked up and saw Old Rabbit and
Doctor Bob laughing uproariously. "We went swimming downstream," Old Rabbit confessed.

I packed up anyway, but they had decided to dive in again. The
rutted path took me past a ripening cornfield on my left. I was distracted by a deeper stretch of river about a mile north. This time I
went swimming with a bar of soap until, for the first time in several days, I felt clean.

At this rate, I would never reach Vermont. I walked further upstream to Stony Brook and the next campsite. It looked too buggy,
so I hiked on, across the road and up Silver Hill. The Appalachian
Trail so narrowed that warnings were posted not to trespass onto
the private land bordering both sides of the path.

At the top of Silver Hill was a comfortable campsite with a wooden pavilion open on all sides, some picnic tables and, most important, an old-fashioned water pump embedded into the rock. The Housatonic Valley lay open to the south. It looked more like a roadside rest stop on the interstate.

Old Rabbit and Doctor Bob, having passed me on my second swim, were already pitching their tent. We took turns at the pump, which sent cold water gushing through the metal spout from a well deep underground. It looked so clean that we didn't need to filter it, which was just as well. When I used my ceramic pump earlier that day, it made a loud popping sound and gave up the ghost.

The three of us talked while we prepared our respective evening meals. I told Old Rabbit and Doctor Bob that I had just retired from the *Times,* and was walking to Vermont from New York City.

"Along the Hudson?" asked Old Rabbit, whose unkempt appearance had been marginally improved by a couple of swims in the Housatonic. Had he held a Styrofoam cup in his hand, Old Rabbit would have qualified for my spare change.

"I started out on the Hudson," I said, "but walked more northeast."

"The French travelers sent back fascinating accounts of life along the Hudson River in the early nineteenth century," Old Rabbit mused. "Inspired a popular wallpaper in Paris."

Old Rabbit was alluding to *Vues d'Amérique du Nord,* a sequence of five murals printed as wallpaper by Jean Zuber in the Alsatian town of Rixheim in 1834, which helped shape how the French imagined early American life. Old Rabbit didn't get around to sharing the details of what he called "this rose-colored view of life in Jacksonian America" until much later, so I was baffled about this turn in our conversation, when everyone else I had met on the trail wanted to talk about stoves, pack weights, and miles just walked.

Old Rabbit turned down the flame under a pot of what looked like couscous, while Doctor Bob sliced and diced some fixings.

"I wrote something on the subject," Old Rabbit said, gently stirring the ingredients. "I'll send a copy if you'd like."

"I don't seem to have my card," I quipped.

"Perhaps I do," Old Rabbit said. He set aside his spoon and rummaged into his pack, from which he produced a bent wafer of cardboard.

"Robert P. Emlen," it announced. "Curator. Brown University. Providence, R.I."

My scruffy companions were not merely employed, but gainfully so. Doctor Bob, it turned out, was David Green, a lawyer in Providence. Every summer their spouses, who sounded as long-suffering as Jaqueline, let them go native on the Appalachian Trail. They were hardly the only trail travelers I would meet who had taken leave of successful lives.

I erected my tent under the trees as a hedge against the prospect of rain, and plumped out my sleeping bag. Trail travel expects self-reliance. If you don't do your own housekeeping, or tent-keeping, cook your own food, wash your own clothes, and sort your own gear, no one else is going to. Your mother won't be around and the elves will be distracted by other outdoor diversions.

The threatened rain held off overnight. Once we rose and were cooking our respective breakfasts, the sky emptied. A couple of strangers trotted in to take shelter from the heavy downpour. They plopped down their packs and shook off the rain like a pair of shaggy dogs, spraying us with droplets. They accepted, gratefully, the dregs of our breakfast coffee.

Storyteller and Jed, as they called themselves, were walking the length of the Appalachian Trail. "Never has so much effort been expended on so little accomplished as walking from Georgia to Maine," drawled Storyteller.

A lanky man with a grizzled beard that dripped raindrops as he talked, Storyteller came from North Carolina. His floppy hat made him look like a hillbilly moonshiner. He was unimpressed by the thru-hikers he had met descending from New England. "We all've sent better people north than they all've sent south," he said.

I had passed Jed sitting on a bench on Kent's main street the previous morning. Jed, who was from Michigan, said he had visited a doctor about a tick bite, and was diagnosed with Lyme disease. Jed exhibited a puffy-looking infection on his left knee below his hiking shorts. The doctor prescribed heavy antibiotics but agreed to let Jed resume walking. There was an abundance of Lyme disease among hikers this summer, he reported.

I asked Jed and Storyteller if they found time to skinny-dip in the Housatonic. "Ah didn't go swimming, Ah took a baaath," Storyteller corrected me. "Ah was naaasty."

No sooner did the rain end than Jed and Storyteller shouldered their packs and strode back into the woods. Old Rabbit and Doctor Bob shortly followed. It took me longer to collect my gear and push it into my pack, which I had reinforced with more duct tape. My destination, the next shelter at Pine Swamp Brook, was a reasonable seven miles north. Old Rabbit and Doctor Bob planned to push on another five miles and camp near Belter's Bump, a scenic overlook. Jed and Storyteller, with Maine on their minds, were desperate to make up the lost day in Kent. We might, or might not, meet again that evening.

I preferred hiking alone, without having to match the pace or patter of companions. Many people, if pressed, will admit to being afraid in the woods, where dangers are less than on a highway. Statistically, you are more likely to get killed driving home from the supermarket than sleeping on the ground under a bower of hemlocks. Catching a cold, or poison ivy, or the attention of a skunk, is another matter.

Today, I decided, would be an easy day. The trail descending from Silver Hill was steep but not precarious. The next paved road led eastward to Cornwall Bridge, less than a mile away. The old Appalachian Trail used to follow it, past a general store where you got a free soft drink when you signed the hikers' register. But the trail was rerouted north a dozen years ago, over hardier terrain.

I had packed out some trash from Silver Hill in a net bag strapped to my pack, but couldn't find any roadside trash can. I crossed Guinea Brook, a pleasant stream said to be named for a freed slave from West Africa who once made his home in these parts.

For all the calories and sweat I expended, there was a seductive simplicity to waking early and walking as far as I could before stopping to sleep. The miles, and the hours it took to cover them, were adding up. I had retired the maps of New York. Connecticut kept shrinking as the superfluous parts of that map were folded under. I neglected to tune in news on my pocket radio. I forgot to nag the *Times* about the missing paychecks. What mattered most was staying rested, fed, and hydrated enough to cover a dozen miles before sundown.

Ahead lay another hot day. The absence of skylight through the trees suggested that the terrain led upward. Traversing it was going to take more than the three or four hours I anticipated.

It had become more useful to think of walking in terms not of miles but of hours. This was how travelers throughout history, or at least before the proliferation of hourglasses, measured distance. Poorer parts of the world still do, because what matters is how long you have to walk, not how far, to get to where you need to go. On the trail, you can cover two miles an hour, plus thirty minutes for each thousand-foot change of elevation. But wristwatches don't tell you how much daylight is left, which is why increasingly I didn't wear mine, instead reckoning the time left by the dwindling gap between the setting sun and the western horizon.

I crossed a dirt road, another brook or two, and started climbing again. A side trail led temptingly downhill to a state park and
campground at Housatonic Meadows, but I couldn't afford to stop
this early. There were more old roads, some logs to take me across
another stream, more ups and downs. The trail dropped to another road, cheating me of what altitude I had gained, and then
rose again steeply. After a few hundred feet, I stopped to catch my
breath.

"You've done the worst." A heavyset stranger called from below,
"It gets much easier ahead."

He said he lived nearby. He was taking his German shepherd on
a short hike.

"Just a little further." "You're nearly there." His continuing encouragement helped propel me up a succession of steep pitches.
Then, with a wave, the stranger and his dog disappeared on a side
trail.

Thanks to them, I pushed on to the Pine Swamp near Easter
Mountain. But the campsite's stream had all but dried up, leaving
enough swamp mosquitoes to carry me off if I was foolhardy
enough to camp among them. Timber rattlesnakes had also been
sighted somewhere near here.

I walked and walked. A side trail pointed to another campsite
near Sharon Mountain, but it had no water either. The bottles I
had filled so casually with spring water from Silver Hill were dry. I
had little choice but to push on.

Trail travel gets reduced to the lowest common denominators
of survival, meaning nourishment and shelter from the rain and
cold. It matters where you choose to camp, how far you travel,
how well you're able to feed and shelter yourself. Eating means
stoking the human furnace. A thru-hiker, in covering fifteen to
twenty miles a day, can burn five thousand calories, or more than
twice the daily expenditure of a more sedentary American.

The sun was setting when I emerged from the woods to a spectacular outlook that seemed to drop straight to the plain below. A wooden ramp, built by local hang-gliders, tilted sharply downhill. Below me lay a circular automobile racetrack, shrunken to the dimensions of a toy. This was Lime Rock, a course popular with the actor Paul Newman and other racing enthusiasts. A faint roar of engines wafted up to my perch.

To the west were the Taconic Mountains in New York and, somewhere along the horizon, shadows of the Catskills and Berkshires. The hang gliding ramp took up what little horizontal space there might have been for a tent. I had no option but to move to the next campsite near Belter's Bump, a couple of miles away. It was growing dark.

A secret to the rhythm of trail travel is growing comfortable with darkness. After sunset, you can squeeze in another hour of travel that would be difficult in a city without lights.

Even so, I was exhausted when I stumbled into the Belter's Bump campsite, tripped up by invisible roots and stones. Old Rabbit and Doctor Bob had been there for at least an hour. Their tent was set up and they had just cooked dinner. In the gloom, I couldn't see much level ground, so I pitched my tent on a slight hillside across the clearing. I tried to start my stove, but it refused to work. I was too tired to fix it. My water purification pump was broken. There wasn't much left to do but climb inside my tent and try to sleep, leaving thoughts of eating and drinking fresh water for daylight.

"We have extra in our pot," Doctor Bob hollered. "How about finishing it for us?"

I pulled my bowl from my pack and crawled over, trying not to act as spent as I felt. I could not find my spoon. My companions scooped into my bowl the rest of their pasta, which had been blended with a tomato sauce as delicately sublime as any you could order in a fine restaurant, which was where it came from. Doctor Bob explained that his adopted son, a chef who presided over one of the best restaurants in Providence, had freeze-dried his special sauce for their hiking trip.

With the cooking spoon they lent me, I wolfed down the pasta and sauce before I realized that Doctor Bob and Old Rabbit had passed up second helpings for themselves. They waved off any suggestion of selflessness.

But later they talked about the phenomenon of "trail magic," how when you felt exhausted or defeated, someone or something appeared to revive you. Their pasta was an example of trail magic. People like the stranger who talked me over the rough spots that afternoon were called "trail angels." Lone Wolf, wherever he was, had gotten this far through blind faith in the kindness of others.

Some readers may think the Appalachian Trail too dangerous for their children. Would they rather have them hanging out with the in-crowd at the shopping mall? That's how ten teenage suburban heroin junkies I interviewed for the *Times* say they started out, totally bored, with nothing more challenging at hand than doing dope.

THE NEXT morning, the trail to the highway ran between cornfields and the river, and I took a wrong turn. I retraced my steps to the last cross-section and hailed a hiker who pointed me in the proper direction. Keeping the Housatonic River to my left, I came upon Doctor Bob fly-fishing. Old Rabbit was drying off from a morning swim. "Watch out for the poison ivy," Doctor Bob called as he reeled in his line. "Lots of it here."

The river looked so inviting in sunlight that I dropped my pack on the sandbar, peeled off my clothes, and jumped in. Here the river ran deep enough to swim, and I paddled into midstream while my companions resumed their hike. Younger, shriller voices were coming from around the bend. I swam hard for shore. The sandbar offered no place to hide, but I pulled my briefs on and my hiking shorts up to my knees by the time one, two, three, and four rafts filled with eleven- and twelve-year-old girls from a local camp floated into view. Once they saw me, I reacted as any mature male instinctively does when caught in a state of undress by a bevy of young females. I sucked in my gut. I would like to report they whistled, but a few only giggled.

I continued past the local high school and back to the river-bank, which now rose thirty feet above the Housatonic. The trail, bordered by stately trees, underwent a transformation. The Appalachian Trail Conference and its Connecticut chapter have created a mile-long loop accessible to people in wheelchairs by leveling the bumps, covering tree roots, and spreading gravel while preserving the vegetation.

I passed some stone slabs, described in a local leaflet as "monuments to an extraordinary vision and instant failure." The stones testified to an epic blunder of the Industrial Age in New England. An intricate network of canals was created at Falls Village more than a century and a half ago to divert the Housatonic to power turbines for a prospective industrial city. At the grand opening in 1851, the crowds gasped as a wall of water surged down the grand canal—and promptly drained away. The stone walls built to contain the diverted water were not caulked with mortar, and leaked. Falls Village remains a village next to the falls, which power three generating units of a plant operated by Northeast Utilities, capable of producing ten thousand kilowatts of electricity.

As I walked toward the plant's switchyard, a heavyset man pulled up in a glossy Buick sedan.

"Seen Rabbit?" he asked. "I'm here to pick him up."

"I camped with Old Rabbit last night," I said, puzzled about a rendezvous. Old Rabbit told me he and Doctor Bob were hiking to Salisbury, and hoped to camp at a campsite north of the village.

"This Rabbit's young," he said. "He's with Phantom."

"I never heard of Phantom," I said. "Sure it's not Doctor Bob?" How many Rabbits were in motion out there, I wondered. Dozens? Hundreds? From what little I knew of rabbits, there had to be thousands. Did rabbits have trail names, like Bad Hare?

"Rabbit said he would be with Phantom." He sat back to wait.

I walked on. When I looked back, the driver was waving at two young hikers emerging, rabbitlike and phantomlike, from the woods.

I crossed the narrow iron bridge. Below me, downstream, more camp kids were squeezing into river rafts. At the end of the bridge, a blue-and-yellow sign warned: "State Police and Neighborhood Watch Protected." Maybe from paddle-by shootings?

The flow over the Great Falls at the small hydropower station looked sparse, though the bedrock had been scrubbed bare by torrents of years past. I followed the river road uphill to another Appalachian Trail sign and turned into the woods. Ahead lay another climb, this time up Prospect Mountain, which proved easier than my vertical workouts of the last two days.

I emerged from woods into a meadow strewn with yellow wildflowers. Among the grass, now grown nearly thigh-high, were tenacious stalks of wheat or rye sown back when the land was worked. I sat down and ate the last crumbs of a cupcake I had bought at the bakery in Kent two days earlier. The morning sunshine gave way to threats of rain and the soft rumble of thunder. I removed my boots and stretched my legs. I was feeling not only sorry for myself but also a little foolish. This was retirement?

After four nights on the trail, I was whipped. Both feet were blistered. The load of my pack had rubbed my shoulders raw and raised a rash across my lower back. Even the soles of my feet felt tender as I massaged them. And after hearing Jed's graphic account of Lyme disease, I worried about a semicircle of tiny insect bites that appeared overnight inside my left forearm. I was ready to stop, not for good but overnight in Salisbury, the next town, where there would be a doctor if the bites swelled into an infection. This close to the Appalachian Trail, Salisbury would surely have a camping store to replace my broken water filter.

Before resuming my slog up Prospect Mountain, I dug out my cell phone and dialed the White Hart Inn in Salisbury. The phone couldn't find anything from the dead space I occupied. This motivated me to climb higher. After three tries along the ascent, I got through to the inn and booked a room for that night. The White Hart was well recommended, and could set me back a couple hundred dollars.

That was a new downside of retirement—paying from my pocket what used to be covered by the expense account. When the *Times* urged us to economize, it meant flying economy instead of business class, staying in less lavish accommodations where bedtime mints were not imported from Switzerland, routing our telephone calls through a toll-free number, and saving receipts for meals over twenty-five dollars. It did not mean traveling on foot, buying day-old muffins, and sleeping in the bushes.

"I'd like your hiker's rate, please," I bluffed to the young woman who took my reservation. "I'm calling from the Appalachian Trail." If that failed, I could plead for their corporate discount, their AARP senior's discount, maybe their panhandler's discount.

"Hiker's rate?" She paused for a moment to check. "Oh yes, that would be eighty dollars." In other words, a fraction what I had expected to pay.

A craving for crème brûlée seized me. Energized by the prospect of a dinner, bath, and bed worthy of an expense account, I pushed over the fourteen-hundred-foot top of Prospect Mountain. It wasn't quite a summit. The woods, primarily maples and pines, were filigreed with delicate green ferns. The trail snaked over and around the mountain into more woods carpeted with dead leaves and past more stone walls. To the northeast was a village, but it didn't look like Salisbury.

Three quarters of this land was cleared and cultivated in this corner of Connecticut by the time of the Civil War. I was looking at the regrowth of woodland on the neglected slopes. A week earlier I had been lamenting the destruction of woodland for suburban housing tracts in Westchester County. Yet here in Connecticut, and further north as I walked, the forest had silently taken back what people no longer used. Forestry experts called it a "succession," and I felt like applauding.

A brisker wind blew up. There was rain hidden in the dark clouds sweeping low overhead. I headed for the shelter of the woods. But the shower was brief and lacked thunder or lightning.

The vistas improved during my descent westward. Rand's View, an outlook named after a local farm family, presented a panorama of lush meadows sloping down to bales of recently mown hay. Beyond the tree line, more meadows stretched to green hills in the distance. A slight mist rising from the valley, still glistening from the rain made it look like a painting by Constable.

The view so enchanted me that when it came time to leave, I couldn't remember from which direction I had left the trail. The sun was no help because the sky had clouded over. It could set me back several hours if I turned the wrong way.

My indecision brought back a nightmare of a ride on a police helicopter from the Peruvian town of Ayacucho, over the Andean cordillera and into the Upper Apurimac Valley, to meet some coca growers who were being arm-twisted to embrace the alternative development of respectable crops. Our helicopter, a clumsy Russian-built crate, skimmed the bare peaks and dropped through layers of heavy clouds into wet jungle. The cloud cover seemed to follow us, pressing the old helicopter into some kind of box canyon. The pilot spiraled deeper into the vortex of jungle as he kept banking, seeking an exit, until we were so hemmed in that I thought I could touch the passing vines. With each new direction, another wall loomed out of the mist. The cop beside me vomited on his submachine gun. It seemed it would be a matter of minutes, or seconds, until the helicopter snagged and crashed. With no room left to maneuver, the pilot chose a creek and followed it through the clouds until we broke free and emerged into the open valley of the Apurimac River. The pilot was grinning with relief when we climbed out.

Here in Connecticut, the guessing was easier. I used my compass to shoot a series of azimuths to prominent hills around me and imposed them on my map to confirm which way to walk. Thereafter, whenever it was time for a break, I left my trekking poles pointing in the direction I was headed.

Was it Will Rogers who said, "It isn't what you don't know that gets you into trouble, but what you know that ain't so"?

I stopped at Billy's View, named after a relative of the property's former owner. It looked past a few maple trees down to the Salmon Kill Valley. The trail continued over a curious eminence known as Barrack Matiff, possibly a corrupted Dutch phrase; my guidebook didn't know the origin. The descent from the last ridge was rugged, on a narrow path broken by sudden switchbacks. At one point, I found myself hanging apelike from a log ladder.

My walk out of the woods and down Lower Cobble Road into Salisbury took me past the railway bed of the bygone Central Northeastern Railroad. Back in 1871, according to the sign, it traveled from Hartford, Connecticut, to Millerton, New York, and later to Poughkeepsie, near the Hudson River. It was the prime means of transport in those days, with special picnic trains for family outings. Its telegraph line carried news of the outside world.

Today, Salisbury is an upscale tourist destination and a haven for second homes of affluent city dwellers. But it was incorporated in 1741 as a farming settlement and source of iron ore mined from the local hills. Salisbury's foundries contributed cannons and cannonballs to the American Revolution, the War of 1812, and the Civil War. The local iron industry went out of business about a century ago.

The White Hart Inn, a pretty white building, lies at the northern end of town, near the village green. A sweet lass at the reception desk found my reservation. "We have a nice room for you on the second floor," she said. "Oh, you forgot to fill in your car license."

"I don't have a car," I countered. "And how about a room on the ground floor?" I doubted that I had enough strength to lug my pack up the narrow staircase.

She found me another room in a ground-floor annex, with a double bed, floral wallpaper, and a television set that seemed locked on C-SPAN. I spent the next half-hour under a hot shower, scrubbing off dirt. Then I pulled my damp sleeping bag and tent from my pack and spread them over the desk and chairs to dry. I dumped old bread and sausage into the wastebasket. Within minutes, my chintz-filled room smelled like a shelter back on the trail.

I headed back to the reception desk and asked the sweet lass to recommend where I might buy a water purification pump. She suggested the Village Store. It was a five-minute walk down to the store, where I found sun hats, leather walking shoes, women's blouses, pedal pushers, pastel T-shirts, even a pair of Rollerblades, none of them in my size. But when I flashed my broken pump, the clerk recoiled.

"We don't have that," she said. "What is it?"

"A hand pump to filter drinking water," I said. "Where can I buy another?"

"Great Barrington?"

"Where's Great Barrington?" I asked.

"Massachusetts?"

Since this was still Connecticut, I gave up and headed across the street to buy bread and other trail provisions.

After seventeen years abroad as a foreign correspondent, I continue to be dazzled by the inexhaustible bounty of an American supermarket. Living four years in the old Soviet Union, we never found enough fruit and vegetables, fresh or frozen, except in the ubiquitous form of cabbages. One winter, there was no juice anywhere in Moscow, including the dollars-only stores reserved for foreigners. Pickings were better in Cairo, though the milk our kids drank came from water buffaloes. In Beijing, we toted frozen orange juice and breakfast cereal back from Hong Kong as carry-on luggage.

But nowhere did I find anything to approach the cornucopia that Americans take for granted in a supermarket, even in a village as small as Salisbury. Russian friends who visited the United States talked foremost about shelves overstocked with delicacies, and none of it rationed! I knew communism was on the skids when I watched a queue of Muscovites jostling to buy watermelons hardly more than a mile from where the tanks and missiles paraded on Red Square.

And so in Salisbury, when a shopper ahead of me in the checkout line whimpered about the caloric content of something in her cart, I wanted to snap, "Lady, the rest of the world never had it so good."

The cornucopia of junk snacks displayed in the Salisbury supermarket reminded me how hungry I was. I could have made a three-course dinner by ripping open the pretzels, corn chips, and

Oreo cookies and devouring them on the spot. Jaqueline had warned me about the perils of shopping on an empty stomach.

After hovering over the gallon jugs of orange juice, I limited my purchase to food that I would eat on the trail. Even so, my grocery bags felt ominously heavy when I hoisted them from the checkout counter and lugged them back to my room.

I tried to call Bruce Bernstein, one of my college classmates who had offered to hike with me after I hit Massachusetts. I left a message on his answering machine, then went downstairs and loitered outside the dining room until it opened, wearing a shirt that my wife made me pack and wrinkled khaki trousers. Two elderly couples well into their seventies walked in a little later, making me feel less alone though no younger. The early bird crowd had arrived.

"May I offer you a cocktail?" prompted the waitress.

"A cold Long Trail lager," I said. "Better make that two Long Trails," I added, though I had three in mind.

I scanned the fancy menu.

"Okay," I wanted to say, "start bringing it out."

Instead, I pretended I wasn't famished. "I'll have the herb-grilled salmon fillet with Nicoise olives, whole-grain Dijon mustard, and asparagus served over Italian orzo," I said, reading from the menu. I didn't want them to omit a single olive, asparagus tip, or mustard seed.

"And to start"—I skipped over the selections of soups and rabbit-food salads—"the chicken-and-cheese quesadilla."

"The quesadilla's very filling," the waitress cautioned.

"Yes, the quesadilla." Here, a mock pause. "And for dessert, your banana pudding pie." It was the closest the kitchen had to crème brûlée, and I didn't want them running out.

The waitress filled her little pad. "You may bring the bread and butter right away," I hinted.

When I returned to my room after devouring everything on my

plate, Bruce called back. He was still in New York, he said, but would drive up to the Berkshires tomorrow. He proposed picking me up between noon and one P.M. If I walked north from Salisbury along Route 41, he would spot me and stop.

"I'll be wearing—"

Bruce's laughter cut me off. "You're sixty-five years old and carrying a big pack? You won't be hard to find."

I slept no worse than anyone else might after trudging eleven miles over mountains, downing three beers, grilled salmon, a chicken quesadilla, and a banana pudding pie, then stretching out on a queen-size inner-spring mattress in a darkened room in front of C-SPAN.

THERE MUST be something metabolic in hiking that diverts the primal urge from sex to food. I kept recalling some memorable dinners as a foreign correspondent, from pangolin on Hainan Island in the South China Sea, to horse sausage and fermented mare's milk in Central Asia, bear nostrils in Manchuria, forest rat in West Africa, snake in Canton, and slimy sea slugs elsewhere in coastal China. (As for what pangolin, a scaly anteater, tastes like, if you ever tasted defeat, you've tasted pangolin, because eating it seemed not unlike eating crow.)

These were exotic delicacies, not necessarily delicious, but in no way inferior to the culinary delights at your McDonald's or Taco Bell.

During the Vietnam War, one of my best meals was in a fishing village south of Danang, where an aging French army veteran in shorts and flip-flops ran a café on the pier that served boiled lobster and shrimp freshly caught, to be dipped in melted butter and consumed with crusty French baguettes and raw Algerian wine.

Still, for ambiance nothing beat a four-hour dinner with an

opium warlord in Yangon, which used to be called Rangoon before the military junta misruling Burma renamed the country Myanmar. My host, Luo Xinghan, was blamed for originating the bulk of heroin smuggled into the United States through the 1960s, back when he was sought as Lo Hsing Han. (The discrepancy has to do with different pinyin and Wade-Giles transliterations of Chinese.)

Three of us reporters—from *Newsweek International,* the *Christian Science Monitor* and the *New York Times,* had secured rare visas to investigate opium cultivation, which the junta claimed to be trying to suppress.

We went into the heart of the Golden Triangle, on the mountainous Shan plateau east of the Salween River, where everyone looked twelve years old and barely five feet tall, though you refrained from pointing this out because everyone was also armed to the teeth. We visited a village of friendly Baptists who went to church and sang hymns you would recognize, when they weren't out growing opium themselves and puffing or peddling it. And we choppered into a remote poppy field that the government said it had seized. The slender white flowers were slit and milked of their precious sap by the time we arrived.

When we returned to Yangon we resolved to look up Luo Xinghan, and Khun Sa, another opium warlord who had also retired to the capital.

We never heard from Khun Sa, who was reported in poor health, though it improved enough once a week for him to play golf with some junta generals. But we got a message from Luo, or Lo, promising to meet us that night at a luxury hotel downtown. We had anticipated a modest interview that would wind up before the hotel coffee shop closed, but when we asked for Luo, we were ushered into a private dining room. The circular table was heaped with Chinese appetizers.

Luo showed up wearing a simple white shirt and black trousers. He looked older than in the wanted posters. He waved us into chairs around the big table and sat down with his small retinue, including his younger brother. White-jacketed waiters paraded in with steaming platters of chicken, pork, beef, whole fish, shrimp, sea slugs of course, and other delicacies whose origins were best left unexamined. Our host served the first round, reaching around the table with his chopsticks to choose samples from various platters and drop them on our plates, his gold Rolex encrusted with diamonds waving over my plate. "Chi ba, chi ba!" our host urged in Chinese. Eat please! It became evident that Luo had not rented the dining room. He owned it, and the kitchen and hotel too.

The quantity of food matched the quality. I counted up forty different dishes and appetizers before losing track. Deferential waiters kept replacing the platter. They transferred the contents to our plates and topped off our glasses of beer.

Our interview lacked only an interpreter. Luo was Kokang Chinese, an ethnic group from the Burma's borderlands with China, and spoke not a word of English. Little Brother jumped in with his rudimentary English, and I dredged up my rusty Chinese, which the *Times* paid for me to learn before I was posted to Beijing. Our translations sounded more like a game of charades.

It was awkward asking our host how he had gotten rich in one of the world's most violent and depraved lines of work. But Luo evinced neither hesitation nor shame as he described moving opium by the ton into northern Thailand to be refined into heroin. "My mule trains extended three miles through the mountains," he recalled, nostalgic over the memory of so much dope bound for the American market.

Luo claimed that he trafficked in opium to stop greedier traffickers from ripping off his people, who grew the poppies to feed their families. His mercenaries guarding the caravans were, he said, Burmese patriots who fought Chinese communists before going commercial. And his eventual capture in Thailand, his extradition back to Burma for trial, and the death sentence hanging over him were based on misunderstandings. Reprieved from the gallows, he went home and saved for retirement with a bakery here, some teak logging and jade mining there. He no longer trafficked in drugs, he contended, having discovered that they were hazardous to his customers' health. With each self-deprecating gesture, his diamond-studded gold Rolex sparkled under the chandelier.

I couldn't figure out why he wanted to tell us this, until he got to the point after four hours. Luo was shocked when one of his sons, who ran a murky trading company from Singapore, had been refused an American visa. Luo himself wanted to visit another son now living in Los Angeles, though he couldn't remember the address. Would we put in a good word with the United States authorities?

After all, he asked us, "Have I done anything wrong?"

AFTER A breakfast of bacon, eggs, and coffee at the White Stag Inn, I loaded my pack, filled my water bottles from the sink, paid my bill, and headed north out of Connecticut. Walking was easier now that the spell of hot weather seemed to have broken. My blisters still hurt, despite the moleskin patches I had applied.

I considered lounging on the grass and waiting for Bruce on the outskirts of Salisbury. But walking to Vermont meant walking every inch of the way. I needed to cover as many miles as possible before Bruce overtook me.

The locals refer to the stretch of Route 41 running north into Massachusetts as Undermountain Road, because it runs along the base of a prominent mountain ridge. It was pleasant to abandon the Appalachian Trail, at least for a while, to discover more of rural New England.

Old farmhouses along Undermountain Road were renovated elaborately, and at great expense. Some had hung hand-painted signs out front coyly identifying them as "Farm." But it was a few more miles before I came upon a field of corn ripening in the sun.

Almost every old house had been gussied up with modern add-ons at a total cost that would bankrupt a small developing nation. Behind the manicured hedges I passed were new brick walkways, stone patios, imported lawn furniture, satellite dishes, tennis courts, and swimming pools, sometimes all clumped to-gether, as though the architectural simplicity bequeathed by the original builders of these homes fell short of self-sufficiency. Play-ing at shepherd and shepherdess on country weekends these days can set you back a lot of money. The Chinese describe such excess as "drawing a snake and adding feet." Occasionally, a homestead had evolved from a trailer or humble cottage. Several cottages had signs out front announcing "Sale Pending." They looked more valuable for the land they occupied.

A handsome woman in a sleeveless black turtleneck swung her enormous black SUV across my path, smiled an apology, and en-tered a long dirt road leading to a house somewhere out of sight. A kid in sweatshirt and shorts darted out at me on off-white Rollerblades, executed figure-eight turns on the road until a car appeared, then glided back to the safety of his asphalt driveway. An oncoming green car stopped and a man in a blue shirt leaned across from the driver's seat. "Would you like a ride?" he asked. "I'm turning around shortly."

"No thanks."

He looked at my pack. "Are you sure?"

"Yes," I said, "but thanks anyway." It was the first time that anyone had stopped to offer me a ride, and the only time that a stranger would do so on my journey.

A man in gray shirt and shorts who was picking up along his property stood and stretched as I walked by.

"A cool day," he called. "How are you doing?"

"Fine," I said. "How far's Massachusetts?"

"Just over the bridge." He pointed to an inconsequential bridge spanning a creek that more or less defined the state line, a hundred yards north.

Massachusetts

There was always more in the world than men could see, walked they ever so slowly; they will see it no better going fast.

John Ruskin

Four

THE JOURNEY of ten thousand miles begins with a single step, says one of those venerable Chinese sages. Two weeks of walking had enlightened me to a painful corollary of this ancient wisdom, which was that a single step should never begin without expensive socks.

The socks I wore were cheap cotton. They were chafing fresh hot spots on whatever skin on my heels and toes had not turned raw. A few miles into Massachusetts, I sat down on the roadside grass and peeled off the sweaty socks to inspect the damage.

"Tell those who worry about their health that they may be already dead," Henry Thoreau quipped. His feet probably weren't hurting when he wrote it.

The road I walked into Massachusetts had been recently black-topped, with a newly painted double yellow line. As I massaged my sore feet, I saw rolling pastures to the east, broken by a line of old trees; the countryside rolled down to a long open valley. To the west, behind me, rose the long mountainous ridgeline followed by the Appalachian Trail, which I had temporarily abandoned.

I had just finished applying fresh strips of moleskin when a black Grand Cherokee stopped and Bruce Bernstein jumped out. He still had the powerful shoulders and arms of a collegiate swimmer, and even with his trimmed graying beard looked younger than I was feeling.

Bruce, a clinical psychologist, was about to fetch Herb Roskind, another classmate who was flying in from Martha's Vineyard and would land his Beech Bonanza on a private airstrip in Great Barrington. Bruce invited me into his car, until I reminded him that I was walking to Vermont every inch of the way and didn't want to cheat. In the end, I tossed my tent, sleeping bag, and stove into the back of his Grand Cherokee. We agreed to rendezvous later at the Berkshire School.

With my pack stripped closer to the weight that I had toted from New York City to Pawling, I felt as though I was flying down the road, my feet barely touching the ground. They were still taking a beating, so at a trail leading to the Race Brook Falls, I pulled off my boots and tied them to the back of my pack, and put on my rubber sandals. The Tevas, designed for river running, gripped the asphalt. Even flip-flopping down the road, I began covering better distance.

It was a good day, slightly overcast and cool, with encouraging patches of sunshine. Roadside splashes of daylilies glowing with orange flowers swayed in the pleasant breeze, which was just persistent enough to discourage the mosquitoes.

There were more of New England's historically ubiquitous stone walls, but these were well tended and maintained, unlike the walls I had encountered falling down in the woods.

"Yard Sale Ahead," announced a homemade cardboard sign. I was moving into country where frugal families clean out, fix, and polish stuff that they no longer need and someone else might buy. Most of what I saw for sale on lawns as I walked north would have been discarded in New York City or Scarsdale. But here and there were pretty teacups, and other china and glassware glistening on blankets and tables. At a yard sale in Vermont, I once snapped up an old-fashioned school desk for thirty-five dollars. But there was no way to carry what I was passing, not even a mirror in a potentially antique hardwood frame that would have looked great in our Vermont hallway.

An old farmer wearing a windbreaker limped down to his woodpile and stopped to wonder what I was doing near his driveway. It was a matter of years until I looked like him.

Time for an energy boost. I unwrapped a chunk of baker's chocolate from my pocket. For a continuous walk, few snacks taste better than semisweet chocolate. Food writers can be a pretentious, irritating lot, and no more so than when they disparage chocolate desserts as sinful or decadent. Sin and decadence are words that define the human condition, not desserts. Sinful? Dropping poison gas on the Kurds when you're the despot of Iraq is sinful. Decadent? Ordering forty-dollar entrées and sixty-dollar bottles of wine in an exclusive restaurant in Manhattan is decadent, when the less privileged are sleeping on the grates outside.

Chocolate is merely delicious, and what's the sin in that? Its bad rap boils down to a frivolous complaint about calories that could be burned off easily, if not effortlessly, by hitting the Appalachian Trail for a few hundred miles. It's an idea worth a few bucks. While I walked, I imagined a commercial like this:

"Hello there. I'm Melissa, and I want to tell you that there is a way to lose weight without having to go on a diet. Like so many of us fuller-figure girls, I had a hard time saying no to that second helping when I visited the buffet table at our country club. Sometimes after we went to bed, I'd sneak down to the refrigerator and dip into the double-chocolate-fudge frozen yogurt. When I had to graduate from a size fourteen, George said he loved me enough to enroll me in this exercise program that simply melted off the pounds. The caring counselors dropped me off way up north in the Pemigewasset Wilderness of New Hampshire, and said I wouldn't see my husband till Massachusetts. As I walked south through the lovely woods, a counselor would surprise me daily with another fat-free tofu bar and tell me to stop sniveling. When George finally hugged me on top of Mount Greylock, he couldn't stop raving about my figure. And all those tears of self-pity left my complexion feeling soft and fresh. Now every time the girls at my bridge club ask how I managed to lose forty pounds without actually going on a diet, I say to myself, 'Thank you, Appalachian Trail!'"

And here the voice-over: "For weight loss without dieting, try the Appalachian Trail. It's more than just mosquitoes and companions who haven't bathed. It's sweating your way to success!"

WHEN I met Bruce and Herb at the Berkshire School, a choral festival was in progress. Lush voices emanated from within the gymnasium. Mentally marking the spot where I would resume walking the next day, I climbed into Bruce's car for the short ride to his house in Egremont. Two other classmates, Joel Mitchell and Dick Bohanon, were driving up from New York. I hardly knew these guys in college, but they were coming to hike along with me the next day.

They insisted on taking me to dinner at the Old Mill, a popular restaurant, where I remedied the day's calorie deficit with chilled melon soup, swordfish, and flourless chocolate cake with unstinting whipped cream.

We returned to the Bernsteins' weekend house, where Bruce's wife, Lita, had prepared for me a cushiony futon with down pillows in a quiet basement bedroom. Unable to keep my eyes open or carry on a coherent conversation, I retired and collapsed until morning.

Lita was hesitant to join the five of us on our hike. "I don't want to be in the way," she told us. Ah, but how could Lita, with her sublime gift of cooking, ever be in the way? She had grown up in a hotel family in the Catskills, Bruce explained, and she knew hospitality. While we lounged around the living room, our spines sagging against the cushions of the sofa and chairs like indolent sophomores, Lita whipped up a fantastic breakfast frittata of eggs, cheese, tomatoes, peppers, and zucchini, waving off with her spoon our insincere offers of assistance in the kitchen. She called us to the table and served the sizzling frittata with a fresh fruit compote, bagels, and coffee.

Unable to postpone gainful exercise any longer, I announced my return to the Appalachian Trail. Herb offered to accompany me, having attended the Berkshire School and worked on the satellite trail leading to the AT. Bruce proposed that he, Joel, and Dick enter the trail from the north and hike toward us.

"There used to be a great view here," Herb said as we gained the ridge. "It doesn't look right. Those trees didn't used to be there."

"Perhaps because that was forty-eight years ago," I ventured.

As we paused to watch a chicken hawk stealing a ride on the air currents, Bruce and Joel hiked up to meet us. Dick, a federal judge, had exercised judicial prudence and turned back when pain in his problematic knee counseled against continuing.

We stood cluttering up the Appalachian Trail when from over the horizon of Mount Bushnell a lissome maiden floated toward us in a snug T-shirt and skimpier shorts. Brushing back long chestnut hair, she asked directions to the shelter at Sage Ravine, on the Connecticut state line. I volunteered with my trail map. She thanked me with a flutter of her wide blue eyes, tugged on the pack straps bracketing her admirable bosom, and wafted away.

As we watched her tanned legs disappear into the brush of Mount Everett, it was left to Bruce to express aloud what we sexagenarians were thinking.

"That's an awfully big pack she's carrying," Bruce said. "What do you suppose it weighs?"

"An apparition," interjected Herb.

Our day went literally downhill from there. The descent from Jug End was steep and exposed, dropping through outcrops of sheer rock. This was not a time to develop a painful cramp, which Herb now felt in his thigh, all but immobilizing him. Bruce tried to help, then announced, "My knee's gone on me."

Joel passed them and took the lead. "What do you call that muscle in your leg that you use to stop from going down too fast?" he asked.

"The braking muscle, I think," I said.

"That sounds right," Joel winced, "because I just pulled mine."

My own right ankle felt stuffed with broken glass, reminding me that I had forgotten to take my Vioxx. Our gallant expedition was presenting enough physical afflictions to convene a medical convention of geriatrists.

In our chauvinist limping and groaning, we quite forgot about Lita, who, having demurred, "Don't let me get in the way," was back in the Bernsteins' kitchen whipping up fresh ingredients from a local farm into a magnificent dinner. The feast she prepared for our less-than-triumphant return was enough to feed every thru-hiker on the Appalachian Trail that day.

When we finally sputtered to level ground, my ankle felt better. To accumulate more distance, I proposed continuing alone a few miles to a roadside parking lot where Joel had parked his Subaru. I crossed Curtis Road into a pine forest, emerging onto a busier road with a farmhouse. The trail crossed through a turnstile, to keep cows from escaping, into a meadow.

At the turnstile, someone had left a frosty unopened can of grape soda as encouragement to a wayfaring stranger—trail magic. With less than two miles to go, I left the donation for a thirstier traveler.

Traversing the swamp that followed, I balanced on a series of narrow walkways, called puncheons, that rested on partly submerged logs or concrete blocks. A plump black-and-yellow snake sunning on one puncheon regarded my approach with annoyance, then flopped into the water. A more solid bridge carried me over Hubbard Brook.

Within minutes, I saw an eroded stone marker on the other side of Sheffield Road. "Last battle of Shays rebellion was here," the inscription announced, and added a date, "Feb. 27, 1787."

This otherwise unremarkable field on the Sheffield Plain marked the final gasp of an agrarian revolt led by Daniel Shays, a defiant veteran of the battles of Bunker Hill and Saratoga in the American Revolution. The insurgents, impoverished to the point of desperation, tried to shut down local courts to stop foreclosures of their farms and other property. It was here the ragtag rebels formed up to be defeated by a superior Massachusetts militia. The state Supreme Court condemned Shays to death, but he fled north to Vermont, which would not join the Union for another four years. Shays eventually was pardoned and settled prudently across the border in New York, where he lived to a respectable old age on his veteran's pension. You wouldn't learn any of this from the terse inscription on the stone battlefield marker, which lacked even the grammatically requisite apostrophe.

The journalist in me wondered how Shays's rebellion, which threatened the stability of the new United States, had played in the newspapers of those post-revolutionary days. On the front page? Or back with the used-harness-and-saddle ads? The uprising was worthy enough of news, but did the editors find it newsworthy?

THERE IS a difference between what seems worthy of news and what becomes newsworthy. Suppose you get offered an exclusive interview with a politician who has little to say beyond his own self-promotion. Accept, and you get trapped between the politician's flack, who asks how soon his master's platitudes will be splashed all over page one, and your unimpressed editors, who ask why this kind of drivel, exclusive or not, should run at all. For that reason, I tended to be skittish of interviews with unelected leaders of small countries, except in Yemen, where I had no choice.

I had returned to Sanaa after traveling for a week in the wild backcountry, and booked a scarce seat on a flight back to Cairo, where I was based at the time. The night before my departure, I received a call from a government flunky.

"Your interview with our president has been approved," he said.

The news took me by surprise. "I didn't ask to see your president," I replied.

I had already interviewed the Yemeni prime minister and the foreign minister, neither of whom said anything interesting enough to clamber onto the front page. Sanaa's police chief, on the other hand, was definitely newsworthy. He had solved the city's illegal parking problem by marching down the main street with a bat, smashing in the windshield of every car that gut instinct told him didn't belong there.

"Your interview with our president is scheduled for ten o'clock tomorrow," the flunky said.

I lunged for my excuse. "Oh dear, that won't work," I said. "My flight to Cairo leaves at eight."

"Your flight to Cairo has been delayed for technical reasons," the flunky said.

"For how long?" I asked.

"Until after you finish your interview."

I was escorted the next morning into the presidential palace, through corridors filled with armed soldiers. The president rose from behind a large desk to greet me. He wore his army uniform, with a pistol jammed in his belt. He read from a sheet of answers crafted for questions that I hadn't posed. The English translation handed to me afterward confirmed that the president had said nothing newsworthy beyond his bold assertion of historical friendship between our two peoples. The interview wasn't a total loss, because the president presented me with a sack of fragrant coffee beans and a curved ceremonial dagger on an embroidered belt.

His aide tugged at my sleeve before I could ask more questions. "Your flight is leaving," he said.

I was hustled into a jeep filled with soldiers waving AK-47s and driven much too fast from the palace out to the airport, whose shimmering tarmac looked about to melt in the hundred-degree heat. A solitary Yemeni Airways jetliner sat at the far end of the runway. I staggered up the ramp, juggling my luggage, coffee beans, and dagger—no time for security checks—and took the only vacant seat. It was hot inside. The other passengers, from an American tour group, had boarded in Nairobi under the illusion that their flight went directly to Cairo, and had been sitting in Sanaa all morning.

"You kept us here four goddamn hours, you son of a bitch," shouted one man, the most soft-spoken. "Satisfied?"

"I was interviewing the president of Yemen," I said. "He gave me this coffee."

Fortunately, their seat belts restrained my fellow passengers during takeoff. Once we reached cruising altitude, the co-pilot whisked me into the cockpit, and cleared the flight engineer's seat for me.

"We almost had a mutiny there," the co-pilot said. "You're safer with us."

*   *   *

BEFORE BREAKFAST the next morning, Bruce and I sat talking about the days when Dartmouth, like some other Ivy League colleges, maintained an unspoken quota limiting the number of Jews it admitted. To be admitted to Dartmouth, Jewish classmates like Bruce had to be not only smarter than the rest of us but also more competent.

At Dartmouth, Bruce had been a varsity swimmer. It got him into Sigma Chi, an exclusive fraternity whose rules in those days barred Jews and blacks. The Dartmouth chapter had ignored the national discriminatory policy. He didn't reflect on his exceptional status, he told me, until he took some summer courses at the University of Wisconsin and visited the Sigma Chi fraternity there. Its Aryans-only culture made Bruce so uncomfortable that he felt guilty about having joined Sigma Chi at Dartmouth. He wondered if he had pledged out of pride, he said, to prove he could be welcome where other Jews were not.

I hadn't joined a fraternity at Dartmouth because none of the ones I wanted would have me. It upset me at the time, though looking back, I can't recall the Greek letters of the houses that rejected me. I threw myself into learning Russian, which landed me eventually in Moscow for the *Times* and launched me as a foreign correspondent. How would life have turned out if I had been goofing around a fraternity house instead?

Lita mentioned a local country club near their Berkshires house that finally opened up its tennis courts to Jews, but not its golf course. She figured the discrimination was rooted in dollars and cents. The club members feared that Jews would drive up membership costs by demanding good food, better service, and central heating.

The influx of weekend people into towns like Egremont had created a two-class system, of people from New York and Boston who brought in the money, and the local residents, a lot of whom wound up working for them. Bruce said his neighbor quit his job driving a beer truck because he could make as much doing jobs for more affluent part-time residents. The neighbor had just built a wooden bridge for Bruce over a marsh in a corner of his property.

The Bernsteins despaired that the ambience that had attracted them to the Berkshires was changing because of an influx of New Yorkers who had wearied of the resorts on eastern Long Island and their high prices and traffic jams.

"Now they're coming here from the Hamptons," Lita said, "and they're bringing their habits with them."

Bruce counted off five restaurants and shops in Great Barrington that now featured sushi. "Ten years ago," he recalled, "people here were saying, 'Who wants to eat raw fish?'"

I HAD shed five pounds from my pack, dumping the overweight into a box that I mailed home from the Egremont post office. As I struggled into it again, I realized that the pack was no lighter because I had bought a week's worth of food and a new pump.

As we formed up on Shays's battlefield, Lita urged me to stay over another night. "We're going out to a nice restaurant."

There is a siren appeal to sloth. Lita's invitation was tempting, but if I didn't get back on the trail, it would become even harder tomorrow. We walked for a couple of miles together before my friends bade me a final farewell. After they drove off, I discovered that I had left my Teva sandals in Bruce's Jeep.

Here the Housatonic flows graciously between tree-lined banks. The afternoon had turned hot. Before crossing the next bridge, I considered cooling off in the river's inviting water as I had done back in Connecticut. My eye caught the sign nailed to a tree: "WARNING," it said in bold letters. "Housatonic River Fish Contaminated with PCB's. DO NOT EAT fish, frogs or turtles from the river."

The sign did not tell me to avoid swimming in it, just to avoid other creatures who did. But since the Housatonic was polluted enough to render fish, frogs, and turtles unfit for human consumption, I walked on.

It took a while to slide back into the rhythm of the trail. A hot afternoon hike into the Berkshire highlands took me over some exposed ledges offering good views of the Taconic Mountains I had crossed in Connecticut the previous week and, further to the west, the Catskills in New York.

After a few hours hiking over East Mountain, I reached the Tom Leonard shelter at the base of a short cliff. The shelter was named for a "ridge runner," a volunteer trail patrolman, who had died in 1985 of an undiagnosed neurological illness. The ample shelter, including an overhanging loft added to the sleeping platforms, was built in 1988 using wood and other material airlifted in by a Massachusetts Air National Guard helicopter. "Please enjoy this structure but leave it in good condition for others to enjoy," a sign said.

Buttermilk Ski Area lay on the other side of the ridge, according to my map, but the shelter felt so isolated that it could as well have been perched on the far side of Baffin Island. My search for water carried me a steep quarter-mile downhill to a small spring.

I had the place to myself, but it seemed a little spooky and, worse, it attracted mosquitoes. I felt safer in the woods. I pitched my tent near the rim of a cliff that offered sweeping views to the south. This reduced the odds that some deranged intruder would bludgeon me to a pulp while I slept; he would stumble over the edge first. My concern was irrational, of course, because homicidal stalkers are unlikely to be obsessed with you once you get older, and in any case seldom climb hills in the dark.

I felt too exhausted to sleep right away. Before buttoning up in my tent, I sat outside at the top of the cliff and scanned the first stars in the immense night sky. Stretching back against the rock, I shut my eyes for a while, then stared again at the canopy glittering overhead. I sought out the Big Dipper and followed the line of its lip to the North Star.

These were the same glorious constellations I had studied one night in the Ogaden desert of Ethiopia, out with a band of guerrillas who were at war with the government. The other journalists included a foxy young French freelance photographer and a lusty Dane who seemed bent on seduction. I'm not sure what he saw in her beyond her beguiling resemblance to the actress Juliette Binoche and her aversion to brassieres. "Tu á finis?" ("Are you done?") she teased between kisses as they nuzzled beneath the canvas tarpaulin that the guerrillas had supplied for all of us to keep warm. Sharing their space under the tarp, I hoped that passion, once ignited, would not embolden the randy Dane to pounce recklessly and miss his Juliette, landing on me instead. I fell asleep through what followed, but her fetching smirk and his sullen silence the next day when the guerrillas took us out to inspect some burnt-out battle tanks suggested that the Dane had been outfoxed.

Here in Massachusetts, these stars would have looked no different to the first explorers in New England, or to the Native Americans who already lived here, or for that matter, to Jesus on the gospel road. Whatever changed and decayed on earth, the stars would be there to chart a constant course for the next hiker, unless man's infernal ingenuity caused the galaxy itself to disappear in a permanent haze of auto exhaust and acid rain.

On the horizon, a light twinkled from a radio tower atop a mountain to the south. Another light blinked from an aircraft high overhead. Its faint drone faded into silence. Absolute silence seems blissful when you've been living in the city, but when solitude and darkness surround you, it can become unnerving, even ominous. There comes a point at which the absence of noise no longer helps you to sleep, and the mind plays tricks. Was the rustle of leaves against my tent the feather step of a mountain lion or, far more likely, a chipmunk? I opted for marauding chipmunks and dozed off, finding clarity at last in the power of silence.

I awoke at dawn and boiled water for two packets of instant oatmeal, leaving enough for tea. My pack still took too long to load, and I didn't hit the trail until the sun had cleared the eastern hills.

I worked my way around the rocky edges of Ice Gulch, a deep glacial gully that trapped the winter snows and ice for well into late summer. This was not a place to slip and break an ankle, because it didn't look possible to climb out. I leaned over the edge but could not see a bottom to the darkness. A cold breeze wafted upward as if from an air conditioner.

I crossed Lake Buel Road, up over a pile of rocks, and across some bog bridges. Destruction was still visible from a tornado that hit the area in 1995. The Massachusetts Conservation Department cleared up its share of deadwood, but the U.S. Forest Service left the tornado damage a jumble. I passed through an area roughly the size of two football fields where trees had been destroyed or felled. Beavers had since built dams, blocking the stream. At a decaying concrete dam, I ran into a day hiker, Vince, who offered me some granola from his bag.

I stopped at Bearstown State Park picnic area for a refreshing swim in Benedict Pond. Sitting waist-deep in the small lake, I washed away two days' accumulation of trail dirt. The state park had clean indoor rest rooms for campers and, outside, a drinking fountain where I filled three water bottles.

Sitting alone at a picnic table, apart from several families on holiday, I ate an early lunch of peanut butter smeared thickly on bread. I felt skittish about mixing with other people when I felt grungy and unshaven. An unwashed appearance and a bulky pack—where do you park it?—makes it awkward to rub shoulders with ordinary tourists. For the same reason, I decided not to call Jaqueline's college roommate and her husband, who had a weekend house in nearby Monterey.

I returned to the trail through a forest of hemlock large enough to block the sunlight and leave no vegetation on the ground. More old stone walls meandered across the forest floor. How long had it taken the early settlers to build the walls on what must have then been newly cleared pasture land?

While rural areas like upper Westchester County in New York were filling up their outdoor space, here in the Berkshires and further north, farms and fences had been abandoned to the woods. Alexis de Tocqueville suggested that the phenomenon was characteristically American.

"The traveler frequently discovers the vestiges of a log house in the most solitary retreat, which bear witness to the power, and no less to the inconstancy, of man," Tocqueville wrote in 1848. "In these abandoned fields and over these ruins of a day the primeval forest soon scatters a fresh vegetation; the beasts resume the haunts which were once their own; and Nature comes smiling to cover the traces of man with green branches and flowers, which obliterate his ephemeral track."

I squeezed through another breach in the stone wall, into another expanse of woods carpeted knee-high with leafy ferns. I managed to go over Wilcox Mountain before the weight of my pack sent sharp pains and twitches down my spine and through my rib cage. My back had rebelled against the unaccustomed burden, and I still had five painful miles to walk before dark to the next campsite.

I could not imagine going that far, though I did. My father told me as a child, "You don't own things; things own you."

* * *

I CAMPED alone again, beside the stone ruins of a barn in a bygone Shaker colony near Tyringham, Massachusetts, in what
must be the mosquito capital of that state. So many mosquitoes
were about that I enveloped my head in a net to cook supper. It
was a hasty meal of instant spinach soup, with some canned
chicken to add bulk. I spooned it into my mouth through a small
gap in the net, which was soon saturated with bits of spinach and
chicken.

Darkness overtook me while I pitched my tent and climbed inside. The mosquitoes hummed against the zipped mesh fly. Somewhere below me was a road, but camping by myself, I felt only
isolation. I liked hiking alone through the day, but on nights like
this, solitude conspired against me. In the distance, a dog barked.
The sound was not unwelcome, since it might keep any coyotes at
bay.

What I learned about the Shakers who lived around Tyringham, a town incorporated two hundred forty years ago, comes on
good authority, from some signs at the campsite. Their pious
neighbors assaulted and whipped the Shakers to discourage the
peculiar practice of their faith. Still, hard work and frugality
helped the Shakers to persevere and, in 1792, to build a village of
their own on Fernsdale Road, a couple of hundred yards from
where I camped. They thrived by cultivating all kinds of seeds for
sale, storing them in a seedhouse five stories high. They also
tapped the local maple trees, over five thousand of them by 1846,
boiling down the sap to refine into sugar.

In 1858, twenty-three Shakers defected back to "the world,"
triggering an exodus that ended eighteen years later with the sale
of the last Shaker property. Some historians speculate that economic hard times brought on the colony's demise; others say it
was the Shakers' commitment to celibacy.

From my own field research, I would ascribe the vanishing of

the Shakers,
non: mosqu
since the p
featured da
helped prev
for the ins
owed its di
mosquitoes
dles and ox
as chair leg

It was s
against my
ering the w
in the rain a

Christopher S. Wr

Sierra mountains and released. W
ground, the bear was back ca
Yes, there are bears in
them. I set out before th
lighter since I had
parka had been
branches.
I passed
mount
of t

Striking camp at daybreak was soggy business. I dismantled my tent and stove, jammed them into my pack with the sleeping bag, enveloped the whole sodden lump belatedly in a rubberized rain cover, and took refuge in the outhouse until the rain let up. A notice inside acquainted me with another potential menace: black bears. One hundred fifty to three hundred males and one hundred eighty females were estimated to be in the general area. Thinking I could always climb a tree, I read on:

"They climb trees with great agility and speed," the notice warned. "They can attain and maintain a speed of 25 to 30 m.p.h. over short distances. They are intelligent, have good long-term memory and are capable of recalling the location of plentiful but periodic food sources several years after their first visit."

It was not encouraging news. I was using my son's length of cord to hoist my bag of food high on a tree limb before bedding down for the night. But I remembered Chris telling me of a bothersome bear who was caught and tranquilized at a campground in Sequoia National Park, where Chris was a ranger, trucked into the

hen Chris returned to the camp-
ging food.

ne woods, but you don't need to meet
e rain had stopped. My pack looked a little
ut the black rain cover over it. I wish my rain
as useful at keeping off wet leaves and dripping

through a narrow turnstile, ineffectually meant to bar
ain bikes, and checked my compass and map. This stretch
ail seemed to be leading me back south, when I wanted to go
orth.

I donned my poncho over my rain jacket, which only made me sweat harder, and hiked toward the road to Tyringham through open meadows. The hills ahead were shrouded in mist. I crossed a pasture and gingerly climbed some wooden steps over a barbed wire fence, taking care not to snag my trousers.

The rain had let up slightly when I negotiated a marshy bog, walking on slippery puncheons that led me to a small bridge over a stream. My water bottles were empty but I decided against stopping to fill them. My map showed a serviceable spring a few miles ahead. So I ignored one of the rules of the trail, which is not to pass fresh water with an empty canteen.

I crossed the Tyringham road and started climbing my way out of the valley. The canopy of tall hemlocks, pines, and red maples formed a natural umbrella that protected me from the rain. With my trekking poles, I propelled myself uphill over rocks and a muddy slope, setting a rhythm of three steps to every breath I took.

To take my mind off the miserable rain and soggy trail, I devised aphorisms pertinent for hiking but platitudinous enough about life to turn a profit on a motivational greeting card. These I panted into the tiny tape recorder that I carried for times, like now, when it was inconvenient to rummage for my notebook.

"Kipling's lesson, 'He travels the fastest who travels alone,' may no longer be true. He who travels alone today usually travels encumbered with far more weight than if he were traveling with someone else, because he carries the whole load."

Too wordy. That would require an extremely large greeting card.

"You don't need so much stuff. Lighten up—physically and emotionally." More harangue than advice, and still too long.

"Come prepared for storms. It isn't always sunny hiking." Nope, though it might work for sailors.

"You're going to make dumb decisions. Deal with them and learn to leave them behind." Yes, at least that's the idea.

"Don't be too hard on yourself. The world will do that for you."

I gave up, overlooking the larger truth. Even with too much baggage, ineptly hydrated oatmeal and undercooked noodles, drenching rain and a night spent dancing with mosquitoes, I had gained another several hundred feet in elevation. Yesterday's problems were fading into just that. For all the self-pity, I was still in motion, nearly two hundred miles closer to Vermont than I had been a few weeks earlier starting from Times Square. The lesson I was learning late is that life does not require you to be perfect, that guilt lies in not trying to finish what you began.

After pausing to plunder some blueberry bushes, I descended toward a small spring off a poorly defined side trail. Despite the rain, the trickle from the spring was muddy and unproductive. I filtered enough through my hand pump to squeeze out less than a pint before I gave up, unwilling to waste further energy. As I screwed on the lid, stones clattered behind me.

A lanky hiker was loping down the trail. He had shaggy red hair and what looked like a United States Marine Corps tattoo on a freckled arm under his wet T-shirt. He hadn't bothered with a rain parka. I estimated his age at thirty. He introduced himself as Pandora. He was traveling the Appalachian Trail from Springer

Mountain in Georgia to Mount Katahdin in Maine. He had set out more than three months earlier and had another few months to go. And so far today, he had walked from where I started out yesterday.

Pandora filled his bottle from the spring more adeptly than I had and set off without further small talk, dancing across the slippery rocks like a tightrope walker, with his trekking poles outstretched for balance, and was soon out of sight. I slogged on alone toward my destination, a cabin on Upper Goose Pond south of the Massachusetts Turnpike that promised bunk beds. I did not want to spend another night sleeping in puddles.

The rain glistening on leaves flashed me back to a night long ago in a Vietnamese rubber plantation, where I joined some American draftees in the 1st Infantry Division on a planned ambush. The Vietcong ambushed our side first, mortaring the American fire base a quarter-mile behind us. We hugged the ground, not knowing where to run as incoming shells whined over our heads from both directions. A helicopter gunship loomed through the darkness, spraying the rows of rubber trees with tracer bullets that flashed like red rain—and missed us. The firefight lasted just a few minutes, but we did not dare return to base until it was light.

There was another night spent with a Special Forces patrol out in the Central Highlands of Vietnam, when I sat in a heavy downpour tending a young Montagnard fighter bitten by a green bamboo viper, trying to suck the poison from his foot with a suction cup. We were too wet and cold to sleep. At daybreak, we saw wisps of smoke rising from across the jungle clearing. The Special Forces captain leading the patrol believed the smoke came from breakfast fires lit by some North Vietnamese soldiers infiltrating from the Ho Chi Minh Trail across the border in Laos. We were not in friendly territory.

I hitched a ride out that morning on a dustoff, a Huey helicopter dispatched to evacuate the Montagnard, whose leg had puffed up by now to twice its normal size. I came to no harm in either episode, which paled when compared to what most GIs underwent in combat.

Still, it distressed me that wet leaves in the rain could seem ominous after so many years. Walking alone in the woods would not get easier unless I forced my mind to dismiss such memories.

I kept losing the trail, which doubled back on itself so often that when I checked my compass, I seemed to be heading back south again. The trees closed around, offering scant topographic clues. I stopped to wait for the next hiker but no one showed up. Calling for help seemed humiliating. Pandora was by now well beyond earshot.

Then water glimmered through the trees to my left. It had to be one of the ponds near the cabin. Between the water's edge and the trail stood the stone hearth and chimney of a dwelling destroyed by fire. Compass in hand, I stopped to listen and was rewarded with a faint rumble of trucks rolling down the Massachusetts Turnpike to the north. I walked on, until the trail intersected with a footpath that turned westward toward Upper Goose Pond.

The wooden cabin there had a red roof of corrugated metal and an elegant steel stairway descending from the second floor. I wonder what fire inspector hiked in to mandate the addition of a fire escape. Inside the cabin were a dozen bunks upstairs and a fireplace and bedroom downstairs, which the caretaker shared with two sons and a large brown dog named Amber.

"His mom was a beautiful black Lab," the caretaker, Kathy, said. "His dad was a terrier. Or a poodle."

A hearty blond woman, Kathy had just paddled back from across the lake in a canoe laden with dozens of gallon jugs of fresh spring water. She invited me to fill my bottles.

"It came right from an underground spring," she said, "but we're supposed to tell you it hasn't been filtered."

I took out my pump and started squeezing water through the

filter. But my throat was parched, and nobody else was taking pre-cautions. I let the raw water trickle down my throat. It was cold and reassuringly tasteless. Water springing from within rock tends to be safer because animal or human waste cannot contami-nate the source. Feeling guilty, I filtered the second bottle.

I climbed to the second floor of the cabin and found a vacant bunk with a dirty rubber mattress where I dumped the contents of my pack. I took the wet tent and sleeping bag outside and spread them over the stairway to dry.

Upper Goose Pond is said to be the only undeveloped pond left in the Berkshires. It was still layered with mist from the latest rain. In the center rose a solitary islet. I walked down to the dock, stripped off my clothes, despite the refusal of the sun to reappear, and jumped into the bracing water until I had scrubbed off the mud caked to my skin.

"How's the swimming?" someone asked.

"Pretty cool," I explained.

"Cool?" he said. "Hey, man, cool."

"Cool," I agreed.

"Cool," echoed a cluster of thru-hikers who sat around the wooden picnic table. But they were discussing stoves, the weight of their packs, and how many miles they had walked. They were averaging fifteen to twenty miles a day on foot. I refrained from saying that I felt lucky to cover ten.

To get some respect on the Appalachian Trail, walking twenty miles or bragging about your stove was not enough. No, you had to cover your twenty miles at a run in pelting sleet or ankle-deep snow, pull into camp after dark wearing your battery-powered headlamp, purify and drink a gallon of water to replace the fluids lost to diarrhea that morning, and then show off your stove.

Pandora sat among his admirers, explaining the fine points of a tiny stove that he had welded himself. It looked more like a hand grenade, ran on some form of alcohol, and weighed mere ounces, not pounds. He waved off compliments from the other hikers, who looked to be in their late teens to late twenties and considered Pandora their guru. It was left to me to bring a real generation gap to the occasion.

Many trail travelers you meet are walking not merely for the exercise. Probe deeply enough and you'll find travelers who are between jobs, marriages, schools, or bad checks. They are walking toward emotional or spiritual fulfillment or away from stress and worse problems they don't want to talk about. Trail names do have their own logic.

I still could not guess Pandora's age. He was older than he first looked to me, probably well into his thirties. He was indeed an ex-marine, another hiker told me later, and a lawyer who walked out of his law firm one day and hit the trail.

When stoves are the subject of conversation, can pack weights be far behind? "I had a tent," Pandora said, "but now I have a tarp, mostly so I can stay in shelters."

Ghostbuster, a bearded young hiker from Connecticut who espoused the philosophy of traveling light, agreed to check my gear. He looked at me as though I were a pack mule.

"Carry two tent stakes instead of six," he advised. "Three Band-Aids instead of six."

I did not tell Ghostbuster that it took at least seven stakes to save my tent from collapse. I did point out that discarding three Band-Aids was unlikely to lighten my pack by as much as an ounce.

Ghostbuster shook his tangle of dark hair. "Little things add up," he explained. "Clothes are where people can usually lose the most weight. I don't have a change of clothes. The worst thing is getting up in the morning and putting on wet things."

He paused and corrected himself. "I have Spandex underwear, reduces chafing. I have one extra pair."

I looked around the cabin porch. Sure enough, everyone was

still wearing the grimy T-shirts they arrived in. Ghostbuster must have packed one more change of underwear than the rest of them owned collectively, while I had no fewer than three. My clean T-shirt made me conspicuous.

Ghostbuster stared at my footwear. "Lose the boots and go to sneakers," he said.

I was about to explain that my boots were on doctor's orders, but this would not impress Ghostbuster, who was covering a lot more miles. He expressed shock that some items in my pack were pristine after two and a half weeks of walking.

"If you haven't used it yet, you don't need it," Ghostbuster reproached me. "I've used everything in my pack several times."

"Take what you have to have," he advised, "then put the rest in the hikers' box."

Ghostbuster threw up his hands at the sight of my nested aluminum cooking kit, plate, and assortment of eating utensils. "Hey, man," he said, "all you need is a pot and a spoon."

"I carry ramen," interjected Animal, an amiable blond youth whose trail name was acquired from his lifelike imitations of a fruit bat. He boasted of surviving on nothing but those bland little rice noodles.

"That's phenomenal," Redneck marveled, "and you're not dead?" It was Redneck's twenty-fifth birthday, though no one had bothered to pack him a cake.

We all looked to Pandora. "I've got everything all wrong," he demurred in a Zen master's self-deprecation. "I've been hiking since April fourth and I still don't know what I'm doing."

The real secret of traveling light, some agreed, was a reliable support group—worried mothers were considered particularly diligent about this—to mail food and clothing parcels to the post offices you expected to pass. Pandora, I was told, had an attractive lady friend who kept him periodically supplied.

I had suggested such a role to Jaqueline, who evinced a conspicuous lack of enthusiasm. "That's what credit cards are for," she told me.

Ghostbuster was bragging about how he had slashed a pound off his pack weight by not carrying any stuff sacks. That seemed logical because so far as I could tell, he hadn't taken enough stuff to put in them. His basic pack weighed a mere twelve pounds.

Redneck countered that his basic pack weighed eleven pounds. "I carried the full pack for a week," he said. "All the straps I didn't use I cut off." Eliminating them had slashed his load by as much as four ounces.

I was calculating what I could lose. One of my can openers? The nail clippers? Spare flashlight? Sweater, fleece jacket? Rain parka or poncho? Orange plastic whistle? My cell phone with its plug-in recharger? Even, heaven forbid, my paperback of Thoreau's *Walden*? The weight of each was inconsequential; together, they had conspired to push my pack weight above fifty pounds.

Henry Thoreau sided with the minimalists. "Most of the luxuries, and many of the so-called comforts of life, are not only dispensable," Henry sternly reminded me, "but positive hindrances to the elevation of mankind." He was right when it came to climbing these hills.

The very familiarity of possessions makes them difficult to abandon. However trivial their usefulness, they evoke the bonds with a distant home and family. I had covered refugees fleeing wars and famine but only now understood why the meager possessions they carried included basic items—a child's blue plush rabbit in Croatia, a worn wooden tablet inscribed with faded Koranic verses in the Horn of Africa—that an outsider's logic deemed not worth the nuisance.

I was not the only hiker on the trail who found it painful to empty his pack. "I started at sixty-five pounds," Finn confided.

"Now I can't get below forty-five pounds. I've seen people with half that much, and they seem pretty chipper."

Finn had quit his job as a stonemason in New York to hit the Appalachian Trail, explaining that he didn't need the stress. He was hiking with Beatle, a fan of the Fab Four who scribbled trivial facts that never occurred to you about the Beatles in the campsite registers.

I started to tell him that I had once met the Beatles, well, had squeezed into the second row of one of their news conferences in New York. But I decided to say nothing because it took place before these guys were born.

What the trail travelers refused to carry, they were more than willing to scrounge. A couple of hikers returned from paddling a borrowed canoe out to the islet on Upper Goose Pond. They had surprised a local swain and his lass in an intimate picnic and, in return for going away, were paid off with some wine and cheese. Their success prompted our crowd to swap tips for foraging opportunities ahead, much as hoboes are said to do at a jungle camp in some railroad yard.

A southbound hiker told me about Marilyn, who lived near Becket, a day's walk to the north. She baked chocolate chip cookies, hundreds of them, for thru-hikers like us. Knock on her door, and Marilyn would give you a few cookies, sometimes warm from the oven. She had a garden hose for refilling your bottles with clean water. And maybe her husband, Roy, would let you camp overnight if you asked nicely.

And Tom, another guy who lived in Dalton, a further day's walk away, allowed thru-hikers to sleep on his front porch or in his yard, though you couldn't use the bathroom inside. The Appalachian Trail went past Tom's house on Depot Street, right through town.

The directions my companions gave for finding Marilyn and Tom were vague. I copied them down anyway, though I didn't expect to stoop to begging cookies or pitching my tent in a stranger's yard.

"Down south, people are more hiker-friendly," Ghostbuster told me. "There's much more trail magic in North Carolina, Tennessee, and Virginia."

He, like Finn and Pandora and almost everyone else here, as far as I could tell, started their journey in Georgia.

"Where did you start?" Ghostbuster asked.

"New York City," I said.

There was a hush as they all turned to stare. Even Pandora looked up from his stove. "How did you get out of New York City?" he asked.

"I walked," I said. "From Times Square."

"Cool," Pandora said again. "How?"

"Up Broadway, through Harlem." I was finally getting some respect here.

"Times Square, like, that's so cool."

"Awesome, man!"

"Through Harlem, wasn't it dangerous, dude?"

A walk out of New York City struck me as neither awesome nor dangerous. My secret was putting one foot in front of the other. Still, I accepted their compliments with a shrug.

Most of these guys had already covered a thousand miles or more, slogging through snow and rain, ascending and descending peaks loftier that I would encounter, wandering for days past dens of rattlesnakes, bears, and mountain folk who mated with cousins at family picnics. Yet something as straightforward as walking out of New York City to the Appalachian Trail struck them as awesome.

Now, by the time you turn sixty-five, you no longer have illusions about your place in this world. When you hit thirty, you forfeit your right to wear your cap backward and blame problems on your parents. And when you hit sixty, you turn pretty much invisible. My age was triple the years of the younger hikers, yet it mattered more to them that I was walking their walk.

Having cooked and eaten my candlelight supper—a bouquet of canned tuna served on a moist bed of reconstituted noodles drizzled with a coulis of powdered cheese sauce and trail dirt—I tramped out back to wash my cookware, then into the woods to pay nature's call on the outhouse, which came highly recommended.

There are privies, and then there are privies. This newfangled model was called a moldering privy and required some dexterity. It had two holes side by side, one for peeing and the other for Number Two, the sign said.

The instructions posted on the plank wall warned not to confuse the two, implying that the courteous user should slide seamlessly from one toilet seat to the other.

"Obviously, it is impossible to retrieve urine which has been accidentally deposited in the #2 pit," the sign scolded. "If you don't understand these instructions, please take your business elsewhere." Tacitly acknowledging the frailty of humanity, a large slotted spoon, labeled a "pooper scooper," was provided to correct mistakes.

I returned to the cabin, collected the tent I had spread out to dry, and was climbing into my sleeping bag when there was a commotion outside. A headlamp sliced through the dusk and bobbed up the trail toward the cabin. The other hikers clustered around the new arrival.

"Mojo's here," the cry went up. "Mojo's here."

I headed back down the fire escape, curious why anyone named Mojo would excite this crowd. Mojo turned out to be a pretty, dark-haired young woman with an impish smile, though this was hard to confirm at first because she wore a black watch cap pulled over her head and down to her eyes.

"I met really old ladies hiking—in their seventies!" Mojo reported with much amusement. I chortled along with the others at the notion of a generation of women whom I had lusted after in my youth tottering along the Appalachian Trail.

"Mojo's going swimming," the call echoed, and even I turned out to watch. To the general disappointment, she appeared in a demure two-piece tartan bathing suit, displaying her trim figure only briefly before flinging off the cap and diving into the pond. The chilly water didn't deter her from taking a proper swim.

Mojo was one of a score of women I encountered who were walking the complete trail between Georgia and Maine. The daily exertion left them tanned and slim. They glowed with good health and defiant independence, which made them not only attractive but a little intimidating too.

Lechers must have hit on Mojo before. I couldn't quite hear what one whispered tonight, but she snapped, "I am not a trail slut!" I couldn't conceive how anyone hiking fifteen or twenty miles a day with a pack had enough energy left at night for hanky-panky.

The next morning, we were discussing pack weights again over our breakfast stoves when Mojo stopped by on her way back to the trail, wearing what looked suspiciously like a clean tank top. She waved off my curiosity about how much her pack weighed.

"I try not to think about it," she replied in the same tone she would have used to dismiss a query about diets.

"I carry what I need," Mojo said, and from the size of her pack, she didn't need much.

Five

MY COMPANIONS clustered overnight around Upper Goose Pond notwithstanding, the Appalachian Trail does not offer the kind of diversion that draws crowds. Some days on the trail, I met only a couple of hikers, and that was in passing. There were a couple of days when I saw no one.

If the nights turned lonely, my days of solitude seemed a blessing. Sometimes I sang as I walked, belting out childhood hymns or country music oldies. I tried to summon up all the verses about the mother who tells the prison warden that she's not in his town to stay and will soon be on her way, she's just here to get her baby out of jail.

I recalled the zeitgeist of the trail in Townes van Zandt's ballad about Pancho and Lefty, and wearing your skin like iron, your breath as hard as kerosene.

When I left the cabin at Upper Goose Pond, the weather had turned sunny but cool, perfect for walking. Sunlight filtered through the trees, oak and something close to aspen, along the trail. Soggy leaves squished under my feet. Along the trail, some orange fungus blossomed, looking like tie-dyed cauliflowers.

The faint roar of the trucks on the Massachusetts Turnpike over the ridge was now less than a mile away. The turnpike, a major artery connecting New York to New England, had become my psychological point of no return, halfway home on my walk to central Vermont. I hadn't given much thought to crossing the six-lane turnpike, beyond hoping that I wouldn't have to sprint.

I was again wearing yesterday's grubby East Chop Tennis T-shirt, which Herb had brought me from his exclusive country club at Martha's Vineyard. I had put away my clean T-shirt of the previous evening because the tennis shirt remained so soggy from sweat and rain that wearing it seemed the best way to dry it out. I hung five wet socks on the back of my pack—the sixth had disappeared to wherever socks go—hoping these too would dry in the sun; wearing them wet would only bring more blisters.

I passed two white-haired women and a man on hands and knees, pruning roots protruding from the trail. A cheerful woman, whom I put in her seventies, said they were volunteers from the Berkshires section of the Appalachian Mountain Club. If they were past hiking the Appalachian Trail, they did not consider themselves too old to maintain it.

The trail dropped sharply, revealing through the trees a concrete footbridge about ten feet wide spanning the divided turnpike, with wire mesh running up either side of the overpass. The trail led down the eroded median strip that divided the eastward and westward lanes, and then up over the second set of lanes. A sign put the New York state line at less than fifteen miles to the west.

The reimmersion into civilization lasted just a few minutes before the trail delivered me back to the woods, past sumac and maple trees to Greenwater Pond, a small lake with boats bobbing in front of summer cabins. A bridge led over a stream flowing out of the pond. I had to jog across a smaller road to avoid a red pickup truck.

From here, it was a sharp climb of about five hundred feet to the plateau. I had cinched my pack tightly over my hips to take the strain off my back. Now the hip muscles were hurting too. I needed a "zero day," a total break that thru-hikers take occasionally to avoid burning out. But I would postpone that until I reached the summit of Mount Greylock, a few days ahead.

Another long climb over 2,178-foot-high Becket Mountain brought me to succession of less discrete summits. The trail, muddy in places, meandered around the deserted Finerty Pond, where the water rippled from the breeze. I filled my bottle from a stream flowing out of the pond, and moved into a hemlock forest carpeted with fir needles, past rocks and ferns. The trail dropped through a grove of deciduous trees as pale as aspens.

I was losing track of time. I woke up with the sun, stopped for lunch when hunger gnawed, and bedded down once the sun set. Life with this circadian rhythm no longer required a wristwatch. To estimate the daylight left to the next shelter, I needed only to extend my arm and measure with my flattened hand the gap between the sun and the horizon, reckoning fifteen minutes for the width of each finger.

But today, with barely nine miles under my belt, I had no choice but to stop at the next shelter beyond October Mountain. The rest of the Upper Goose Pond crowd had long since breezed past. Fresh muscle spasms triggered flashes of pain along my back, forcing more frequent stops. My hope of covering a decent fifteen miles faded, even though the three hours of daylight remaining were sufficient to cover six more miles before dark.

My descent over October Mountain in the afternoon heat was rewarded by trail magic. Something silver gleamed among the stones in a mountain stream.

A can of Coors Light lay in the swirling water. I called for its owner but no one answered. I looked around and scooped up the can. The water had chilled it to perfection.

I hurried on toward the shelter a hundred yards away, to make sure that the can's owner was not about to retrieve it. No one was there. My pack thumped on the shelter floor. The beer was quaffed in a succession of delicious swallows. My sagging spirits revived. The hard wooden floor felt therapeutic against my sore back.

Whether it is beer chilled in a stream, or a cold can of grape soda at a pasture turnstile, or granola shared by a young hiker, small generosities are reminders that some people don't think what you are doing is frivolous.

I had this campsite to myself, not including the porcupines who had chewed up the threshold of the shelter's small porch and started munching on the picnic table. Hikers' entries in the loose-leaf shelter register reported finding porcupine droppings on the table overnight.

I decided not to pitch my tent on the ground and risk a nocturnal visit by porcupines, or perhaps a skunk. Black bears had also been sighted in the area. I moved into the three-sided shelter, where the mosquitoes in residence turned out to meet me.

The shelters look appealing when you stagger in exhausted from the trail. But close up they are seldom clean, and they attract rodents, who scamper in to feast on whatever overnight hikers drop, or chew through food bags that the visitors neglect to hang beyond their reach.

Besides potential rabies, don't overlook the rarer but as fatal hantavirus, which my *Appalachian Trail Guide* reported was spread by an infected rodent's evaporated urine, droppings, and saliva. Some precautions proposed in my guidebook included "Don't sleep on mouse droppings (use a mat or tent)" and "Don't handle mice." No mouse-fondling tonight?

An inspection of the shelter on my hands and knees turned up what looked like some peppercorn-size mouse pellets, so I swept them out and partially erected my tent in the loft. Pitching a tent inside a shelter is considered poor trail etiquette, and not a little wimpish, but I did not want to spend another night harried by mosquitoes, or rodents. As I stretched out with my copy of *Walden* to read before boiling up dinner, I knew that Henry Thoreau would have disapproved.

"It would be well, perhaps, if we were to spend more of our days and nights without any obstruction between us and the celestial bodies," Henry nagged, "if the poet did not speak so much from under a roof, or the saint dwell there so long. Birds do not sing in caves, nor do doves cherish their innocence in dovecotes."

All well and good, Henry, I thought, but you didn't write that while swatting mosquitoes, or stepping on a porcupine when you went out for a post-midnight pee, or bumping into a bear, or a randy skunk. And you never heard of hantavirus.

Just before dusk, two high school students from southern New Jersey, Dan and James, hiked in to the lean-to. They had neglected to bring a water filter, so I lent them mine to fill their bottles at the stream. In return, Dan gave me a few heat tablets suitable for cooking, because the fuel canister on my stove was running low.

After pleasantries over our respective suppers, we hung our food bags from the shelter eaves, high enough to keep them away from porcupines and bears, mice and rats and ants, and then turned in. I called out a good night.

"Good night, sir," Dan and James chorused.

MY DISTASTE for rodents was not philosophical, though the mice at October Mountain were unlikely to be as formidable as some rats I encountered during the Vietnam War. I spent a week at a

Special Forces outpost tunneled into a jungle hillside ouside a Montagnard village called Dak Pek. During the requisite poker game on my first night there, a couple of Green Berets pulled up their shirt between poker hands and stabbed their stomachs discreetly with hypodermic needles.

"Rabies vaccine," the team medic explained. "Just a precaution when you get bitten."

"You have rabies here?" I asked.

"Rats," the team sergeant said in a thick Mississippi drawl. "Rats live in these tunnels and there's lots of them. Stay around long enough, and you're gonna get bit too."

"Why not requisition some cats from headquarters in Kontum?" I asked.

"We did," the sergeant said. "Rats killed the cats and ate them."

"How about traps?"

"Tried them. Traps weren't big enough. Rats couldn't fit in them."

"Exterminators?"

"Can't spray these tunnels, we gotta live here too."

I said that there had to be some solution.

"There is," the sergeant said. "Tuck in your mosquito netting, keep the rats out while you sleep."

The team found me a cot belonging to a soldier away on long-range patrol. His cot was squeezed into a dank log bunker at the end of a tunnel. Mosquito netting was draped over the cot's wooden canopy frame. A machine gun mounted at the observation slot that passed for a window blocked the flow of air. I was issued a blanket and a .45-caliber pistol, and told which way to escape and regroup if the North Vietnamese overran us during the night.

I tucked the mosquito netting in firmly, but lying in the cot in the dark, I wondered if I had seemed too gullible. I hadn't seen any

rats, after all, so maybe the story was made up. I had no choice but
to play along with the joke.

I was awakened sometime after midnight by the rustling of the
mosquito net. A faint scampering around my cot was followed by
something live chasing something else up the netting. Squeaks
and squeals followed, the passionate sounds of rodents in lust.
The frame began to sway. Not only were there rats in the tunnel, I
concluded, but a pair were copulating over my head. If their ec-
stasy tore my net, I'd be sticking a needle into my stomach too.

I pulled the pistol from under my pillow and pointed it upward,
but I couldn't see what or where to shoot. A shot would trigger a
false alarm that the North Vietnamese were swarming over the
barbed wire.

Fortunately, the netting held until the rodents' ardor had cli-
maxed and the passionate lovers made their postcoital getaway
down the netting. I don't know whether the earth moved for
Mickey and Minnie, but it sure did for me.

Nobody would believe this back home. But there was no skepticism when, feeling foolish, I mentioned it to the Green Berets
the following morning.

"Mating season," one of them said.

THE NEXT morning over oatmeal and tea, James inquired politely,
"May we ask how old you are?"

"Sixty-five," I told them. "The same age as your grandfathers."
Dan and James looked at each other and nodded. I didn't want
them offering to assist me down the trail, so I let them depart
ahead of me.

I walked back to the stream where I had found the chilled
Coors, to filter fresh water. In the muddy gravel was the unmis-

takable paw print of a bear. The paw looked like it belonged to a large bear. I retreated with my bottle unfilled.

I wanted nothing more than to get out of there. Maybe a chocolate chip cookie, if I could find one, would calm my nerves.

The morning had a pleasant breeze. The trail was muddy but flat. I crossed a dirt road flooded by beavers, who had dammed up the adjacent stream with sticks, mud, and even some small logs, backing up the water nearly three feet high.

I walked out of October Mountain State Forest to Pittsfield Road, where, according to my directions, Marilyn the cookie lady lived. A southbound hiker pointed me eastward a hundred yards. The cookie lady was away, he said, but her husband, Roy, was there.

And here I was, capping my retirement from forty years of globe-trotting journalism by walking up to a stranger's house to panhandle for some cookies and a drink from the garden hose.

The Wileys' two-story, brown-shingled house was set back from the paved road, just behind an old yellow house that looked prematurely abandoned. The family dog sauntered out to greet me. He was part chow and part golden retriever, with reddish fur. Roy Wiley wore bifocals and a battered cap. He stood by a brown picnic table, chatting with Solo, a park ranger from Alaska who was hiking south. Solo, husky and taciturn, wore Indian-style leather leggings over his boots. He had come to beg for cookies too.

Roy explained that Marilyn had been visiting her family in Iowa but was due home soon. He was leaving soon to pick her up at the airport if I cared to wait. I declined.

Sensing my disappointment, Roy went inside and emerged with a basket of Marilyn's cookies, or what remained of them, and some tiny packets of dried prunes. Roy apologized for having to ration the cookies to three per hiker until his wife could whip up a fresh batch.

Roy had moved to Massachusetts from upstate New York fifty-one years earlier. He and Marilyn had lived in their brown house for seventeen years, and grew blueberries for a hobby. Roy was also restoring an old Piper Clipper plane and had built a dirt runway two thousand feet long behind the house.

I bit down on the first cookie. It was still moist, despite the baker's week-long absence, and densely studded with chocolate chips. I asked Roy how long his wife had been baking for hikers.

Roy didn't know for sure. It started when the first hiker knocked on their door.

"We just got into it." Roy shrugged.

Just got into it? Tons of chipped chocolate. Mountains of butter and rivers of sugar. Mega-kilowatts of electricity to bake scores of thousands of cookies. It was no big deal to the marvelous Marilyn and her soft-spoken husband, Roy.

Several more hikers hove into view. Word had spread far about the cookie lady, as far as Alaska and New Brunswick, Canada, which was where one young woman was hiking from. A kid wearing a cotton kilt that looked more Burmese than Scottish followed. Roy Wiley was so busy apologizing to the grubby, grasping hands about the three-cookie limit that he did not hear my thanks. I filled my water bottles from his garden hose and slipped away, saving my last cookie.

The trail wound for several miles through marshy woodland that belonged to the watershed for the city of Pittsfield, ten or so miles to the west. A sign warned me to stay within the narrow corridor of the Appalachian Trail, which seemed hardly wider than ten feet.

I was packing several days' accumulation of garbage since Benedict Pond, with no place to dump it. I looked for a trash can at the next roadside parking lot, but there was none. Doubtless, emptying such cans made too much work for the city of Pittsfield, but so did picking up trash dumped on the roads by people who didn't want to be bothered carrying it. Hikers would tote more of it off the trail if we knew that a dumpster awaited us at the next road.

Back when I worked in Moscow, I learned from *Pravda* that Russian city dwellers each discarded on average six hundred and sixty pounds of garbage a year—less than half of what New Yorkers junked—and that Leningrad, as St. Petersburg was called in those days, had an experimental plant for composting nearly a quarter of the city's garbage. I was intrigued enough to ask to visit it. Suspicious city officials grilled me face-to-face about my intentions. "Can't you find something better to write about?" the deputy mayor snapped.

I wanted to shout that there wasn't much point in lofting Russians and Americans into orbit together if they had to fling their disproportionate trash out the spaceship hatch every morning. Instead, I argued that New York City could learn a few things from how Russian cities were run. So the deputy mayor grudgingly authorized my visit to the dump, where I watched Leningrad's garbage piled into giant rotating drums and fermented for two days before being distributed as valuable compost to city hothouses for growing winter vegetables.

If we all had to tote our garbage around for a couple of days, as I was doing on the trail, we'd think up even more ingenious ways to be less profligate.

In the parking lot on Blotz Road, a hiker was unlocking her car. She shook her head when I asked if she had seen a garbage can, then offered to drive my bag of trash home (try handing your trash to a New Yorker). Depositing my fragrant rubbish in her car trunk, she introduced herself as Green Turtle. I gave my trail name as Super Tortoise, which I was desperate to shed because it hit too close to the truth.

I stopped to lunch on bread with plenty of peanut butter at the top of Warner Hill, which was crowned with blueberry bushes, a rock cairn, some other rocks to sit upon, and a few hardy trees for shade. To the west were factory or storage sheds in Pittsfield, across the valley. To the north lay the long table of Mount Greylock, which I would climb tomorrow. I peeled off my shirt and stretched out on a flat rock for a nap. It was here that I must have dozed through my tick bite.

The vegetation was nearly waist-high in the vertical clearing for power lines that I crossed next. It offered an even better view, clear to the Taconics in New York state. Back into the woods, I waded through a sea of green ferns. On one of the passing birches, someone had carved the name "S. Krol" and the date "1985." I wondered if the defacer of birches was as big a jerk today.

I checked my map. A climb over Day Mountain separated me from my night's destination, the small town of Dalton. It had no shelters or campgrounds, and the local inn was likely to be expensive. Where had I written the name of the man who let hikers sleep on his lawn?

I was adjusting my pack in preparation for a strenuous climb when a pair of trail travelers breezed past me and stopped. They carried small, light packs, barely one-third the bulk of mine. They introduced themselves as Flash and Knute. I said I was hiking alone. They invited me to join them.

Henry Thoreau would have refused. "I never found the companion that was so companionable as solitude," Henry claimed. "To be in company, even with the best, is soon wearisome and dissipating."

But I welcomed Flash's and Knute's company, if only to goad me into adopting a faster pace. When I explained that I was sixty-five years old and would only slow them down, Flash shrugged a so-what. "Yeah, I'm sixty," he said. So, as it turned out, were more than a few other trail travelers I met.

A small, wiry man with big glasses and an unruly mop of gray hair, Flash moved with a suppleness much younger than his sixty years. Like me, he was walking into retirement, from a career administering state programs in Ohio for the developmentally disabled, or mentally retarded.

Knute, who looked barely into his thirties, had a strapping body and Nordic features framed by a bandanna tied snugly over his head to absorb the dust and sweat. Originally from Minnesota, Knute had been driving tractor-trailers out of Laredo, Texas. He wearied of long-distance driving and hit the trail to give himself time to figure out something better to do.

Flash and Knute seemed an odd pair to be traveling together from Georgia to Maine. They met hiking the same stretch of trail, and their easy camaraderie was forged vying with each other to go faster. Thru-hikers tend to self-segregate according to speed. Arriving at the same shelter at night bonds them together.

"So many bears down in Tennessee that we found cage doors on some shelters to keep the bears out," Flash told me while we hiked. "That attracts more bears, of course, because the hikers get lazy about hanging up their food."

"Of course," I gasped, struggling to keep up.

Unwinded by the exhausting uphill stretches, Flash offered nonstop observations on just about everything, which on our walk into Dalton included reminiscenses about past perils narrowly avoided.

"Plenty of rattlesnakes in Pennsylvania out sunning themselves on the rocks," Flash reported a little later. "We had to step around them.

"Miles of poison ivy down in Virginia," Flash said, moving so briskly that his feet hardly stayed on the trail. "One woman got poison ivy so bad hiking that they put her in the hospital for a month."

Knute, who set our brisk pace, was as taciturn as Flash was voluble. He said he enjoyed his companion's running commentary. "Helps pass the time."

Flash's narrative helped us make short work of Day Mountain. Before I realized it, we were descending into Dalton. We were held up at the railroad track until a long freight train passed, going east.

All Americans carry a piece of Dalton in their wallets. Dalton is the home of the Crane Paper Company, which has been printing paper used in United States currency since 1879. Zenas Crane arrived here in 1797 and built his first mill two years later, using hydropower from the Housatonic River to make a superior paper from hand-cut rags and cotton. Today, Crane banknote paper is trucked under state police guard to an armory in Springfield, to be sent down to Washington for engraving.

Flash and Knute headed for the same backyard I had heard about. Its owner, Tom Levardi, lived in a two-story gray clapboard house with a wide veranda on Depot Street, about a block away from an old paper mill on the Housatonic. Tom, who looked in his early fifties, came out wearing a T-shirt. He had just returned home from his job at a supermarket. He had been letting hikers sleep on his property for about twenty years.

"It's on the Appalachian Trail," Tom explained. "There used to be a laundromat next door where hikers stopped to wash their clothes. One of them asked me where he could camp, so I let him use my backyard."

He added, "Sometimes they also sleep on my porch."

Tom agreed to let us pitch our tents out back. He laid down only a few rules: no use of the bathroom inside, no trash left behind, and no noise after eight P.M. He retired shortly after seven, because he had to get up at four the next morning to open the supermarket.

Tom kept a loose-leaf book with recommendations on things to do around Dalton, including some menus of local restaurants. He had another register to be signed by hikers staying overnight. The comments consisted mostly of effusive expressions of gratitude.

He waved off my offer of a donation. "I'll have some ice cream waiting if you're around before seven," he said.

I wondered whether the neighbors complained at the impromptu tent city that sprouted on Tom's lawn every night, but they confessed to enjoying the transient backpacker parade.

Flash carried a one-man tent like mine. We pitched ours against Tom's backyard hedge, staking out turf against later arrivals. Instead of a tent, Knute used a lighter bivouac sack, a glorified sleeping bag with a cradlelike hood and mosquito netting.

Pitching my tent, I noticed what looked like an insect bite turning red on my upper arm. I hadn't felt the bite and it didn't hurt. I resolved to keep my netting zipped tighter.

Then, famished, we headed out to eat. We settled upon Benny's Family Restaurant, because it was close and cheap. I stuffed myself with fried chicken and French-fried potatoes, lots of bread, coleslaw, and a brownie with ice cream. Benny also served Michelob beer on draft for only two dollars a pint. How could I afford not to drink two?

The small-town porch lights glowed softly along Depot Street, guiding us homeward to Tom's backyard. But Tom had turned in for the night. We did too. When we woke up about six A.M., several more tents had sprung up alongside ours. For a couple of dollars, we ate bacon, eggs, home fries, and coffee at Duff & Dell's, a small but bustling delicatessen. Regular customers were finishing their coffee and joking with the waitress before heading on to work.

The Appalachian Trail turned left onto Main Street and over the Housatonic River. We trudged past All Saints Episcopal Church, which had a crenellated tower instead of a steeple, a Methodist church, and a Cumberland Farms outlet, then turned right up High Street, across Park Avenue and back into the woods.

This was what Earl Schaeffer, the patriarch of the modern Appalachian Trail, had envisioned when he became the first hiker to complete the entire trail in 1948: a national walking trail that would connect towns and villages rather than avoid them, as the trail designers tend to do today.

"They go out of their way to run you up and over every nondescript hill," Knute complained while we walked. The result is that thru-hikers have so few opportunities to rub shoulders with the locals that the relationship becomes one of mutual suspicion. Dalton, where hikers walked right through town, was an exception.

In a couple of hours, we arrived at the turnoff to the Crystal Mountain campsite. While Flash and Knute filled their water bottles in the stream, I hiked a couple of hundred yards to the campsite, whose setting was less interesting than its name implied. Several hikers were lounging outside their tents.

Inside the privy, a torn Bible lay on the toilet seat, not, however, for use as a source of contemplation. Previous users had worked their way up to the Book of Nehemiah in the Old Testament. It reminded me of the contemptuous desecration that I had witnessed on display toward religious objects in China and the former Soviet Union. I walked back to the main trail. Only later did it occur to me that I should have rescued the Bible, but where would I have carried it?

We passed a beaver dam and in a few miles a succession of quartz outcroppings named the Cobbles. Below to our left was a slender but substantial reservoir. In the distance loomed Mount Greylock, our destination for the night. What we saw first was Saddle Ball Mountain, a satellite peak, though viewed from the south it seemed higher.

Mount Greylock is thought to be named for a Mohawk chief. Its long silhouette reminded Herman Melville of a great white whale when he wintered over at Arrowhead, a farm in Pittsfield, writing *Moby-Dick*. You could see the similarity, sort of, in the massif's curved flanks and rounded summit to the north.

Melville lived close enough to Mount Greylock that when he finished *Moby-Dick*, he celebrated through the night with his friends at a party on the summit. He also picnicked on Greylock with Nathaniel Hawthorne, who described the undulating surroundings as "huge mountain swells heaving up" and subsiding like waves on a vast sea.

Thoreau spent a chilly night on Mount Greylock in 1864, sleeping with his head turned to the campfire. He said he covered himself with boards for lack of a blanket to keep warm. Even Edith Wharton ascended Mount Greylock. Her chauffeur, as she told it, became the first driver to take a motor vehicle to the top, in 1897. Now, of course, thousands do it on a paved road winding up the mountain.

As we hiked down North Mountain into Cheshire, a small pond shimmered like a mirage through the trees. It turned out to be a backyard swimming pool, protected by a wire fence.

Two centuries earlier, Cheshire secured its niche in American history as a record producer of Cheshire cheese, and specifically a massive slab weighing more than twelve hundred pounds. Elder John Deland, described as an "eloquent preacher and influential patriot," presented the cheese extravaganza to President Thomas Jefferson in the White House on New Year's Day of 1802, or so the carved stone monument on Cheshire's village green says. Members of the Congress and the Supreme Court assembled in the East Room of the White House for the occasion. They were reportedly allowed to carry chunks of the cheese home.

Cheshire appeared to have gone out of the cheese business by the time we arrived at the junction of School and Church streets. I read the inscription only because of the stone monument, carved in the form of an oversize cheese press—how Andy Warhol would have envied it—on a swatch of grass across the street from the post office. Knute was picking up a supply package mailed by his parents. I sifted through the contents of my pack, looking for items to mail home.

I bought a small box at the post office and threw into it my floppy sunhat, which always snagged on branches, and any clothes I hadn't worn more than once.

I thumbed through my paperback copy of *Walden,* reluctant to jettison its wisdom for the weight of a few tent pegs.

My copy of *Walden* had been a constant companion on my walk. It was also taking up too much room. At nearly eight ounces, it weighed more than the tent pegs.

"Simplicity, simplicity, simplicity!" Henry was shrieking inside my head. "I say, let your affairs be as two or three, and not a hundred or a thousand; instead of a million count half a dozen, and keep your accounts on your thumbnail."

Henry convinced me. Bidding farewell, I chucked *Walden* into the box. All I wanted to see again were my lost Tevas. As soon as Bruce Bernstein found them, he had called Jaqueline for instructions. "Then he'll just have to go barefoot," my helpmate advised. She did buy me new sandals later in Vermont.

Knute was performing a hasty triage on the parcel he had picked up from his parents, throwing some items into his small pack, offering others to me, and casting the rest into the hikers' box in a corner of the post office. Gleaning behind him, I picked up a couple of candy bars and some squares of baker's chocolate.

My arm was hurting. The mysterious bite had spread into a reddish splotch across my right biceps. I pulled out some suntan cream and smeared it on top of the infection. Redneck, who had ducked into the post office too, stared at my swollen arm. "Looks like you got Lyme disease," he said.

Ahead of us lay a strenuous climb to the summit of Mount Greylock. Knute, bandanna tied around his head to soak up the sweat, set his customary brisk pace as we cut through a freshly mown pasture and over a stone wall. Flash tucked in behind him and I brought up the rear. We crossed Outlook Avenue and charged the mountain's southern approach.

The trail rose almost straight up, climbing nearly eight hundred vertical feet over the next mile, switching back and forth up the contours of the ridge until I lost sight of my companions. I had misjudged Mount Greylock, which does not figure prominently in the annals of American mountaineering; because Melville and Thoreau had preceded me, I assumed that it would be a romp.

By the time I finally overtook Knute and Flash, they were finishing a short pee-and-water break and eager to move on. If they slowed down to my lagging stride, we could arrive at the summit lodge too late for dinner. Stripping down our pack weight left us with insufficient food to cook a proper meal.

"Go ahead without me," I told them. "Ask the lodge to save me something to eat. I'll be along."

"No," Knute said firmly. "We're traveling together and we're going to walk into that dining room together."

Flash, Knute, and I had barely met, and now my companions—we didn't even know each other's real names—were determined not to leave me behind. They moderated their pace and I stepped up mine to make sure they would not go hungry. I have not done as much for some people I knew better, or had them do as much for me.

Once we had achieved Saddle Ball Ridge, the steep trail leveled off somewhat, then rose and leveled off again at a more reasonable pitch. We left birch and maples behind and ascended into a dense belt of balsam fir stunted by wind and cold. We climbed through vegetation that presaged what lay to the north.

At last we emerged through the trees and onto paved asphalt. I had forgotten that Mount Greylock, which nearly defeated me lower down, had a paved road running clear to the top. I had been dodging branches, now it was back to dodging automobiles. Statistically, you're less likely to be done in by a hungry bear on Mount Greylock than by a speeding Mustang.

I imagined what literary introspection the hikers' register on Mount Greylock might have revealed in its less trammeled days. Henry Thoreau would have waxed as expansive about his summit bivouac as he did in a subsequent essay:

"But as it grew colder towards midnight, I at length encased myself completely in boards, managing even to put a board on top of me, with a large stone on it, to keep it down, and slept comfortably."

Melville would have signed his trail name: "Call me Ishmael."

And Wharton might have confessed to a little slack-hiking: "My chauffeur brought me this far."

The wind-battered trees gave way to a meadow that opened up the summit. Our destination, Bascom Lodge, was a cavernous building constructed from the local schist back in the 1930s, with a sloping roof and stone chimney, and two similar wings. The lodge could sleep several dozen overnight guests, most of them in simple bunkrooms; the overflow was left with sleeping bags on the floor.

And thanks to Knute's steady pace, we did arrive just in time for dinner, which was curried chicken with rice and overcooked stringbeans, served family-style at a long table by an amiable Ukrainian student here on a visitor's visa.

At the other end of the table, I spotted my Connecticut trailmates, Old Rabbit and Doctor Bob. I expected them to be several days ahead, but Old Rabbit explained that they had lingered in Dalton to visit the Crane Paper Company's paper and currency museum.

The view from the summit was spectacular in every direction. By day, you could see parts of Vermont, New Hampshire, New York, and Connecticut, as well as Massachusetts—all five states through which I planned to walk.

At night, the panorama was washed out by a blinding lighthouse beam on a memorial erected in 1931 to honor the Massachusetts men killed in the First World War.

The garish glare, more befitting the exercise yard of a maximum-security prison, ruined an otherwise unimpeded view of the pristine night sky. Persistent flickers penetrated from a few bright stars. Walking away from the lighthouse, I had better luck looking down on a carpet of lights sparkling, like strands of a long diamond necklace, from towns along the valley of the Connecticut River.

BREAKFAST tasted better, with lots of blueberry pancakes, bacon only slightly charred, and coffee. The pancakes were snapped up as fast as they appeared. These were customers who would burn off a day's calories before the next meal.

My arm looked, if anything, worse. The infection was streaking toward my armpit, an ominous sign. I called the local hospital. The receptionist advised me to come right in, never mind an appointment.

"Your taxi driver knows where we are," she said.

But taxis didn't cruise Mount Greylock. "I'll be hiking down," I said. I wasn't in bad enough shape to call an ambulance.

Knute and Flash were packed up and straining to travel. They told me where they hoped to camp that night, well inside Vermont, and I promised to catch up if the doctor let me continue. This time, they knew not to wait. I never saw them again, but I like to think they made it to the Appalachian Trail's finish line atop Mount Katahdin.

Several years earlier, brass plaques were bolted onto the summit's rocks as part of a renovation to make Mount Greylock more tourist-friendly. One from *A Week on the Concord and Merrimack Rivers* recalled the night Thoreau spent on Mount Greylock. Waking at dawn, he pushed aside his makeshift wooden coffin and climbed a small observation tower erected by students from nearby Williams College. He found himself surrounded by "an ocean of mist, which by chance reached up exactly to the base of the tower, and shut out every vestige of the earth, while I was left floating on this fragment of the wreck of a world, on my carved plank in cloudland.

"It was such a country," Thoreau concluded, "as we might see in dreams, with all the delights of paradise."

I doubt that Thoreau's envisioned paradise from Mount Greylock would have encompassed a golf course, a convention center, and clusters of new vacation homes linked by more asphalt roads and sewer lines. Such plans are afoot to carve a resort into the majestic northern slopes at an estimated cost of $125 million.

Thoreau himself observed, "If a man walks in the woods for love of them half of each day, he is in danger of being regarded as a loafer, but if he spends his whole days as a speculator, shearing off those woods and making earth bald before her time, he is esteemed an industrious and enterprising citizen."

I set off from the summit in the familiar company of Doctor Bob and Old Rabbit, without bothering to sign the hikers' register. It took about three and a half hours to descend over Mount Williams, 2,951 feet high. There were brief but rewarding views

of the valley as we dropped 2,500 vertical feet down an occasionally precarious trail, through sugar and red maples, red oaks,
white and yellow birches, and more stands of spruce and hemlocks, into North Adams.

North Adams was a prospering mill town before the textile
business fled overseas to cheaper factories, leaving it and other
New England towns to founder. North Adams had lost one third
of its population in the last fifty years according to local news reports, prompting the state department of environmental management to come up with the plan for a resort.

Old Rabbit's wife, Laura, had driven up from Rhode Island to
meet him, and was waiting at the end of Phelps Avenue. A nurse,
Laura took one look at my arm and ushered me into the Emlen
family Volkswagen for a drive straight to the hospital. We followed blue highway signs marked with a white "H."

The North Adams Regional Hospital was perched on a hill
above town. It was cool inside, and all but deserted. The staff
seemed used to seeing hikers stagger in from the Appalachian
Trail.

A young nursing student, Amy, escorted me into the emergency ward. Amy was slim and blond, with a white coat that
highlighted her summer tan. She sat me down on a bed and took
my temperature and pulse with nimble fingers, displaying a
sweet solicitude.

The doctor on duty appeared. With a businesslike felt-tipped
pen, she traced the outline of the crimson blotch on my arm, including the direction of the pinkish streaks.

"Looks like you were bitten," she told me.

"Lyme disease?"

The doctor glanced at my muddy shorts and boots. "Where
were you hiking?" she asked.

"From New York City. I just came over Mount Greylock. I think

I got bitten near Pittsfield." I added, "I'm trying to get to Vermont."

"It's definitely infected, probably from a tick or spider bite," she said. "But it doesn't look like Lyme disease."

The swelling characteristic of Lyme disease, she explained, presented itself in concentric red and white circles, like the bull's-eye on a shooting target. Still, my guidebook had warned that one in four infections from a deer tick did not manifest the classic symptoms of Lyme disease.

"We won't take chances," the doctor said. "I'm giving you antibiotics by intravenous drip to fight the infection right now. Then I'll prescribe a regimen of cephalexin, four times a day for ten days."

But would she let me keep walking with a suspected case of Lyme disease? I pictured myself escaping back to the Appalachian Trail, only to fight off waves of dizziness, shortness of breath, irregular heartbeats, facial paralysis, shooting pains through my arms and legs, and the other dire symptoms enumerated in my guidebook, while my mental faculties took an extended holiday, leaving me baffled about what I was doing in the woods anyway.

Or I could call Jaqueline to come and fetch me, in effect conceding that I had tried and failed in my journey, just short of the Vermont border. Would the hospital confine me in its intensive care ward? How soon would my wife show up? Would I still recognize her in the galloping dementia of Lyme disease?

"Can I go back to the trail?" I asked the doctor. Once I was chock-full of antibiotics, she might let me finish the last few miles to Vermont.

"Not today." The doctor shook her head. "I want you to check in to a motel, at least overnight, to see if the swelling on your arm goes down. You need the rest. North Adams has some good restaurants, by the way.

"Tomorrow, if the infection hasn't spread beyond the outlines of my pen, you can start hiking again. But don't push yourself, and keep taking the antibiotics every four hours until they're gone. If the infection looks worse tomorrow, come right back here. And if it doesn't get better while you're hiking, go to the nearest hospital."

A nurse set up an intravenous drip and inserted the needle into the back of my hand. I spent the next hour under Amy's supervision, listening to her stories about teaching aerobics and, inevitably, having a boyfriend.

After the doctor discharged me from the emergency ward, I found a telephone in the reception area and started calling motels listed in the Yellow Pages. They were full, until I found a room at a modest motel on the road west toward Williamstown. The proprietor promised to hold the room for an hour before renting it to the next arrival. The motel was a few miles from the hospital, he assured me, maybe ten minutes by taxi.

I couldn't afford to wait for a taxi. By now it was late Saturday afternoon, and I rushed downhill to the nearest pharmacy, on Eagle Street, before it closed. Since I didn't want to walk back uphill, I lugged my pack along.

The pharmacist filled my prescription for forty pills of 500mg cephalexin. I walked on to a supermarket, to stock up on food in the event that I was up to hiking tomorrow. My heavy pack rode in the market's wire cart while I made the rounds of the shelves, plucking groceries that added another six or seven pounds. By the time I was ready for a taxi, I couldn't find one.

There was nothing left but to start walking again, for what seemed a lot more than a few miles. I didn't reach the motel until nearly six P.M. A couple of loud guys in T-shirts peeled up in identical black pickup trucks, bearing cases of beer and bottle-blond girlfriends. They checked in to the room next to mine. It was shaping up into one raucous Saturday night.

I was tempted to indulge in a brief nap, but I was as hungry as I was tired. I took a hot shower instead, put on my only clean shirt, and walked across the road to an Italian restaurant where the food wasn't very good, but the cold beer was.

I walked back to the motel, turned on the air conditioner, soaked a towel in hot water, and slapped the hot compress on my arm. I couldn't see any change in the infection. Too weary to embark on anything as ambitious as watching television, I collapsed on the bed.

I slept ten hours, right through the party next door.

IT WAS a relief to find my swollen arm still attached to the rest of me when I awoke. The infection had not receded from the ink parameters outlined by the doctor's pen. But it had not spread either, which I took as implicit permission to resume walking. I was going to call a taxi to carry me back to the trailhead until I discovered that my room had no phone. I walked across the gravel yard to use the phone in the motel office, but it was locked and empty.

I returned to my room, which seemed dark and claustrophobic after my exposure to the morning sunlight. I filled my water bottles from a bathroom faucet, shouldered my pack, and ventured out in search of breakfast.

In the old expense account days, I would have scoffed at the notion of walking a couple of miles to eat breakfast cheap at a fast food franchise. But my immediate priority was enough carbohydrates to jolt me back into motion.

It took nearly an hour to walk to the red-roofed Friendly's restaurant I recalled seeing along the highway the previous afternoon. Again, there was the problem of what to do with my pack while I ate. I should have painted a large smiley face on it so I could plop it in a chair across the table as my dining companion.

But the thud it made when I dumped my pack near the cash register was loud enough that several customers turned around to see whether anyone they knew had keeled over.

Friendly's had filled up with a Sunday morning crowd of golden-age regulars, some of whom had come from mass at a Roman Catholic church just down the road. None of them looked capable of hoisting my pack, much less scampering away with it. Having the pack stolen no longer seemed such a calamity. Still, I transferred the fat plastic vial of antibiotics to my pocket before occupying a newly vacated table against the wall.

A fireplug of a woman was sitting in the booth across the aisle. "Mildred just had the shingles," her husband announced loudly to passersby, as though his wife had changed her mind about ordering the pancakes with imitation maple syrup.

"I felt it right here," Mildred chimed in, "and then it worked down over here—" Her graphic details, having to do with tingling and twinges of pain in sundry body parts, were better left for a doctor's examining room. But so were the other ailments volunteered by acquaintances who stopped to chat.

These were people who relished entertaining one another with their physical complaints. Migraines, cataracts, hernias, constipation, cranky prostates, varicose veins, incontinence—nothing seemed off-limits for breakfast conversation. I considered rolling up my T-shirt sleeve and flexing my inflamed biceps for the edification of my fellow eaters, with a shout: "Second opinions, please?" This was the right place to come for unsolicited medical advice on a Sunday morning.

But the waitress distracted me by setting down a platter with scrambled eggs, bacon, link sausages, and toast. I asked the waitress for more milk for my coffee. She plopped down a handful of those irritating plastic cuplets of dairy product that defy opening, except with your teeth or a Swiss Army knife.

The gentle folks around me, for all the health problems they described, were tucking into breakfasts as hearty as mine. Their ailments did nothing to diminish their appetites. Nor did my tick infection, which now sounded not so bad after all. And I was escaping to the Appalachian Trail.

I topped off the last slice of toast with a red-and-white 500mg capsule of cephalexin, swallowing it in full view of the other customers. My furnace stoked, I retrieved my pack and traced my steps back to the bridge over the Hoosic River. The Appalachian Trail's white blazes took me down a back street, through someone's yard and uphill along Sherman Brook. For a couple of hours, moving at a steady if slow pace, I climbed the last miles to the Vermont state line.

I wasn't convinced that I was there until I turned around in the small clearing to read the sign I had just passed: "Welcome to Massachusetts." I had indeed walked to Vermont. But a couple of weeks' traveling still separated me from retirement to my home in central Vermont, more than a hundred miles north and thirty miles west as the peregrine falcon flies.

I sat down on a large boulder and toasted my arrival in Vermont with a bottle of L'eau de La Faucet d'Motel Toilette and the second antibiotic pill.

THE INFECTION on my arm looked no kinder in the unfiltered sunlight, but I consoled myself that there had been a time when disease left me sicker than this.

During the Angolan civil war, I lived a week and a half in the bush with Unita insurgents as we traveled north toward Cuito Cuanavale, where Unita, with South African artillery support, had fought government troops and their Cuban allies to a standstill.

Andy, my fellow traveler from the Associated Press, and I lived relatively well, considering that a war was on. Mattresses were found for us to lounge in the back of a South African truck, while the guerrillas—hard, disciplined men in plain olive drab uniforms—squatted in rows on the bare metal. A foraging party returned nightly with fresh antelope meat, which was cooked up with spices into a pungent stew. Where the antelope came from wasn't clear, since the war had slaughtered most of the wildlife in which Angola once abounded. The skeleton villages we saw had little left to show beyond tattered posters extolling the demagogic leader of Unita, Jonas Savimbi.

The government fighter-jets patrolling overhead never descended to examine the reddish pillars of dust thrown up by the battered truck in which we jostled along. Their Cuban pilots were wary of the Stinger missiles that Unita had reportedly acquired from the CIA.

Our truck's frequent breakdowns came as a relief, when we could dismount, shake ourselves off, and breathe in cleaner air. The dust caked my face and glasses. When I spit to clear my mouth, it looked as though I were chewing tobacco. We passed inviting ponds, but I had been warned not to swim in Africa's still waters because of the risk of bilharzia, a snail-borne parasite that causes a potentially fatal disease called schistosomiasis.

After several days of hard travel, we forded a clear, fast brook and stopped to refill our canteens, to which I added prophylactic iodine tablets. I peeled off my clothes and stretched out in midstream, where the cold currents flowed swiftest, washed my hair and scrubbed down my skin. The water's chill was invigorating in the languorous midday heat. I climbed out and back into my dirty clothes, and we drove on.

A month later, I was reporting from Mozambique, on the other side of southern Africa, when a wave of headaches, fever, and chills overwhelmed me. I flew back to Johannesburg, where my doctor said I showed classic symptoms of malaria. I was taking antimalaria pills regularly, and a series of blood tests detected no malaria.

The fevers and chills persisted until my doctor, baffled, referred me to a leading South African specialist in tropical medicine, Benjamin Miller. He diagnosed bilharzia, his speciality, and put me in a military hospital, where he administered a new medication so powerful that the nurses kept monitoring my blood pressure and pulse. Dr. Miller put me through the treatment again a month later, to kill off whatever parasites survived the first blast.

From my hospital bed, I complained to Dr. Miller, "I thought you couldn't catch bilharzia in cold running water."

His bushy eyebrows furrowed. "That's the first myth," the good doctor said.

Vermont

Ascend our rocky mountains, let thy feet fail not with weariness, for on their tops the beauty and majesty of earth, spread wide beneath, shall make thee to forget the steep and toilsome way.

William Cullen Bryant

Six

In 1827, a New Englander named S. R. Hall published a book titled *The Child's Assistant to a Knowledge of the Geography and History of Vermont,* in which he exhorted his young readers to go out and enjoy the Green Mountains. This was bold advice at a time when most Vermonters had no choice but to walk. To them, these mountains were obstacles to going almost anywhere, too steep to clear and plow and too densely vegetated to yield a profitable run of maple syrup.

"From the summit of many of these mountains, the view is delightful," Hall enthused as though he had been there, "and will richly repay any one able to endure the fatigue, for the time and effort required to ascend to their tops."

Vermonters tell of an old farmer, when asked by a muddled tourist how to find a town he had already arrived in, snapping back, "Don't you move a goddamn inch!" A small sign in this modest clearing where I now stood told me to go no further to find the Long Trail, which runs two hundred seventy miles up the spine of Vermont's Green Mountains, from Massachusetts to the Quebec border.

The Long Trail, which extends into another 175 miles of side trails, is called Vermont's "footpath in the wilderness," an understatement that gives little hint of the wilderness's wild and rugged character. The trail wends its way over the highest peaks in Vermont, traversing expanses of national forest as well as privately owned pastures and woodland.

Thru-hikers should thank a Vermont school principal named James Taylor, who, like Hall eighty years earlier, wanted to "make the Vermont mountains play a larger part in the life of the people." Taylor was thirty-eight years old when he and his friends started carving out the Long Trail in 1910. The final ten or so miles to the Canadian border were completed in 1930. The achievement was celebrated with flares simultaneously set afire along the chain of summits traversed by the finished trail.

"The Long Trail is an invitation," Taylor explained once. "It entices all the world to walk a mountain-high, tree-embroidered, free, open and easy path that begins where Vermont begins and ends where Vermont ends."

As the country's oldest long-distance hiking trail, the Long Trail predates by more than a decade the Appalachian Trail, which follows it for a hundred miles before swinging eastward toward New Hampshire. The Appalachian Trail was not conceived until 1921 and was finished in 1937.

As I started the Long Trail, it seemed inexplicably more benign than stretches of the Appalachian Trail I had been traveling. I descended somewhat through shady groves of bright birch and hardwood maple trees. A bed of lush ferns to my left was interrupted by a scattering of large rocks. It was tempting to stop and stretch out among the ferns, but a half-dozen more miles remained before the next spot to camp for the night. I walked along a large beaver pond and, balancing on a large log, crossed the brook flowing out through the wall of accumulated logs, brush, and mud.

The *Long Trail Guide* lays out some travel rules with admirable bluntness. "If you packed it in, pack it out." "Take only pictures.

Leave only the lightest of footprints." "Don't carve into trees or shelters. People don't care who loves Sally or where Joe stayed when." The enforcement of this common sense falls upon the thousands of hikers themselves. I met more than a few capable of bludgeoning into unconsciousness anyone caught willfully defiling their wilderness.

Rules seem friendlier and easier to remember if you arrange them into haiku, that delicate poetry of seventeen Japanese ideograms. For example, this philosophical conundrum in the *Long Trail Guide:*

> Keep pets on
> leash and away
> from water
> sources.

Or a reflection from my Appalachian Trail map:

> Stay on
> trail lands
> if you wander
> too far you
> may be
> trespassing on private
> property.

I bought the trail guide a few months earlier when I joined the Green Mountain Club. Vermont has no dearth of country roads; indeed, I had to cross quite a few of them. But I thought that taking the Long Trail would better evoke what the pioneers must have felt when they arrived on these trails worn by the original Indian inhabitants and marked by French trappers.

The Long Trail represented the progressively contrarian mind-set of the state where I wanted to retire. Vermont abolished slavery in 1777, before the rest of the United States. Vermonters got a head start on the American Revolution. Ethan Allen and his Green Mountain Boys captured Fort Ticonderoga from the British in 1775. Another Vermonter, Solomon Brown, was the first to draw British blood, in the Battle of Lexington on April 19, 1775.

Vermont remained a self-declared republic until 1791, mostly because New York and New Hampshire, who coveted its territory, refused to let it join the original thirteen colonies forming the United States.

When Congress passed the Fugitive Slave Act in 1850 mandating the return of slaves to their owners, the Vermont state legislature responded by enacting heavier fines plus five years in jail for anyone caught sending back a slave. During the Civil War, Vermont dispatched more volunteers per capita to fight for the Union than any other state. At the Battle of Gettysburg in July 1863, one Vermont regiment fixed bayonets and countercharged Pickett's Charge, splitting the Confederate assault. Then the Vermonters, country boys on nine-month enlistments, went home to prepare to harvest their crops.

Other states prohibit same-sex civil unions but not the clutter of highway billboards. Vermont did the opposite. And no other state is represented by a politically independent senator in Congress and a socialist in the House of Representatives.

It was nearly nightfall by the time I arrived at the Congdon shelter, somewhere in the hills southeast of the town of Bennington. I had walked fourteen miles since breakfast back in Massachusetts. In the dark, it was hard to find ground flat enough to accommodate my tent. It took more time to refill my bottles from the brook without muddying the water before I pumped it through my filter.

I was tired. I fired up my stove and boiled enough water to cook a package of noodles, which I spilled over my shorts as soon as I sat down to eat. I made a supper as best I could out of what was left in the pot.

On the far side of the brook, another solitary traveler had set up a black tent, in contrast to the vivid colors characteristic of modern tents. His pack was black. He wore a black T-shirt bearing the logo of the FBI Academy in Quantico, Virginia. He introduced himself as Gatorman, though he looked more like Harrison Ford.

The man in black drew my attention for another reason. He must have been in his forties, but lean and hard enough to be mistaken for someone younger. Not many men find time to walk about in the prime career years between thirty and sixty. Gatorman was the exception. Most travelers on the trail, he and I agreed, were between jobs or had yet to find one.

"I was a deputy police chief in Florida," Gatorman said when I asked where he came from, and named a wealthy suburb near Miami.

"I was a cop for twenty-one years. I gave it up because of the aggro."

"Aggro?"

"Aggravation," he explained. "Being a cop was a good career when I started out. But today it gives you nothing but aggro. So I quit."

The disgruntled cop flew north, re-created himself as Gatorman, and started walking south. "I'm going to meet some friends in New Jersey," he said. "Or maybe I'll keep going to Pennsylvania."

Gatorman walked away and crawled into his tent without inviting more questions.

THE NEXT day dawned bright and cloudless. Gatorman headed off south—trail etiquette did not require him to say goodbye—

while I cooked my oatmeal, without spilling the pot this time. The sun was above the fir trees when I started north again.

An hour's walk along the ridge took me up Harmon Hill, a little more than 2,300 feet high. The trees on the hilltop had been chopped down long ago, to be replaced by wild ferns and bushes that grew waist-high in parts. It was a lovely site for a picnic, with fine views west to New York and, five miles away, to the town of Bennington.

The town's skyline was dominated by a slender monument to the Battle of Bennington in August 1777, which marked the first major defeat of British troops in the American Revolution. The Battle of Bennington was actually fought across the border in New York state. But Bennington had the nearest respectable tavern and got credit for the victory. Its stone pinnacle is said to be the tallest battle monument in the world, and so it looked from where I sat eating some peanut butter on bread in the meadow atop Harmon Hill.

The descent, steep and rocky, dropped me nearly a thousand feet down to Route 9, a disheartening loss of altitude that would have to be regained. Traffic rushed toward me from both directions as I trotted across the highway, which links Vermont with New Hampshire to the east and New York to the west. The Green Mountains run north to south, limiting the number of roads across the state.

I paused for a while to watch an almost unbroken procession of big trucks roll by.

Though I railed earlier against sport utility vehicles bullying pedestrians, I harbored no such resentment toward the big eighteen-wheelers that now whizzed past in a blast of wind that left no doubts about who owned the road. Truck drivers can be a decent, considerate lot if you give them room to do their job. I encountered them at their finest in Bosnia.

I had wangled permission from the office of the United Nations High Commissioner for Refugees to ride one of its humanitarian convoys across Bosnia during the war. The convoy I joined carried American grain, Italian cooking oil, and Scottish sleeping bags to Muslim refugees in Tuzla. The drivers were mostly Norwegians who had driven long-distance rigs in Europe before volunteering to work in Bosnia.

We set out from the UNHCR warehouse in Metkovic, a Croatian border town. The convoy's leader, a taxi driver from Lillehammer named Roy Finstad, led the way, briefing the other drivers by radio on the conditions and hazards ahead. He told us when to put on our flak jackets and helmets where there was danger of fresh fighting. We donned flaks and helmets six times on the run to Tuzla and back.

Roy had me ride with him. He apologized for smoking too much, a habit acquired in Bosnia that he wanted to quit. Roy had made about eighty round-trips into Sarajevo, under siege. Today the shelling was too heavy for a convoy to get through. So we headed further, for Tuzla.

To stay beyond range of Serbian artillery, Roy took the convoy over a precarious mountain road hardly wide enough for the bigwheeled rigs. The drivers followed, grinding uphill past outposts guarded by French soldiers in battle gear. At one treacherous hairpin turn, I looked over the cliff and saw a big white truck snagged upside down on rocks several hundred feet below. Part of a Danish food convoy, it had slid over the edge a few weeks back.

"The driver lived," Roy reported, "but he broke every bone in his body."

The Norwegians, who traveled unarmed, slept overnight inside their cabs, buttoned up at a warehouse compound in Zenitsa. Three British aid workers, Roy explained, had been ambushed some months back by rogue Arabs who had come to fight for a

Muslim Bosnia. One Brit died instantly. The others, wounded, jumped into the nearby river and rode it downstream to safety. Their stolen vehicle was later recovered near Sarajevo.

As we drove onward, Roy heard over the radio that another UNHCR vehicle had been hijacked. We saw it parked in a gritty little town the next day, with its UN insignia peeled off. Roy ordered the convoy to keep rolling.

Wearing helmets and flaks, we followed a road for a few miles down the middle of the front lines separating Serbs and Bosnians, past the incinerated carcasses of three civilian trucks destroyed earlier.

After our trucks were unloaded in Tuzla, we stayed the night with a Norwegian medical unit, drinking beer into the early hours. A driver told me about coming under fire once from the Serbian guns, and accelerating into a tunnel before another shell exploded where he had just been. Another said he had last traveled to Tuzla in snow, marooned in the storm for two days.

After a few hours sleep, the Norwegians climbed into their trucks and barreled back across the border to Metkovic, where they dispersed for sleep, a hearty dinner, and a swim in the nearby Adriatic.

"What's next for you?" I asked.

Roy lit another cigarette, coughed, and said, "We do it again."

VERMONT is said to have fewer roads today than on the eve of the Civil War. Some vanished in the regrowth of forest. Others I walked over had been reduced to little more than trails or logging tracks.

I crossed a picturesque brook on a small bridge and began the circuitous climb to Glastenbury Mountain, the first major peak in southern Vermont. The trail, which seemed long and tedious, led me upward through the narrow cleavage in what had looked like a monolithic cliff, then beneath a power line and later into a swampy stretch of woodland. My back again rebelled at the cumbersome pack, sending spasms through my body.

"I have walked myself into my best thoughts," boasted Søren Kierkegaard, the nineteenth-century Danish philosopher, "and I know of no thought so burdensome that one cannot walk away from it."

Sure, but nothing dampens the pleasure of thought like the burden itself. The accumulated weight of possessions compels you to keep looking down to avoid tripping up. Your outlook on the world gets restricted to rocks, tree roots, puddles, and slick leaves underfoot. The wider reality becomes harder to discern.

In woods this deep, all nature begins to look pretty much alike. I sometimes wondered if nocturnal elves were relocating the same scenery further down the trail while I camped.

We might grow less addicted to stuff if everything we bought had to be carried on our backs. Was it Socrates who said several thousand years ago that those who are happiest and nearest the gods are those who need nothing? I had wearied of my burdensome pack, whose center of gravity kept shifting below my buttocks. Little could be done about the tent, but my sleeping bag was too heavy and so damp sometimes that I could wring it out like a dishrag. I resolved to buy a new pack and sleeping bag during my rendezvous with Jaqueline in the village of Manchester in a few days.

I rested on the wooded ridge in a clearing called Porcupine Lookout. The porcupines were off doing whatever porcupines like to do on summer afternoons. But the views were spectacular. To the east below me stretched unbroken forest, then several undulating rows of mountains, and, to the southeast, a hump that I took to be Mount Greylock, which I had descended the day before yesterday.

The name bestowed on Vermont by French explorers in the early seventeenth century holds true. Samuel de Champlain is said to have cried, "Voilà, les vertes montes!" ("Behold, the green mountains!") I have seldom seen so many shades of green coexist in such harmony. From where I sat at Porcupine Lookout, the green needles of wind-stunted balsams and spruce took on a yellowish hue against their driftwood gray branches. The beech and maple leaves were bright emerald against the darker jades of hemlock and other firs. Sunlight had turned the ferns a luminescent chartreuse. There were other chlorophyl shadings in the seedlings and undergrowth sprouting along the trail. And the shadows of passing clouds turned entire swaths of green forest momentarily black.

There was not a shopping mall or a highway in sight. This was how the land must have looked to Champlain and his companions, before the settlers later walked into what they called New England. Only the eastern horizon was interrupted, by four thin white towers rising like windmills in what had to be New Hampshire.

The final push up Glastenbury Mountain felt like climbing a steep staircase or, to be more accurate, a succession of staircases improvised from rocks and logs. For all the strain on my quadriceps, the stairs were less strenuous than sliding on the mud-slick trail lower down. The climb was over when I saw cold water trickling above the trail from a metal pipe planted in an underground spring. I filled my empty bottles. At a shelter a hundred yards away, some hikers were eating supper.

The Goddard shelter, a sturdy stone dwelling named after a former Green Mountain Club president, was open on its southern side to an uncluttered view and a breeze brisk enough to keep mosquitoes at bay. There wasn't enough flat space near the shelter to pitch my tent, but sleeping inside the shelter seemed appealing, especially without mosquitoes. A vacancy opened up after several hikers announced they were moving on to spend the night on the mountaintop.

I shared the shelter's plank sleeping platform with five fellow travelers, among them a blonde and an equally attractive brunette from Brattleboro who had hiked up another trail. There were also a quiet graduate student at Indiana University named Tom and a redheaded young man who charmed the ladies by addressing them as "ma'am," and whom in turn they respectfully called Captain, and Storyteller, the North Carolinian with whom I crossed paths in Connecticut.

I expected Storyteller and his partner, Jed, to be well ahead by now. But Storyteller, it turned out, also landed in the emergency room in North Adams. Jed kept walking.

"I had a high fever and heart palpitations," Storyteller said. After his heartbeat and temperature returned to normal, he was discharged with the same caveat I was given. "The doctor said if I had any more heart trouble or fever to head for the closest hospital," Storyteller said. The hospital did a brisk business restoring ailing thru-hikers with antibiotics and putting them back on the trail, where they insisted on being anyway.

I shook out my sleeping bag next to Storyteller's. His bushy gray beard, floppy hat, and rural Southern twang made him look more than ever like a backwoods moonshiner.

"What put you on the trail?" I asked.

"I just retired," Storyteller said. "Had my own business servicing computers. I was ready to give it up."

Stretched out on his sleeping bag, Storyteller began to talk about his daughter coming home to live in North Carolina.

"She's still in school?" I asked.

Storyteller nodded. "Came back to finish up her Ph.D."

And Storyteller was fast asleep, a man who talked like a hillbilly but fathomed the inanimate perversity of computers and had a daughter working on her doctorate.

Before turning in, I walked downhill to the shelter's privy, where a sign advised: "Pee in the woods." It would have been more useful to tell us that at the top of the trail. Still, it was a relief to get official endorsement of what guys have been doing naturally for thousands of years.

THE NEXT morning, I asked Captain where he was hiking.

"Started in Maine, sir!"

"The Appalachian Trail?"

"Yes, sir!"

"But you're not from Maine?"

"No, sir! South Carolina."

His snappy responses evoked memories of starched fatigue uniforms, spit-shined boots, and tough love from dyspeptic master sergeants.

"Just out of the military, are you?"

"Yes, sir!" Captain said. He kept his old rank as a trail name. It did impress the pretty women.

Captain had completed four years as a transportation officer in the 18th Airborne Corps at Fort Bragg. I told him I'd been stationed at Fort Bragg as a paratrooper too, which he found interesting.

"What are you planning to do as a civilian?" I asked.

"Going into the family business, sir!"

"Well, happy hiking." How long would it take Captain to slip back into addressing his neighbors as "y'all"?

"Yes, sir!" he replied. I half-expected him to salute. "Good hiking to you, sir!"

It took but fifteen minutes to reach the 3,748-foot-high summit of Glastenbury Mountain, which turned out to be flat and heavily wooded. I climbed an abandoned fire tower for the view, which my trail guide promised would extend south to the Berkshire and Taconic ranges and north to Stratton and Equinox mountains in Vermont. But the morning was so hazy that I couldn't see much beyond the outlines of a small lake to the east.

I followed the ridge off Glastenbury for another four miles before breaking to rest at the next lean-to. It was called Caughnawaga and built with logs by kids from Camp Najerog in 1931. The lean-to had badly deteriorated and teemed with thousands of ants. There had to be a lost peanut-butter-and-jelly sandwich somewhere in the lean-to's seventy-year history.

Conceive of some bespectacled klutz of a kid—let's call him Marvin—who dropped his sandwich while his fellow campers were assembling the lean-to six decades ago. Marvin couldn't confess to such clumsiness, so he must have shoved the peanut butter, jelly, and dirt sandwich in the caulking between the logs. Marvin and his chums at Camp Najerog would be octagenarians by now, and given more to losing dentures and the like, so it's a bit late to ask them to come back and clean up. But I wish Camp Najerog realized that it had left for posterity the densest ant colony on the Appalachian Trail.

It was all uphill from the Caughnawaga lean-to, moving north on the ridge. At the first clearing, more lines of ridges and mountains emerged. A wind began blowing up, a harbinger of rain to follow.

Though it was only mid-afternoon, I resolved to stop at the next shelter, near Story Brook. My back was hurting again and Stratton Mountain was too far to climb before dark. It meant doing only nine miles today, after routinely clocking the double digits.

The last two days of fourteen miles left me more enervated than usual, possibly because of the antibiotics I swallowed four times a day. The tick infection on my arm had begun receding.

As my pace dragged, a gossamer black butterfly, speckled white with a scarlet band across its wings, flitted ahead as though it were enticing me along the trail, like the mischievous Tinkerbell. The butterfly disappeared into the trees, then reappeared and finally vanished as I approached the Story Brook shelter.

I was met by an amiable tan-and-white dog, the large sort normally found herding farm animals, though this one wore a red doggie pack. He sniffed me over before admitting me to the shelter, which was occupied by a young woman who introduced herself as Shannon. She didn't look to weigh much more than her dog. Shannon unharnessed his red doggie pack and extracted a plastic bowl and a sack of dry food, which she poured into the bowl. The dog wolfed it down.

"His name is Palix," she told me. "He's a cattle dog. I got him in Oregon."

Shannon lived in Lee, Massachusetts, several days' walk to the south. "I was teaching school but I tired of it." She brushed back her soft dark hair. "I've decided to study to become a wildlife ecologist, maybe in Mexico."

Shannon thrived on the outdoor life. A hiker who burns five thousand calories a day is unlikely to have a weight problem. Shannon was a section-hiker, covering the Appalachian Trail a few days at a time. And she was doing it by herself.

"Don't you feel vulnerable hiking alone?" I asked her. Every hiker had heard about the two young women in Virginia who were murdered on the Appalachian Trail, though it had happened years earlier.

"But I'm not alone. Palix looks after me." Her canine escort panted agreement, exposing some formidable fangs in his powerful jaws. Physically, Palix was equipped to rip the arm off anyone lunging for his mistress.

"So Palix would—" I began.

"Yes," said Shannon, who seemed not uncomfortable about sharing the shelter with someone closer to her grandpa's age.

Shannon was heading back south the next morning, so we left our packs at the shelter and hiked with Palix for an hour or so to check conditions ahead. A hand-lettered sign warned that the bridge over Black Brook was washed out and the brook could only be crossed by wading it. It proposed following an inconvenient detour to the west.

Back at the shelter, Shannon insisted on boiling some water to make us herbal tea. The rain arrived early enough to convince me to sleep inside. I took one end of the wooden platform and Shannon took the other. Palix stretched out at the foot of her sleeping bag and, so far as I could see, didn't take his eyes off me.

The next morning, Shannon cooked breakfast, consisting of instant oatmeal hydrated in instant cappuccino. It tasted better than it sounds. She saddled up Palix and they trotted off together. If this fine weather held, I would climb over Stratton Mountain and camp tonight beside a quiet pond on the far side.

The bridge over Black Brook had been swept away, as the sign warned, but some Good Samaritan had strung a length of clothesline from one bank to the other. With one hand loosely on the line, I crossed the river by hopping from one rock to the next without falling in.

There were more reminders of Vermont's past when I crossed a road to Arlington that followed the old Kelley Stand stagecoach route. Kelley Stand itself lies five miles west, and the old tavern where travelers spent the night is long gone. Following a smaller gravel road took me through a lumber camp, also vanished, called Grout Job.

The trail returned to the woods and cut back and forth in a succession of rugged switchbacks up Stratton Mountain. I paused to filter more water from a spring spilling onto the trail.

A fire tower atop Stratton Mountain, 3,936 feet high, offered unimpeded views of the previous two mountains I had traversed, Glastenbury and Greylock, and two more mountains ahead, Killington and Bromley. To the east in New Hampshire, rock outcrops were gleaming on Mount Monadnock. Despite the sunny, pleasant weather, a brisk wind keened over Stratton's summit, rattling the skeletal tower.

Stratton Mountain has a transcendental significance for serious hikers, who view it as the inspiration for the two most prominent trail systems in the United States. James Taylor said that the idea of the Long Trail came to him while he waited for the mists to dissipate from Stratton's peak. Stratton is said to have motivated another patriarch of the outdoors, Benton MacKaye, to create the Appalachian Trail as "a footpath for those who seek friendship with the wilderness."

My musings on the mountain's significance were interrupted by the splash of a fifteen-year-old in a baseball cap announcing his arrival by loudly pissing all over the summit rocks, much as feral dogs do when marking their territory. Fortunately, the balsams on Statton's summit were too scraggly for carving initials. But the right to pee in the woods should not extend to clearings where other hikers stretch out to eat their lunches. The youth was accompanied by more than a dozen other noisy adolescents who had been bused from Albany, New York.

Several of the girls joined me on the fire tower, emitting banshee screams whenever the wind caused it to sway. They squealed in mock fright as though Stratton's lovely summit were an amusement park and they were riding a roller coaster. I would have pointed out the whalelike silhouette of Mount Greylock that inspired Melville, but these kids might take *Moby-Dick* for a punk rock group.

Once down from the fire tower, I sought out their chaperone, a young woman who acknowledged her inability to restrain her charges by shrugging and rolling her eyes.

It is too easy to infer from such louts that all teenagers are obnoxious. Chalk it up to a generation gap widened by the acceleration of technological change. Only twenty years earlier, we toiled as foreign correspondents without computers or cell phones. Kids like these are hard put to conceive of a world that lacked either.

The adolescents on the mountaintop had barely started school when the Soviet Union collapsed; I wondered if they knew who won the Cold War. They were not conceived when I covered the Vietnam War, or the peace accord between Israel and Egypt, or the captivity of diplomats at the United States embassy in Tehran.

Was I being dismissive? Thoreau would have thought so. "Age is no better, hardly so well, qualified for an instructor as youth, for it has not profited so much as it has lost," Henry reproached, having reached this sage conclusion in his thirtieth year. "One may almost doubt if the wisest man has learned anything of absolute value by living," which is true enough for many of us when it comes to programming the VCR.

But in Thoreau's time, teenagers hardly existed as such in Vermont or other parts of rural America. There was no time for adolescence. Girls and boys started work earlier, married earlier, birthed or sired their children earlier, and died earlier. Their schooling, such as they received, came in winter, because their labor could not be spared during the spring sowing and autumn harvests. They still managed to drive their elders to despair, I'm sure, but they had less time and money to do it. Today, American-style adolescence remains a luxury that much of the world still cannot afford.

For now, I was anxious to distance myself from these ill-behaved trolls and tune out their prattle about Britney Spears. One of the dispensations of growing older is that you're excused from having to know, or care, who Britney Spears is. Call me old-fashioned, but I assert unequivocally that there hasn't been any-one really worth listening to since, well, John Fogerty and the best rock group ever, Creedence Clearwater Revival, and, maybe, the Beatles with *Sgt. Pepper's Lonelyhearts Club Band* before Yoko Ono came along to muck them up, and I shouldn't overlook Sun Records' rockabilly lineup of Elvis Presley—the early Elvis—Johnny Cash, Carl Perkins, and Jerry Lee Lewis, and Buddy Holly too, for that matter, though Dire Straits has a great guitarist in Mark Knopfler, and the Grateful Dead sound most mellow when you don't crank up the volume. I once interviewed Jerry Garcia, who was charming if unquotable because he was stoned at the time. I even met Janis Joplin. That's all I'll say about the de-plorable state of music today.

I passed up continuing to the mountain's satellite northern peak, where Stratton's ski lifts converge, and instead took the Long Trail directly downhill. There would be more time left for skinny-dipping in the bracing waters of Stratton Pond. And tomorrow would take me into the town of Manchester, where Jaqueline had agreed to meet me.

Stratton Pond is the elegant sort of miniature lake that gets cel-ebrated on travel brochures. As one of the most popular sites on the Long Trail, it attracts several thousand visitors in the summer, in part because of a convenient access trail and parking lot. I in-tended to claim one of the tent sites set aside on the wooded northern shore. But by the time I arrived, the shoreline was overflowing with a church group from Michigan that had booked all the campsites for the next four days.

The tenters were amiable enough, though more numerous than the ten-camper limit imposed by the Green Mountain Club on organized groups, and not inclined to shift for a stranger. Their menfolk stared at me in the grudging way that the ancient Is-raelites must have watched a disoriented Philistine who strayed too close to their campfires. The women were friendlier. One loaned me her biodegradable shampoo when I went for a swim, though in my hiking shorts rather than naked as I had hoped.

When I asked where I might pitch my tent, one pointed to a hollow between two pine trees, which was ample enough to squeeze in a hiker arriving without legs, and good for sopping up drinking water.

I was grilled about where I came from, theologically as well as geographically. When I identified myself as a newly retired news-paper reporter (and, I added, an Episcopalian), a chatty blond woman took it as an invitation to share her reading tastes.

"I just finished this novel by a Christian author where the world ended and everyone got saved in the Rapture and were gathered up into Heaven," she told me, "except for two sinners unworthy of redemption. And do you know that one of them was a journalist?"

Yes, I nodded, that sounded about right.

I packed up and walked back to the Vondell shelter on the other side of the lake. Scruffy thru-hikers with names like Lefty and Stray Cat were settling in. They salted their conversation with what my old newspaper euphemistically calls barnyard obsceni-ties. But they were willing to share. While we fiddled with our stoves, Stray Cat complained about having hiked once to a shelter in bad weather to find it claimed by a Boy Scout troop from Mass-achusetts. "The scoutmasters sealed off the shelter and wouldn't let anyone else in," he recalled. The memory of being turned away still enraged him. Lefty grunted sympathetically. Trail protocol dictates that when a newcomer shows up, everyone should move over. The *Long Trail Guide* directs: "Please fit fellow hikers in."

Stray Cat wore a bandanna pulled tight over his skull. He had covered twenty-eight miles that day, compared with my eleven. He had previously walked Vermont's Long Trail twice from Massachusetts to the Canadian border; that's two hundred and seventy miles end-to-end each trip. This summer, he was bound for the White Mountains in New Hampshire. "I'm doing the Whites," he explained. The rest of the year, he worked in an outdoors store in Massachusetts.

"Why do you enjoy it?" I asked my usual question.

"It's a simple life," Stray Cat supposed, giving more thought to his stove than to my question. "You don't have to think about anything but hiking and eating."

I wanted to quip that I thought about blisters and an aching back. Instead, I nodded in empathy with Stray Cat's wise reply. My body was cooperating better than I had reason to expect. I had forgotten about my arthritic ankle and never did strap on the eighty-dollar brace prescribed by the surgeon in New York. My age no longer mattered, not to the likes of Stray Cat and Lefty. I wasn't walking as fast or as far as they, but I was walking as fast as I could, more than three hundred miles so far. My wife and kids were gentle on my mind, and it had been days since I had fretted about lost *Times* paychecks, about e-mail piling up unanswered, about bills going unpaid. After forty years as a professional news junkie, I had lost interest in tuning my tiny radio to the latest news, or turning it on at all. I was clueless about the stock market and the New York Yankees. The cell phone stayed inside my pack, with my pepper spray. My daily fears involved Lyme ticks, poison ivy, and damp matches.

Filtering drinking water fresh from a natural spring, coaxing enough flame from the fuel canister on my ministove to cook one more supper of noodles and canned tuna, finding a dry patch to pitch my tent and a cool lake to jump in—such triumphs defined contentment. Indulgence was measured out in squares of semi-sweet baker's chocolate. I could not recollect all the things that I no longer craved or needed. Well, at least not until tomorrow, when I planned to pull off the Long Trail for a zero day—no mileage—in Manchester.

Jaqueline promised to meet me with some clean clothes. She had reserved a room at a comfortable inn in the village, where I could sleep in a bed and eat meals cooked by folks who knew what they were doing. I would buy a better pack and sleeping bag. I resolved to lighten my load by cutting back on everything else.

Stratton Pond is one of a handful of popular spots on the Long Trail where the Green Mountain Club dispatches a caretaker to collect an overnight fee, in this case five dollars. Lefty, who had been minding his own business, was cooking up a fragrant mess of pasta and beans. He promised the caretaker that he would move on once he had eaten. And true to his word, Lefty packed up and left, telling us that he was damned if he would pay five bucks to sleep in what was a national forest already subsidized by the taxpayers. My guess is that Lefty did a stealth camp in the woods a mile or two up the trail. Though they sleep where they are not supposed to, stealth campers leave fewer traces than most legal visitors.

Stray Cat could only come up with three singles, and the caretaker said he didn't have change for anything larger. I paid Stray Cat's two-dollar shortfall along with my own fee. He reimbursed me with a couple of packets of instant oatmeal, which pass for currency on the trail.

I asked the caretaker whether he had collected from the tenting Christians on the other side of the lake. "Not yet," he said, "but I know there's ten of them camping for the next four days."

"Only ten?" I said. "I don't think so." Based on my experience doing crowd counts as a reporter, there were a lot more souls dug in over there. They may have booked ten places, but they were proliferating like the loaves and fishes shared at the Sermon on the Mount.

But, I hastened to add, the tenting Christians across Stratton Pond were decent enough folk. And if the trumpets of Judgment Day sounded before their reservation expired, they would get transported to the Pearly Gates in the apocalyptic Rapture, leaving the lake's prime tent sites to be divided up among us sin-sodden trail travelers.

I WAS wakened about four o'clock by the pounding of heavy rain. It slammed the shelter's slanting corrugated roof with such force that I dreamed myself in the engine room of a ship tossed in a hurricane. Had I pitched my tent in that soggy hollow across the lake, I might have ended up listed as a freak drowning in the local newspaper.

I got up as soon as there was light to move about, and boiled up my two packets of instant oatmeal. Stray Cat was sucking dry oatmeal flakes into his mouth directly from the packet. I offered to cook it for him, but he insisted between chews that oatmeal didn't taste that bad raw. He was anxious to hit the trail. He was also stopping in Manchester for the day, to wash clothes and stock up on groceries for his assault on the Whites. I packed more slowly with the rain in mind, making my pack as waterproof as I could. Stray Cat had vanished into the rain by the time I started walking, having waited in vain for the torrents, punctuated by thunder, to let up.

It was the kind of downpour that had motivated Noah to get out of bed and start hammering together his ark. I was soaked even before I crossed the Winhall River and made my soggy way through sometimes dense vegetation into a three-mile stretch of primitive forest called the Lye Brook Wilderness.

The deluge obscured where the trail led, and several times I had to retreat. It was difficult to distinguish streams of rainwater in the marshland from the true path through the wilderness, poorly marked under the best conditions. What had been dips in the terrain now filled with puddles and deeper pools. I negotiated the flooded trail by straddling its shoulders and balancing on my trekking poles. I slipped on the mud and sudden pain jolted up my leg. I had twisted my bad ankle.

And still the rains came down, transforming the woods into faux–tropical rain forest. Every leafy branch I passed dumped more water down my neck until I was soaked to the skin. My rain parka seemed to be holding in more than it was keeping out. I had started out wearing gaiters to keep my boots and heavy socks dry, but they too became hopelessly waterlogged before I emerged at last from the Lye Brook Wilderness.

The driving rain did not end until I had peeled off from the trail and was walking down the stony Rootville Road into Manchester. The sun came out, bringing a mist rising from the steamy woodland. Hypothermia can pose a risk even in summer, and I found myself shivering. I pulled on my soggy fleece jacket, which did warm me up. But my trousers, heavy with water and caked with mud, slapped against my legs.

I managed to squish up ahead of Jaqueline at the elegant Inn at Manchester. The friendly staff pretended that my scruffy appearance was not unusual among their guests, some of whom were sitting outside on the manicured lawn, dressed down in tennis whites and crisp sundresses. "We've had hikers before," the receptionist said. But I was not discouraged from unlacing my boots and carrying them upstairs.

I didn't have time to shave before Jaqueline drove in, but managed to put on a wrinkled change of clothes, which were drier though no cleaner than what I peeled off.

We headed out to do Manchester. I was abandoning America's least desirable activity—walking—for its favorite pastime—discount shopping. Manchester calls itself "Fifth Avenue in the Mountains." As soon as I entered Brooks Brothers, a nattily dressed older salesclerk headed me off.

"May I help you?" he asked pleasantly.

"I'm looking for a shirt," I said, and pointed to a display rack of dress shirts at forty percent off. "Maybe in blue."

"We seem to be out of blue in your size," he said after rifling through the rack. "Let me look down in the storeroom."

He returned, smiling, with a blue shirt.

"Would you like anything else?" he asked. "Feel free to look around."

I had forgotten that such retail outlets exist for profit, not exclusivity. Had I walked in from the trail wearing the pelt of a freshly slaughtered bear, it would not have raised an eyebrow.

Jaqueline and I drifted across the street to Burberry, where I bought another blue shirt, steeply discounted. My support team succumbed to a red fall coat in her size, lined with Burberry's trademark plaid. Accumulating shopping bags, we wended our way through Nicole Miller, Garnet Hill, and Peruvian Connection. Among the Armani, Donna Karan, Anne Klein, Versace, Perfumania, and Liz Claiborne outlets are a spectacularly good bookstore, Northshire Books, and a couple of outdoors stores.

The real clash of civilizations was occurring outside at Malfunction Junction, as the locals call their busy three-way intersection of Routes 7A and 30. Traffic control at Malfunction Junction consists of some blinking red lights that offer no hint as to who ought to be yielding way.

A few hours earlier, I had been wandering alone through the wilderness. Now I was in the front seat of our Volvo with Jaqueline driving, mired in the kind of gridlock we had endured for three years in Cairo. Here the delays were caused mostly by cars with New York and New Jersey license plates, which tried to jump the line and succeeded more often in snarling the already chaotic flow of traffic. In New York City, a blinking red light means looking both ways while you accelerate through it.

I saw Stray Cat, his pack loaded with fresh supermarket provisions, rushing back toward the Long Trail like Lot in full flight. I knew how Stray Cat felt. When you've grown accustomed to the trail, a little urban life can seem overwhelming. "Wait for me!" I wanted to shout, but Jaqueline had made a dinner reservation at a recommended restaurant. I hunched down in my seat, embarrassed to let Stray Cat see that I had forsaken the call of the wild.

When I allowed as how my faithful old pack was giving me backaches, Jaqueline, who would rather have browsed the stacks of Northshire Books, told me, "Then throw it away and we'll get a new one!" She swung a detour back to the Eastern Mountain Sports outlet, and made me buy a smaller, sleeker pack and lighter sleeping bag. I scooped up a fresh fuel canister for my Pocket Rocket stove.

My new pack, a Gregory, was deftly fitted to my frame by Brendan McKenna, a lanky salesman who conceived of his job as actually helping the customer. With a thoroughness befitting bespoke tailors on London's Saville Row, Brendan, a seasoned hiker himself, instructed me to hoist one arm overhead, then the other, while he pulled at the pack and tugged or loosened the straps until it felt molded to my back.

We extracted ourselves from Malfunction Junction in time to

get back to the inn and clean up for the Reluctant Panther, where the food is called cuisine and carries Midtown Manhattan prices. It was delicious, of course. Presentable in my new blue shirt, I ordered simple: a Caesar salad enhanced with succulently ripe slivers of avocado, followed by pomegranate-glazed medallions of smoked pork tenderloin with a medley of roasted potatoes, carrots, and asparagus in an apple-cinnamon demi-glaze. (The chef was glazing up a storm that evening.)

For the last few weeks, I had been wolfing noodles from a single pot with my spoon. Now a dazzling assortment of silver forks and knives confused me. I resisted the urge to squirrel away some freshly baked rolls and pats of butter for my return to the trail the next day.

THOUGH the Long Trail skirts Manchester, the town makes no effort to attract hikers, who, after all, may spend less in a summer season than some motoring tourists drop overnight. What used to be a hostel for hikers closed down, leaving the bed-and-breakfast places, which don't like trail travelers soiling their hand-hooked rugs and monogrammed towels, leaving dirt rings around the old-fashioned bathtub, and wolfing down all the home-baked blueberry muffins before the desirable guests appear for breakfast.

For all its outdoor attractions, including nearby Mount Equinox as well as Stratton, Manchester caters to the moneyed class in ski season and out. The demand for second homes even created a labor shortage. A former New Yorker who relocated to Manchester lamented that you couldn't find carpenters, electricians, plumbers, or other useful hands anymore because "people with nothing to do"—her code for the rich weekenders from Boston and New York City—had hired them away at higher wages.

My zero day with Jaqueline was delightful, but I felt like a stranger in Manchester and was restless to return to the familiarity of the trail. By not being welcomed in more towns, the Appalachian Trail was at risk of becoming a self-selecting ordeal for the super-fit, widening America's grand divide between its ironmen, and ironwomen, and its slobs.

Over salads at the Little Rooster Cafe, where the waiting time for a table was a mere hour and a half, Jaqueline reminded me that she had to fly the next weekend to a reunion of her mother's childhood friends in Red Oak, Iowa.

"Will you get to the house in time to feed the cats?" my wife asked with some anxiety. "I don't want to have to put them in a kennel."

In time to feed the cats? I only had to climb over the rest of the Green Mountains as far as Sherburne Pass, then swing east into New Hampshire, walk north along the Connecticut River, then back across the river into Vermont and up Bragg Hill to our home in retirement. As I calculated it, that gave me a week to cover something more than a hundred miles, much of it uphill.

"No problem," I breezily assured her. My walk was winding up as a race against the clock to ensure that her elegant prime cat, Eliza, and spunky little spare cat, Nikki, were overfed on schedule, unless I sprained my ankle, got hit by lightning, or suffered a number of other potential calamities running through my mind that suddenly seemed plausible. I could imagine the elegant prime cat and spunky little spare cat wailing piteously for their Meow Mix while I lay comatose from a bloody tumble down some forested mountainside.

"Of course, I could ask Donna"—our Vermont neighbor—"to look in on the cats," Jaqueline said.

"I said I'll do it."

"You're sure?" she prodded. "And clean the litter box? There is the kennel, I suppose. But all those dogs barking at them—"

I was more concerned about a lawsuit from the owner of whatever yappy dog might be dumb enough to take on our spunky little spare cat. "Mr. Wren," I could hear the kennel owner complain, "your delinquent kitty has been frightening the rottweilers."

"Trust me," I assured my wife.

By the time I was hiking up among the boulders on Rootville Road, it was after four P.M., an hour where I would normally begin looking for a place to camp. The return to the Long Trail went more painlessly than I anticipated. My new pack rode high against my back, as I propelled myself uphill with the trekking poles.

I soon reached the next shelter north, below Spruce Peak, but since I was not tired or hungry, I pushed on toward the next camping area, which my guidebook located at the start of the next climb up Bromley Mountain. An old road led me to a small bridge where a couple of fishermen had set up a tent and were feeding branches into a campfire. Once I crossed the bridge and was back in the woods, I had the trail to myself again. In another fifteen minutes I came upon the tenting area set on the banks of Bromley Brook. I had covered just six miles but it was growing dark.

I camped beside the brook, erecting my tent by the light of my headlamp, and boiled water for some supper. The night turned colder, which was good because it kept away mosquitoes. Silver light from a ripening moon poured through the canopy of leaves. The cold air seemed to suck perfume from the surrounding firs. Sitting in darkness under the stars, eating noodles again, I heard an owl hooting and listened for the more remote reply. Such nights no longer left me uneasy. I hoped that, in Saint Paul's words, I was learning to be content with whatever I had.

"I know what it is to have little, and I know what it is to have plenty," Paul reassured his followers in Philippi who worried about his hard life. "In any and all circumstances I have learned the secret of being well-fed and of going hungry, of having plenty and of being in need."

I put aside the pot and hoisted my food bag over the branches of a nearby tree. I crawled into my tent and snuggled into the fluffy new sleeping bag, still wearing my sweater and jacket, lulled into contentment at the thought of walking again toward home.

I had been disabused of the assumption that contentment is synonymous with plenty when I reported from Mozambique, a country abounding in natural beauty and beautiful people on Africa's southeastern coast. A vicious civil war, exacerbated by the alternating natural disasters of drought and flood, had left the country an international charity case for so long that donor fatigue was setting in. Whenever I went there to work, I wore old clothes to give away before I left. It sounds patronizing, but there was no shortage of grateful recipients. Only in Mozambique did I find refugees in straits so dire that some were reduced to wearing loincloths fashioned from tree bark and vines.

On one such trip I flew with my son, Chris, into an isolated government-held village in central Mozambique that was beseiged by Renamo insurgents. The plane was chartered by CARE. Chris, who had taken a year off from college to join us in Johannesburg, has a photographer's eye and had already published photographs from Namibia and Angola in the *Times*. I doubt that my wife was totally aware where I took him, but Chris was cool under pressure and a good companion in tight spots. And taking him along ensured that I wouldn't do anything reckless.

Our pilot, an expatriate Canadian, made an initial pass over the village. If he didn't see children outside, he explained, something was wrong and he wouldn't land. But enough children were waving here that he banked and touched down on the rutted dirt airstrip with a minimum of bumps. An ancient C-46 cargo plane had landed before us. Barefoot villagers were unloading its cargo of heavy sacks of donated grain. The workers would get paid with a portion of the grain. Some weighed less than the hundred-and-ten-pound sacks they hoisted.

It would take them more than an hour to unload the aircraft, so Chris and I set out to explore the village. Most of its inhabitants had collected along the airstrip to see the grain unloaded and wait for it to be handed out. A few soldiers napped in their trenches. The shacks looked deserted. I didn't want to stray too far, with Renamo guerrillas rumored in the vicinity. We heard a chorus of children's voices and followed them to a derelict wooden building that might have been the headquarters of a bygone Portuguese colonial administrator. Its windows were gone now and most of the peeling shutters had fallen off.

The singsong chorus grew louder as we walked inside, taking care to sidestep missing floorboards. At the end of the long hallway, we pushed open a door. Several dozen children sat half-naked in rows on the floor of the bare room, watching a teacher write on a fragment of broken blackboard with some substitute for chalk. He pronounced each new word slowly, and had the children repeat it over and over. There were no books. The teacher wore no shoes and a shirt and trousers so tattered that they exposed his bony elbows and knees. When the children stopped chanting to gape at us, he stood patiently, waiting for us to leave. I wondered why he hadn't joined the other men unloading the plane. Wouldn't he miss his share of the food rations about to be distributed at the airstrip? Chris raised his camera but I shook my head. We shut the creaking door quietly and walked back to the dirt airstrip. The teacher's voice and children's responses resumed.

Tossing on my bed that night in the muggy heat of a hotel in Beira, I wondered whether what I did counted for anything. CARE let me ride on its plane, hoping that what I wrote might encourage more aid donors. But whether it did or didn't, I would be dining well soon enough in Maputo, the capital. If Renamo overran the village, the teacher might be dragged out and beheaded. The guerrillas showed contempt for education as the Khmer

Rouge had in Cambodia. If Renamo came to terms with the government (as it ultimately did), the teacher would be free to do what—teach more hungry children in abysmal circumstances, without prospect of adequate recompense?

The barefoot teacher seared my memory, leaving little doubt about which of us followed the nobler calling.

Seven

WHEN I first started walking to Vermont, I resolved to write up the day's events before going to sleep, based upon my notes and digital voice recordings. But more often than not, I was too tired and postponed the task until morning, when I could think more clearly. I needed to reflect not just on what I was doing, but also on why. So while I rose shortly after six on this morning, breakfasting on more oatmeal and a fresh loaf of rye bread, enjoying the luxury of a full fuel canister screwed into my Pocket Rocket stove, it took two hours before I started walking.

First, I fleshed out the notes that I had scribbled into my journal by the light of my headlamp the previous evening. Then I dumped out the contents of my new pack and reconfigured the load so the heavier gear would ride higher on my back. I was traveling lighter now, with a change of underwear and two pairs of clean socks in place of all the stuff I had been carrying, but my stove, tent, and fresh groceries still took up space. The chill morning warmed slightly as the first sunlight flitted through the trees. The birdsong to which I had awakened was giving way to harsher sounds of car and truck traffic building on the highway that I had crossed the previous evening.

I filled up my water bottles at the brook. It would not take much more than an hour to the top of Bromley Mountain, which was only 3,260 feet high, though scale is relative in hiking. As the mountain grew steeper, I climbed more slowly. Soon a lean stranger was crowding my heels, and I stepped aside. He paused and extended the scarred bottom piece of a trekking pole.

"Is this yours?" he asked in the burred accent of northern England.

"No, I've got mine."

Mick had come over from Northumberland to do the Appalachian Trail. There were some good walks in England and Wales, he said, and in Spain too—he mentioned the five-hundred-mile pilgrimage to Santiago de Compostela—but none compared in scenic diversity to the Appalachian Trail. He had been walking since Georgia at a pace brisk enough to deliver him to Maine before the first autumn frosts, though looking at his meager pack, I wasn't sure what he was living on. Mike made Flash and Knute, my go-light companions back in Massachusetts, look like beasts of burden.

"Cheers," he called. He sprinted up the trail and out of sight.

I resumed walking but when I jammed my left pole in between the rocks for traction on a steep pitch, the support wasn't there. My pole tip had fallen out—I must not have twisted it tight before setting out—and the end of the shaft was clogged with dirt, which meant that Mick quite probably was carrying the rest of it.

Almost all the serious hikers use trekking poles now, and mine helped keep my full weight off my bad ankle. The damaged pole would be useless unless I could retrieve the tip. I could walk back to Manchester to buy new poles, but that would cost me more than a day. Small mishaps on the trail can add up to large ones, and my missing pole tip evoked the adage about the battle being lost for want of a horseshoe nail. I had to catch up with Mick, which seemed impossible unless he stopped to linger on the summit.

My path merged into a broader ski trail overgrown thigh-deep in summer vegetation. The trail, Runaround, led to the bare mountaintop of Bromley, where lift chairs dangled motionless, unmoved by the slight breeze. It had been years since I skied at Bromley, but I must have ridden the same chairlift.

Unlike the more rugged Alps, Vermont's mountains can look pretty much alike blanketed in winter, when only their vertical drop and labyrinth of downhill runs claim attention. Their personalities emerge after the accumulation of snow has melted. The top of Bromley was treeless and still grassy in parts that had not been trampled bare by the boots of hikers and maintenance crews.

An observation tower offered views in every direction. At its base, I found a packet with my name on it. Brendan McKenna, who had sold me the new pack and sleeping bag, had hiked up the previous afternoon and, as promised, dropped off the package, which had some freebies left from a recent meeting held to discuss prospects for a new hikers' hostel in Manchester. Brendan enclosed a local newspaper account of the meeting, along with a watch cap, insect repellent, a few energy bars, and a packet of Gatorade.

Mick was sunning himself on the front porch of a small cabin used by the ski patrol in winter. It was left open for summer hikers, which explained why no one had wanted to camp below. I explained to Mick that it was my pole tip after all.

"I gave it to Seven-States," Mick said, and pointed inside.

A dark-haired young hiker sat a table wedging my tip into his own battered pole.

"I believe that's mine," I snapped, bracing for a dispute that I was unlikely to win.

But Seven-States obligingly handed the tip to me. He was so gracious about it as to leave me feeling embarrassed. He had lost his tip a couple of days earlier, and when Mick appeared with a re-placement, Seven-States said, "I knew it was too good to be true."

The cabin was bare but for the table, a telephone by the wall, and a couple of sleeping bags, with the usual camping gear scattered around. The telephone was being used by a sandy-haired man with the husky build of a football lineman.

"I love you too," he said and blew a kiss into the mouthpiece.

He turned and offered me the telephone. "It works fine," he said, "but you have to use a credit card."

"I have a cell phone," I announced, before it occurred to me that no other trail traveler I met carried one. Boasting about a cell phone made me sound as though I were pining for civilization. "My wife made me bring it," I explained. That didn't help either.

"I just called my wife in Illinois," he said. "I'm Buzzard."

Buzzard looked built too solidly for long-distance hiking, but he had already walked from Georgia. Pandora, the ex-marine at Goose Pond in Massachusetts, observed that as you hiked, the strength gravitated to your legs, weakening your upper body.

"I'm Hack," I said, "formerly Super Tortoise."

"I used to be Skunkman, but I got sick of it," Buzzard said.

"My real name's Cameron," confessed Seven-States, who added something about coming from Virginia. His trail name seemed relevant to the number of states he covered on foot. I wondered if Cameron would become Eight-States in New Hampshire, but it's not considered polite to pick apart trail names.

Mick allowed as how he was Mick, because everyone he knew back in England always called him Mick, so there wasn't much bloody point in changing from Mick to anything bloody else.

Well, that is as far as confessional group therapy goes on the Appalachian Trail, unless the participants give themselves permission to share their innermost feelings about stoves, pack weights, and daily miles walked.

Buzzard and Seven-States finished packing up their gear. Mick was eager to go. They discussed camping next near Big Branch, a river more than thirteen miles north. I doubted that I would get that far, and would camp around Griffith Lake or Lost Pond, a few miles closer.

Before we parted, I thanked Seven-States for returning my pole tip by giving him my Gatorade crystals, which he dumped into his water bottle and drank down. As a reward for finding the tip in the first place, I handed Mick a couple of energy bars and the insect repellent. He was traveling lean, and accepted them gladly.

Buzzard and Seven-States set off north with Mick in the lead. I preferred to stretch out for a nap on the front porch of the ski patrol cabin porch. But I was short of water and Seven-States said there was none to be found on Bromley's mountaintop. I drained the final swallow from my bottle and resumed my journey, less than an hour behind the others.

It had become another good day for walking. The weather was sunny and warm by Vermont standards, which meant not too hot. The trail dropped steeply, about six hundred feet in elevation, to Mad Tom Notch. At the edge of an unpaved Forest Service road stood an old-fashioned iron pump. Working the heavy pump handle with one hand while filling a bottle under the spigot with the other required some dexterity before my bottles filled.

The trail north led through two primitive wilderness areas, at Peru Peak and Big Branch. There were fewer signs and less trail maintenance. I had to climb back up another thousand feet over Styles and Peru peaks. The peaks involved a pleasant ridge walk through spruce trees but offered almost no perspective on the countryside below.

Griffith Lake, on the other hand, was lovely enough to be inundated with overnight campers who had hiked in to enjoy the lake.

The trail turned marshy, compelling me to step carefully to avoid sinking into ankle-deep ooze. I had already filled my daily quota of human contacts—Buzzard, Seven-States, and Mick—and it was only mid-afternoon. I decided to camp alone at the next lean-to near Lost Pond.

I was intrigued by the *Long Trail Guide*'s description of the lean-to, which was originally built on Cape Cod in Massachusetts. At the behest of its owner, Louis Stare Jr., the lean-to was taken apart into thirteen pieces and trucked two hundred and fifty miles to Vermont, where it was hauled to its present location by a tractor and wagon. "The lumber, exposed to the salty sea breezes of the Cape, once made this shelter especially popular with the local porcupine population," the guidebook said.

But to get there, I had to scramble first over Baker Peak on a steeply angled series of rock ledges, the most exposed I had encountered in Vermont. I would have been more nervous about climbing rocks if I had been wearing my cumbersome old pack. Here were fresh views of the mountains I had crossed to the south and new peaks ahead like Killington, the highest mountain I would climb, to my north. Otter Creek, whose name is popularized by a Vermont microbrewery, coursed through the valley below. Beyond it, an old marble quarry carved into the side of Dorset Peak gleamed like alabaster in the sun.

As I finally approached the lean-to at Lost Pond, I was greeted by the din of recorded country music. A pudgy man wearing heavy glasses was sitting at the picnic table, smoking cigarettes while he fiddled with the reception on a cheap black radio. He looked angry, whether over my arrival or some earlier affront I could not say.

I enjoy country music, but not deep in the woods at full blast, and not the trash that his station was spewing out. Having spotted me, the Country Music Fan turned up the volume.

"Where is the water?" I hollered over the racket. He pointed beyond the lean-to to a wooden bridge over a ravine.

"Staying tonight?" Country Music Fan called. He phrased it more as a challenge than a question. His bedroll was spread out under the eaves of the lean-to, but there was no sign of a stove or food. After the fit thru-hikers I had been meeting, this guy looked so unsuited to the trail, psychologically as well as physically, that I wondered how he had gotten this far.

I saw a small axe near his feet.

Something told me that camping overnight here could be a memorable experience, and not a restful one. At the least, he would play his radio all night while blowing smoke rings and stroking his axe.

"No," I said. "I'm fetching some water and moving on." Whether his rage involved an employer, a woman, the federal government, or imaginary black UN helicopters, it seemed important not to hang around and find out. One of the better survival tips outdoors is to avoid sleeping next to really weird strangers.

Given the number of people who hit the trail to forget their troubles, it is surprising that more are not unstable. But walking is as healthy an outlet as you can devise for releasing frustration, because it requires expenditure of energy. Anyone embarking on a criminal career as a psychopath would find slim pickings in a wilderness short of human prey.

Under the bridge, I scooped cold water from the stream into my two water bottles without looking for my filter pump. To save time, I added a couple of iodine tablets for purification. I shouldered my pack and called out, "Have a nice day." County Music Fan shrugged and lit another cigarette. This wilderness was the most unspoiled, beautiful stretch of the Green Mountains I had seen.

* * *

DOING DUMB things on the trail can cost you hours or days of lost time, sometimes even a broken limb. But I was thinking about doing some dumb things as a foreign correspondent where the stakes were even higher.

My most unnerving blunder happened not in a hot war zone but in the balmy Philippines, following the 1986 "people's revolution" that toppled the dictator Ferdinand Marcos. Looking for stories to pursue, I decided to visit the Moro National Liberation Front, as the Muslim insurgents called themselves, and find out whether the front was more willing to negotiate with Marcos's popular successor, Cory Aquino.

I made contact in a dark Manila restaurant with a radical Muslim activist recommended by a Filipino journalist. After some persuasion, he consented to put me in contact with the rebels on the rugged island of Mindanao. We arranged to meet at a mission hostel in Marawi City, a town where he would introduce me to people who might escort me to one of the front's bases in the jungle. I agreed to come alone, as I didn't want to share the story with another reporter. And I didn't take time to do my homework, to see what I was getting into.

A few days later, I flew down to Iligan on Mindanao's northern coast. I hired a battered taxi to drive me into the mountains to Marawi City, which turned out to be a ramshackle town on a freshwater lake. When I showed up at the address he had given me, I was told that my contact had just left in a hurry. Hoping that he had merely gone to fix my appointments, I went out to explore the town and start asking questions.

Returning to the hostel at dusk, I was met by five Filipino civilians, or so I thought until I saw their pistols and M-16 assault rifles. Their leader identified himself as the local police chief. He told me that as an American, I was in danger. The police had been tipped off, he said, that a hit squad of Muslim militants was shadowing me; whether to kill me or kidnap me for ransom, he didn't know. He also confirmed what I was discovering, that the wretchedly poor backwater was a hotbed of Islamic fundamentalism fueled by Libyan oil money.

The chief said he didn't have the resources to protect me, but he did assign two of his men to guard the hostel door overnight. They complained that robbers might ambush them for their M-16 "long guns," worth fifteen hundred dollars apiece on the local black market. I spent a long night on my cot wondering how to get out of town.

In my early days covering civil rights in the segregated American South, I heard that the safest time to travel in a racially mixed group was on Sunday morning, when the racists were attending church. If this was true, it might work with militants attending noon prayers at the local mosque.

The hostel found a taxi to pick me up at noon. With the call to prayer still sounding over loudspeakers, I told the driver to take me to Iligan, and fast. He sped down the mountain road while I stretched across the back seat, feigning sleep. Fearing that the airport might be watched, I spent that night in a seedy hotel. The next morning, I walked to the bus station and squeezed onto a crowded local bus just departing for Cagayan de Oro, the next big town on the coastal highway. From there, catching a flight to Manila was easy.

A decade later in New York, I covered a terrorism trail of three Pakistanis, subsequently believed to be a cell of Al Qaeda. They had bungled a plot to blow up American airliners when smoke from the explosives they were mixing in their Manila flat attracted the local fire department. Their leader, Ramzi Ahmed Yousef, was later convicted of masterminding the first World Trade Center bombing in 1993. Watching Yousef shake his head in court and swear that, no, he never heard of Osama bin Laden made me grateful that our paths hadn't crossed in the Philippines.

BIG BRANCH, less than an hour away from the Lost Pond lean-to, was an energetic river that tumbled westward between two steep banks. Across a suspension bridge on the far side of the river, downstream from the stone foundations of a vanished mill, I saw Buzzard and Seven-States. They had finished cooking supper and were about to settle down for the night. Mick, they reported, had elected to move on to the next shelter four miles north. There was very little level ground there, but I found enough space downriver to pitch my tent overooking Big Branch's sheer right bank. A steep trail led down to the river, where I pumped fresh water.

I set the water to boil on my stove and went over to chat with Buzzard and Seven-States. Buzzard's tent looked spacious enough to accommodate two people comfortably, in contrast to the rip-stop-nylon coffins the rest of us squeezed ourselves into every night.

"That's a big tent," I remarked. "The extra weight doesn't bother you?"

"I've been hiking with my wife." Buzzard explained that the telephone company he worked for in Illinois had cut back and he found himself retired.

"I wanted to do the Appalachian Trail," he said, "and she joined me until Massachusetts. She doesn't like mountains and went home. I'm used to carrying our tent."

Buzzard asked who I had been hiking with.

"I was mostly alone," I said, "except in Massachusetts, where I joined a couple of guys named Flash and Knute."

Buzzard looked interested. "I met Flash down in Virginia. Where did you leave him?"

"Coming off Mount Greylock," I said. "I lost a day in the hospital emergency room in North Adams."

"I'm going to catch that little bastard," Buzzard announced.

"They were moving fast," I said. "Flash told me they kept their packs down to a basic weight of twelve pounds."

"I'm going to fill his pack full of rocks to slow him down."

"They'll be a few days ahead of you by now."

"My advantage is he don't know I'm behind him." Buzzard chuckled over his strategy.

"You've got another advantage," I told Buzzard. "You're younger. Flash told me he's sixty."

"I'm sixty too," protested Buzzard, who looked about half his age. "I'm older than Flash, because I was born in February, and he wasn't born till May."

Trail travelers keep reminding one another that hiking is superior to nasty competitive sports. "This isn't a race," Knute insisted when I fretted about holding him and Flash back on Mount Greylock. But scratch below the surface of the professed egalitarianism and you invariably strike something that walks and talks and quacks like rivalry. It becomes most apparent among the thru-hikers who start out in Georgia and before long are calculating who will finish first up Mount Katahdin in Maine. Just because hikers go on vacation, human nature doesn't.

I never learned whether Buzzard caught up with Flash, but clearly they knew each other better than I thought.

"This isn't a race," I reminded myself, and went to sleep fuming that Mick, having overtaken me south of Bromley that morning, was bedding down at the next shelter ahead.

I SLEPT Sunday-late, and by the time I crawled out of my tent, Buzzard and Seven-States were gone. I hiked down Big Branch and along Little Black Brook, preoccupied with thoughts about whether to boil up pasta or rice for supper. I was unprepared for Little Rock Pond, a jewel of a mountain lake framed by fir trees and bushes and set against a background of rock outcroppings reaching from the skyline down to the water.

It is one thing to visit a place whose beauty has been acclaimed on picture postcards or Web sites. It invariably looks smaller, or drabber, or defaced by billboards and souvenir stands. It is another to stumble upon beauty so pristine that you stop and gasp in astonishment.

Natural beauty can evoke a range of responses. Some yearn to carve their initials into it. Others want to buy it up and post "Private Property" signs so no one else can enjoy it. And still others pounce in front of you to preempt a work of art with digital video-cameras, especially at museums, as though the *Mona Lisa* or *Whistler's Mother* were about to deliver a sound bite. I didn't photograph the lake because my camera was buried again inside my pack. Anyhow, my snapshots end up sprouting stray telephone poles, detracting from the object of attention. True beauty is celebrated most appropriately with reverence.

"A lake is the landscape's most beautiful and expressive feature," Thoreau reminded me before I had dumped him at the post office back in Cheshire, Massachusetts. "It is earth's eye; looking into which the beholder measures the depth of his own nature."

The lake had a seasonal caretaker, but his tent was zipped tight and no one else was around. So I did what any solitary pilgrim would do. I peeled off my clothes and piled them on a rock. Then I plunged naked into the clear water. It made for cold swimming, but as I splashed around, the sun poked out from behind a cloud. Once I swam to shore and dried out in the sunshine, I found that I had not been alone. A small loon was paddling on the far side of the pond.

I would never feed the cats by dawdling like this. I dressed in my old clothes—no point in putting on a clean T-shirt and underwear because they'd be sweated through again by evening. Continuing a mile or so beyond the pond, I entered a patch of woods that was once known as Aldrichville, Vermont.

A little more than a century ago, Aldrichville had been a pretty typical Vermont village, until it ceased to thrive and was abandoned to the forest. A few stone walls, a rusty iron paddlewheel, fragments of farm and milling implements scattered near Homer Stone Brook—these were scant clues to people a few generations earlier who had felled trees, built homes, tended crops, ground their grain into flour, sung hymns, courted, married, procreated, called one another to supper, quarreled, and died in this utterly deserted place.

Where I now set down my pack there once stood a blacksmith shop, and over there a store run by one Barney Aldrich. The rushing brook powered a mill on its steep banks where the old paddlewheel now lay. Some paces away were traces of a likely schoolhouse and, a little further, four cabins dwelt in by families named Bitourney, La Rochelle, and Bushee, whose forebears would have walked south from French Canada.

Beyond this, I knew nothing more about Aldrichville. I would not have reconstructed this much had not the U.S. Forest Service, with the generosity of the Hayes Foundation, financed an archaeological dig in its Relics and Ruins program and reported the findings on a sign posted near the Long Trail.

As I walked through Vermont, I encountered more stone walls slicing through what looked otherwise like primal forest. It was hard to believe that most of Vermont's woodland, dense and untamed as it looks today, had once been clear-cut for meadows and farmland. The hills were denuded, trees were chopped down and floated downriver, and the water was fouled by runoffs from the textile mills. Villages like Aldrichville returned to forest when farmers headed out west in search of more fertile land and a more generous climate. Of the Vermonters who marched off to fight for the Union in the Civil War, only half came home. Of those who left, half were killed or gravely wounded; the other half headed out where life was easier and the soil more productive.

The climb over the western slopes of another mountain called White Rocks was steep but short. I descended through a dry grove of tall hemlocks to Wallingford Gulf Road, which connects two towns, Wallingford and East Wallingford, that remain very much alive today. This part of the trail had been relocated over Bear Mountain a couple of years earlier. The terrain was steeper and took me five hundred feet higher than the old trail, but the climb was not as strenuous as my map suggested.

I had walked thirteen miles by the time I stopped to camp a couple of hundred feet off the trail, near a shelter called Minerva Hinchey. The shelter, named for a former secretary of the Green Mountain Club, offered an abrupt contrast to the unspoiled Vermont countryside I had just passed through. It was set along an old road, barely a mile from an overhead power line. The corrugated metal privy uphill from the shelter was riddled with bullet holes, probably put there by the local chapter of the National Rifle Association during one of its patriotic beer binges. There were the unkempt remains of old campfires in a nearby clearing.

I pitched my tent near the shelter and carried my empty water bottles down to the spring. As I approached, I heard cries of outrage from a couple of other trail travelers.

"Thoughtless bastard!" one of them screamed, which was the mildest comment on the matter.

The bottom of the small spring was littered with kernels of rice. The thoughtless bastard in question must have washed out his pot in the only available source of drinking and cooking water, and was lucky not to have been caught doing it. Anyone with enough sense to find his way downhill knows that you clean pots downstream and away from running water as meager as this.

Another beautiful moon levitated through the trees as I cooked my gourmet specialty—noodles and pepperoni sausage—at the shelter, letting the water boil longer than usual. I had finished supper when a slender youth walked out of the darkness and dropped his small pack.

"Could you direct me to the spring?" he asked.

"It's polluted," I told him. "Some thoughtless bastard—" I offered him some of my water. He would never spot the rice kernels in the dark.

The youth—I withhold his name for reasons that will become apparent—was a native of Iowa. He said he had just hiked thirty-two miles from the shelter at Spruce Peak, which I had passed two days ago.

"Thirty-two is a lot of miles," I said. It was double what most trail travelers could do, and nearly three times what I was covering.

"My best day was thirty-eight miles," he said.

"What's your pack weight?" I asked.

"Twelve pounds," he said, and that appeared to include his water and food. The lad didn't carry a tent or sleeping bag; they weighed too much. He slept at shelters under a poncho.

I wondered what his secret for distance was.

"Care to share some of the herb?" he asked softly.

"A joint, you mean?"

He shrugged. "Just a toke."

I declined. I prefer a beer or two at night. People I knew who smoked marijuana were not the sort you would turn to for help with the *Sunday Times*'s crossword puzzle. But the lad was the first mannered pothead I had met, and I supposed that the miles do roll by if you're hiking stoned.

No, he corrected me, he only smoked pot to relax.

"Where do you buy your weed?" I asked, having learned the argot from covering illegal drugs for the *Times*. People take drugs for two reasons, to feel good and to feel better. I wasn't sure in which category my companion fitted.

"I ask around," he said. "This is the last of what I bought in Tennessee."

"Don't get caught," I warned. "The Vermont state police have this hang-up about illegal drugs."

He nodded and moved downwind of me to light up. His joint glowed softly in the dark. It was the only recreational drug I had encountered in the counterculture world of trail travel. Vitamin pills would have been my choice for the weight, but the lad was clipping off thirty-two miles a day—and hey, it's what keeps you moving that matters. I felt flattered that he was willing to share his dwindling stash with a graying stranger.

The young pothead from Iowa consumed his joint, rolled up in his rain poncho on the shelter floor, and fell asleep. This was no small achievement, because the shelter attracted the nastiest mosquitoes I had encountered in Vermont. I was grateful to sleep cocooned inside my tent. I needed a restful night because tomorrow I had to propel myself up Killington Peak, at 4,235 feet the second highest mountain in Vermont.

OF THE uncounted places that we drift through in our lives, only the best and the worst get recalled with much clarity.

Once in Russia, I flew from Irkutsk to Yakutsk, two cities in the depths of the Siberian taiga. The aging Aeroflot plane deposited us on an anonymous airstrip for deicing and refueling. My companion, another American reporter, and I were shooed with the rest of the passengers into a midwinter gale that numbed our exposed flesh. Through snow and forest we stumbled, toward the beckoning lights of a cabin pillowed among the snowdrifts. We had to shove hard to open the plank door.

Inside, the cabin looked, and smelled, more like a pigsty. Around the stove milled a surly crowd in heavy coats and fur hats. Most were drunk; some could barely stand. The rancid stench of fried grease wafted from the kitchen, mingling with the sour odors of wet clothing unwashed since the last spring thaw. I hankered for some hot tea, but I couldn't push past a knot of miserable wretches quarreling over the empty vodka bottle they had consumed. A sobbing woman flailed at the slovenly man groping her. In a far corner, a teenager in a vaguely nautical uniform banged on a battered guitar while his well-lubricated comrades sang along off-key. River sailors, another passenger explained, leaving unclear what sailors were doing here in midwinter, when Siberia's rivers were frozen thick enough to drive monster trucks across.

We waited inside the cabin, blowing on our hands and stamping our feet, until the Aeroflot stewardess at last bellowed us back to our flight. As we climbed the ice-crusted ramp, my friend looked toward the cabin, intermittently obscured by blowing snow.

"Well," he sighed, "that's another town I never got laid in."

FOR A change, I was not the last to depart the next morning. The lad from Iowa was gone, presumably with a fresh patch of mosquito bites, but other late arrivals lay stretched out in their sleeping bags. One was snoring loudly enough to scare the chipmunks.

I didn't cook the usual oatmeal and tea because my water bottles were empty and the thought of dipping into the polluted spring discouraged a refill here.

As I left, a new trail traveler approached the shelter. He was lean and shirtless under his pack harness, with a graying beard. We stopped to exchange the usual trail pleasantries.

"I'm Batty," he said, which helped explain the cloth cutouts of black bats sewn across the back of his pack. Batty was stopping for breakfast, so I cautioned him about the spring and moved on, following the trail north uphill behind the shelter.

In an hour or so, I was descending toward the Mill River along a steep ridge that dropped sharply to my left. Below lay the X shape formed by the intersection of two long runways at the municipal airport southeast of Rutland, a city in central Vermont. The only sign of activity was a small plane taking off that had yet to reach my altitude.

The Mill River was spanned by a suspension bridge built of little more than wooden planks and wire. It swayed to my steps over Clarendon Gorge, a dramatic channel that centuries of rushing water had carved through the rock.

I crossed a busy highway to Rutland and the tracks of the Green Mountain Railroad. The Long Trail led me through a pasture and over some fences, where I struggled not to snare my shorts on barbed wire. At the top of a rocky ravine unfolded a gentler ridge and a remnant of road said to have been built in the mid-eighteenth century as a British military route in the French and Indian War. I paused to filter cold water from a substantial brook into my empty bottles.

Batty pulled in and joined me down at the brook. He too was hiking the trail from Georgia to Maine. But he came from Virginia, and had a wife and two grown children, as I did. He used to be a chemical engineer.

Storyteller. Flash. Buzzard. Batty. And me. What we had in

common was that we'd hit our seventh decade, or were about to, without slowing down. Perhaps we weren't all that exceptional. What attracted Batty to the trail was the feeling of contentment that infused those traveling it. "The people you meet feel pretty good about themselves," he said.

That was true. We might get unhappy or angry about the erratic weather, or the pointless ups and downs, or the bastard who cleaned his rice pot in the drinking water. But we weren't stuck in therapy over it.

Batty and I talked as we set out together across Lottery Road, through more meadows and over more wooden stiles protecting fences. We emerged onto Cold River Road to see two houses but no trail. A middle-aged woman emerged from one house to water her flowers. Without looking up, she pointed down the road, to the trail blaze we needed.

Batty asked her whether other hikers got confused.

"All the time," she called back.

We stopped to eat a snack at the next shelter in preparation for the unbroken four-mile push up the southern flank of Killington. In contrast with the customary wood lean-tos, this shelter, named for Percy Clement, a governor of Vermont just after World War One, was solidly built of stone, with a handsome fireplace and a reliable stream nearby that yielded ample water.

At shelters, as well as in other real estate, location is everything. While the Clement shelter is ideally situated for the final assault on Killington, the Green Mountain Club recommends not spending the night there because of the adjacent access road and the lowlifes it invites. "Unfortunately," the club's guidebook notes, "this shelter is subjected to unexpected nocturnal visits by uninvited carousers." You can't get much rest when midnight troublemakers squeal in on pickup trucks to party and hurl their empty beer cans at your sleeping bag or stomp your tent while you are still inside. The safest places to camp tend to be far from the road and the local liquor store, which is why trail travelers seek out inaccessible places to sleep.

We were soon walking again. Batty assured me that he was in no hurry to climb up Killington. But I gave him the lead and, left to his accustomed pace since Georgia, he was soon out of sight through the trees. Now alone again, I could not afford to dally when the climb ahead required a gain in altitude of two thousand feet or more.

I continued up a series of switchbacks that turned into a narrow, uneven path threading, sometimes precariously, along the peak's eastern slopes. Maples, birch, and other hardwoods gave way to spruce forest as I climbed, planting my poles and propelling myself forward at an unbroken rhythm of four steps for each breath I took. I did not dare stop. Lagging too far behind, I could not call Batty for assistance if I tripped and fell, though I suspected he was already beyond earshot. If he was going over Killington, I could too.

In a couple of hours, I broke free of the steep woods and into a less formidable expanse of forest, where I paused to take in the first panoramic views of the Coolidge Range. Having made up my mind that Killington would be strenuous, I was surprised that it went easier than expected.

Bathed in sweat, I finished the satellite peak of Little Killington and dipped slightly into a densely wooded saddle to the final rise up the main peak. A sign pointed downhill toward Cooper Lodge, which at 3,850 feet offers the highest fixed shelter on the Long Trail. The stone building was built below the summit of Killington Peak by the state forest service before World War Two. A lodge conjures up images of snug comfort, but here the spartan interior consisted of a picnic table and four sleeping platforms. The lodge was sturdy enough to withstand a hurricane, but there was no glass in the openings built as windows, and a fresh breeze was blowing in from the west.

I heaved my pack onto one of the shoulder-high upper platforms to claim a space in case I couldn't find a better campsite, and walked back to the main trail to complete the remaining four hundred feet of my ascent. It took only ten minutes to scramble up a steep rock gully to the top of Killington. The wind turned brisker, but the afternoon sun had pleasantly warmed the exposed rocks.

I emerged to find myself alone on the summit plateau, which on a clear day can offer views of five states and Canada. Mount Mansfield, a hundred and fifty feet feet higher than Killington, was visible on the horizon to the northwest. The views in every other direction were no less breathtaking, encompassing the White Mountains in New Hampshire to the Adirondacks in New York. To the south were the mountains I had overcome as far away as Glastenbury.

The green carpet below was part of the Calvin Coolidge State Forest, named for the frugal Vermonter who became a president. He was so economical in his speech that when a woman bet him that she could get three words out of him, he told her: "You lose."

Killington, which dominates the Coolidge Range, is one of the most popular ski destinations in New England, and its summit plateau has been heavily developed. I passed a shuttered weather station and followed a dirt road over to the gondola terminal. Brightly painted gondolas dangled on the terminal racks like giant Easter eggs, rattling in the wind. Nobody else was around.

I tested the doors to the terminal restaurant and snack bar in vague hopes of finding a hamburger and a chocolate milkshake. But the doors were locked. I felt as though the world had been vacuumed of its six billion inhabitants.

I had ridden some of these gondolas to the top of Killington when it was packed with winter skiers who had come for the groomed downhill runs. The solitude left me feeling content rather than lonely. I would have hung around longer on top, but the sun was going down. A chilly evening breeze had me shivering in my damp T-shirt and shorts. Camping on top was illegal, though some hikers did it. But I had no interest in dragging my pack up to the top. Carefully, I descended the gully, which looked steeper than what I had come up an hour earlier. The rock already felt chilled.

Batty had pitched his tent in the limited camping area, and two other tents had been erected, leaving no space for me. I was not unhappy to sleep inside the shelter. There weren't any mosquitoes tonight because the evening had turned cold.

I shared the shelter, built to sleep sixteen hikers, with five overnight companions. There were three teenage girls newly graduated from Fieldstone School in Riverdale, in the Bronx. There was also a high school science teacher from New Jersey who was hiking with his ten-year-old daughter. She was thrilled to be on the trail. He called himself Grumble; she was Bee. It was a clever pun when it comes to trail names.

I cooked up a packet of rice and beans, and mixed in chunks of the pepperoni I had packed for my protein. It was more than I needed, bubbling over the pot after I stirred in the boiling water, but I consumed every mouthful, and not just because I was hungry. A problem with cooking on the trail is that you have to eat everything you cook, or pack out the leftovers. Dumping it in the woods is not only disgusting but also attracts animals you really don't want to meet. But it isn't much fun to travel with a quarter-pound of whatever it is that you couldn't bring yourself to finish the night before.

I offered my extra rice and beans to the three teenagers, but they seemed to be on diets. Grumble and Bee also declined, saying they had already eaten.

Grumble was busy answering Bee's constant questions. She was a bright little thing, and he was a natural teacher.

I asked Grumble whether the hiking wasn't too strenuous for a ten-year-old. They were not striving for distance, he explained, and were content to cover six or seven miles a day from one shelter to the next. Then Grumble excused himself to tuck his daughter, tenderly, into her sleeping bag.

It was a grand night for sleeping. But the air wafting through the fir trees was so fragrant that I went out after midnight and sat on the shelter's stone steps, gazing up into a field of stars so close that they seemed capable of being scooped up in a net like butterflies.

Watching Grumble and Bee relish each other's company carried my drifting memory back to a time when my own two children were small and I was often absent or inattentive, chasing datelines and deadlines.

Oh, there were winter afternoons when we lived in Moscow and I took Celia and Christopher cross-country skiing beside the frozen Moscow River, pulling a sled behind me to haul them home when they tired. On Saturday mornings in Cairo, we rode horses in the desert near the Pyramids. In Beijing, we bicycled around the hutongs, or back streets, or tossed a football around behind our apartment building at Jianguomenwai. But that was when I was around, which wasn't that often.

It was colder now and I was ready to retreat into my sleeping bag. When I stood up, my thigh muscles burned from the day's exertion. Lights were twinkling through the trees from the direction of Rutland, about ten miles away.

DURING the four years we lived in Moscow, we had to request visas from the old Soviet government not just to enter Russia but also to leave it. One week, Jaqueline took Celia to the Finnish orthodontist in Helsinki, an overnight train ride to our family's favorite city. My son, Chris, then seven years old, objected to being left behind, so I proposed that we join the ladies in Helsinki for the weekend. Chris would miss a day of classes at the Anglo-American School, so we brought along his homework.

The next morning, I telephoned a request to the Foreign Ministry for exit visas that same night. Arranging visas normally took several days, so I implied that our sudden departure involved a family emergency. I anticipated bureaucratic objections; to my surprise, our exit visas were forthcoming late that afternoon.

Our trip went well until the train stopped short of the Finnish frontier for customs and immigration formalities. Two Russian customs inspectors headed for our compartment, accompanied by several men in civilian clothes whom I took for KGB. They opened our suitcases and took turns combing through the contents. They carried off every piece of paper, including Chris's arithmetic homework, to be photocopied. One plainclothes agent peeled the lining out of my alarm clock. They dismantled the berths and pulled apart the bed linens.

After an hour, the chief inspector returned and dumped the papers on my suitcase. He jumped off the train before it rolled into Finland. My urgent request for exit visas must have led my Foreign Ministry handlers to conclude that I had something important, perhaps documents or a manuscript, to spirit out of the country, so they had told the KGB to intercept us. I wish the searchers had taken time to correct Chris's math.

I DIDN'T leave Cooper Lodge until the sun had nearly cleared the treetops. This would be an easy day. My destination was the Long Trail Inn, a half-dozen miles down the mountain, near the junction where the Appalachian and Long trails divide. It made sense to sleep in a real bed and scrub down in a shower before pushing eastward for the forty-five miles into New Hampshire. From there I planned to walk north along the Connecticut River to my home just across the river in Fairlee, Vermont.

When I stepped outside the lodge to clean out my cooking pot, Grumble and Bee were departing. Bee wore a floppy hat pulled down tight over her ears. Her pack looked as large as mine.

"That's quite a load you have," I said.

"Oh, my dad carries the heavy stuff," Bee said. The little girl's reply struck me as good advice for parenting. Grumble was indeed carrying the heavy stuff, which he strained to put on his back, but Bee had been taught how to pull her weight.

The trail north had been relocated a few years earlier well west of the next summit of Pico Peak, which at 3,957 feet is only slightly lower than Killington and has its own ski area. Work was underway to link the two ski areas by gondola. But the relocation moved the Long Trail a mile from the Long Trail Inn, which had been in its early days the headquarters of the Green Mountain Club and a place where every trail traveler stopped.

My map was too old to show the relocation, which didn't matter because the new trail was easy enough to follow downhill. It seemed more circuitous but made for easier traveling, because it had not yet been rutted by runoff from rainwater and the underlying roots and rocks had not yet been exposed by hard use.

As I descended, I came upon two work crews of teenagers wearing the green T-shirts and hard hats of the Vermont Youth Conservation Corps, an AmeriCorps program. The boys and girls, of high school age, were working hard with picks and shovels to improve drainage on the trail. They were a different crowd from the ill-behaved adolescents I met on Stratton Mountain. Several called out and waved as I hiked past.

The trail dropped about eighteen hundred feet before bottom-ing out in the tall grass beside Route 4, a main artery across central Vermont. The highway cutting through Sherburne Pass presents one of the major hazards on the Long Trail, which it is obliged to cross. A constant stream of large tractor-trailer trucks and smaller cars and vans held me up for ten minutes.

Once across Route 4, it was easier to walk facing traffic on the highway to the Long Trail Inn. "I'd like a room at your thru-hiker's rate," I said, whatever that was, and dropped my backpack on my floor to authenticate my request. That turned out to be forty dol-lars, and included a hot breakfast.

Grumble and Bee had arrived earlier, and were about to catch a bus into Rutland to shop for groceries and take in a movie. The inn's restaurant was closed, so I had lunch in its Irish pub. McGrath's Pub seemed to be doing a brisker business in draft beers on tap. A line of thru-hikers had bellied up to the bar, when you'd expect them to be out walking on such a sunny day, and showed no inclination to leave. I recognized a few and would have enjoyed a beer with them, but I was afraid it would put me to sleep through the afternoon.

Leaving my pack in my room, I walked back along the highway to the Long Trail and hiked a mile north to Maine Junction, which according to my map marks the point at which the Appalachian Trail veers off from the Long Trail and heads east to New Hamp-shire and Maine, while the Long Trail continues north to the Que-bec border. But the relocation had moved the junction up the trail to a dip called Willard Gap.

I had neglected to bring my rain parka, and was overtaken by a sudden thundershower, which left me drenched. But the storm was the kind of interlude that you would expect in Beethoven's Pastoral Symphony, and nearly as brief. The glistening leaves and bushes along the trail turned luminous in the dappled swatches of fresh afternoon sunlight. By the time I returned to the inn, my soaked trousers were drying and the rain was a memory.

I went back to my room, showered, and changed to somewhat cleaner underwear. Then I stretched out in front of the television set. Did people really spend their afternoons watching drivel this inept when they could have been out walking? Or were they given no choice?

Before my mother died, I visited her in the hospital facility where she was bedridden following a stroke and a broken hip, and found her clustered in her wheelchair with other patients before a giant television set. It seemed outrageous that this clever woman, whose imagination seemed as boundless to me as her love, would end up parked by the nurses in front of a bad soap opera.

What scared me about old age was not the dying part—I believe the Creator of a world conceived so exquisitely as ours would hardly neglect to build in a second act—but the institutional dehumanization that precedes death and becomes a state of vegetation, because it assumes a lack of will among those too weak to protest. I switched off the television set and went downstairs to join the hikers at the bar.

I intend no callousness, but when you have worked long enough at the journalist's trade, death ceases to be a novelty. The hard part is not seeing someone dead, but having to watch them die. When apartheid collapsed during my four years in South Africa, I took my turn covering the violence wracking the restive black townships around Johannesburg. I was in Katlehong for one disturbance when Allister Sparks, a South African friend who reported for the *Washington Post,* called me to join him down the street. "Someone's been shot," Allister yelled. A middle-aged man was sprawled facedown in the nearby intersection, blood from an unseen wound staining the red dirt.

He lay motionless, so I rushed to see whether we could stanch the bleeding. Before I could roll him over, I felt a squat Uzi subma-chine gun pointing into my face. I backed off. Two gunmen were aiming at us, one with the Uzi, the other with a shotgun.

"Police," whispered Allister, though they were Africans in civil-ian clothes. They looked as terrified as I felt, which made them more dangerous.

They kept ordering us to leave. "You are prohibited to be here," the man with the Uzi screamed. "This is private property." His col-league jabbed at us with the shotgun. I guessed that he had done the shooting.

Allister, his face flushed, shouted back at the gunmen, "We will not leave a public thoroughfare." I was merely scared, but Allister was seething, and his mounting anger was contagious.

There comes a time when you realize that you're fated to die sooner or later, and accept that sooner might grant you a little more dignity. We stood our vigil, at gunpoint, for more than a half-hour while the pool of blood widened around the man lying on the ground. The longer we waited, silently, making no sudden gestures, the less panicked the gunmen became. But they never lowered their guns until a yellow bakkie, or pickup truck, ar-rived.

A beefy Afrikaner jumped out. He too wore civilian dress, but a pistol protruded from a holster inside his trousers. The gunmen saluted. Ignoring us, the Afrikaner motioned them to toss the body in the back of the truck. When they picked up the victim, I saw the hole, as large as a softball, that the shotgun shell had punched into his stomach. There would be no way to survive a blast that close. The two cops jumped into the back with their vic-tim and the little yellow truck drove away.

That evening, I called South African police headquarters in Pretoria. They said a rioter had been killed but claimed to have no details. Allister returned to Katlehong once relative peace was restored to assemble the pieces. The man we saw die turned out to be a popular schoolteacher. He had been visiting a friend and took a fatal shortcut home. He had turned the wrong corner, and a cop blew him away, mistaking him for someone from a mob that had torched another policeman's house on the next street.

Eight

BEFORE LEAVING the Long Trail Inn, I ran into a subdued Storyteller. He said the doctors ordered him to stop hiking or risk serious damage to his kidneys. He was waiting for his daughter to drive up from North Carolina.

He had walked this far. I didn't know how to say I was sorry without adding to his disappointment. Storyteller was as natural a trail traveler as I had encountered. "You can come back next year and finish the AT," I told him, though we both knew that it wasn't the same as knocking off all 2,168 miles in a single season.

I left about nine A.M. by a steep trail behind the inn, to the junction where the Appalachian Trail split off eastward. I hit gravel again at the state campground in Gifford Woods, walking past tents, trailers, and fire pits, even a concrete shower building. Luxury! A lake small enough to be called Kent Pond lay on the other side of the highway. Some of the campsites I passed had boat trailers. I followed a dirt road toward the boat-launching beach before skirting the shoreline and entering more woods along a soggy trail. Eventually, this left me on another dirt road where the white blazes on the trees seemed to evaporate. I wondered if I had walked too far.

A cyclist in a blue helmet and tank top was fiercely pumping her way uphill into the sunlight.

"Where am I?" I hollered.

"Thundering Brook Road," she called without looking back. She and her bicycle must have climbed this road fairly often. I found the road on my map and headed downhill. The cyclist flew past me on her descent and saluted with a friendly wave.

At the bottom of the hill lay Ottauquechee River, whose name hinted at the vitality of previous rivers I had crossed. My map put the Ottauquechee's headwaters hardly more than a mile upriver, but here it looked as stagnant as a swamp and nearly obscured by weeds and branches. Several hundred yards down the road were the low buildings of Sherburne township, a logical place for a water spigot, but I had enough water left from the inn. The trail led back into the woods across the road and straight uphill, rising along switchbacks and swatches of old logging roads for nearly fourteen hundred vertical feet. I was unprepared for terrain this steep, having assumed that the hardest climbing was behind me on Killington Peak. The trail at last let up, only to rise higher again.

The relentless ups and downs proved tougher than I anticipated. The contours of the Green Mountains, like the Appalachians, Rockies, or Sierras, generally flow north to south. But walking from west to east meant having to climb up each ridge and down to the next valley, and then doing it again. And again.

A side trail pointed to a shelter at Stony Brook, but it was too early to stop for the night. I dropped down to Mink Brook, topped off my water bottles, and resumed climbing. I had walked eight miles by now, with another nine miles to go before the next shelter, Winturri. What promised to be a lark was turning into one of my longest, and hardest, days. I was falling more and more behind the schedule I had imposed on myself.

I descended to another dirt road, crossed Locust Creek, and climbed up more switchbacks to a more promising ridge. The wood line opened to a view of Lakota Lake hemmed in by green forest hundreds of feet below me. I drained one of my water bottles. I expected to find new water at the next shelter, at least two hours away. It was unlikely that I could arrive there before dark. I began looking for a spot to stealth-camp.

As I walked, more slowly now, along the wooded ridge I noticed a rocky trail cutting sharply to my left, and decided to follow it. It was by now seven, and the next shelter lay more than an hour ahead. The side trail led me to a cabin overlooking the expanse of unbroken greenery in the valley far below.

"Hey man, what's up?" a voice called. I looked up and saw a shirtless blond sunbather on a small observation platform cantilevered atop the cabin roof.

"I'm looking to camp," I said.

"Stay here," the sunbather said. "There's just me and my friend."

"You found a good view," I said.

"It's awesome, man," he said.

Another youth emerged shirtless from the cabin and waved me in.

"Isn't this private property?" I asked. I hadn't seen it on my map.

"Yeah," he said, "but the owners let us use it."

"How do you know?"

"The sign says so."

The cabin was empty inside but for the packs of the two guys and some charred wood in the stone fireplace.

"Any mosquitoes?" I asked. There was no glass in the window frames.

"Oh, not too bad."

On one wall, I saw the notice posted by the cabin's owners, Richard and Teresa Pete of Lookout Farm, a small inn in the valley below. They said hikers were welcome to stay overnight, though private guests had priority. "If you do use this cabin, help us to keep it clean," the Petes said in their note. They asked that hikers carry out any trash left by those "less considerate."

Well, fourteen miles was enough for today, and sleeping on plank floors had become a luxury. The Petes' note on the wall was a relief from all the "No Trespassing" signs I had walked past in New York state.

I climbed up a wooden ladder bolted to the side of the cabin, to the small deck on the roof. The sunbather introduced himself as Joey, from New Jersey.

The view was indeed awesome, extending in all directions, from the Adirondacks to Killington Peak and White Mountains.

"The moon should be nearly full tonight," I remarked.

"I'm sleeping up here," Joey said.

"Where's the water supply?" I looked around for a spring.

"There isn't any and we've run out," Joey said. "Can you spare some?"

"I don't have much," I said, "but help yourself."

As I rolled out my sleeping bag, another hiker, Bad Moon, pulled in, and then a quarter-hour later, a fresh-faced young blond woman. They were low on water too, so we shared what little we had. There was room on the floor for all four of us, since Joey refused to leave the roof. We were strangers living together like a family. Again, no one asked my age or seemed to care.

The setting sun cast the surrounding valleys into shadow. The rising moon, brilliant as a super-trouper floodlight at a rock concert, bathed our small world in a silver glow so intense that we could walk about outside without twisting on our headlamps.

The last moon I had seen this dazzling was two decades ago over Nimule, a rickety town on Sudan's border with Uganda, where I camped in a schoolyard with some Sudanese journalists chasing the same conflict. The hippopotami roaring in the adjacent White Nile made that night even more exotic.

But moonlight in Vermont transcended this midsummer night into an out-of-body experience. "Like it's . . . like it's totally awesome, man," Joey called down from the roof. What more can be said when you've already exhausted the superlatives?

Our night did seem enchanted. A spirited breeze wafted through the open windows. There was no point in trying to sleep. I crawled from my sleeping bag to sit outside on a large rock, mesmerized by the moonglow against the background of stars. Around me, tall grass swayed rhythmically in the breeze.

Below, Lakota Lake had been swallowed up by the black expanse of forest. Tiny pockets of light twinkled from what would have been Windsor and White River Junction and perhaps Woodstock, as though these towns were viewed from twenty thousand feet through a jetliner window. Here at little more than two thousand feet, we seemed to be floating on a cloud. It was the kind of weightlessness that I had felt jumping at night as an army paratrooper, floating through the darkness between the opening shock and the hard landing.

It took the droning of mosquitoes to break the spell. I went back inside and crawled into my collapsed tent to shut out the insects.

THE FRESH-FACED blonde eschewed fanciful trail names. She called herself simply Leslie. She was compact and tough, and wore her sun-streaked hair pulled back into a lank ponytail. Leslie volunteered little about herself beyond the fact that she too had been hiking from Georgia. Early in the morning, she packed up and left us before breakfast.

I balanced my stove on a large rock outside the cabin and cooked some oatmeal into a sludge with the last dregs of my water. Peanut butter was my staple diet, and I smeared some on my last crust of bread. It was hard to swallow with nothing to wash it down. I would have to stop at the next spring.

Joey descended at last from the roof to report that looking up at the stars all night had been, like, totally awesome, man. I told him it had been, like, awesome down below.

Bad Moon chatted affably while we loaded our packs, prompting me to ask if his trail name had something to do with the Creedence Clearwater Revival song "Bad Moon Rising."

He shook his head. "The other hikers gave it to me in Virginia."

I waited for him to explain.

"I dropped my pants and mooned some tourists."

I noticed the owners' note on the wall, asking us to keep the cabin clean. When the others left, I stayed behind to sweep up with what passed for a broom, stacked the firewood, and collected scraps of trash, which I stuffed into a pocket on my pack. The cabin looked tidy again.

A wooded rise, called the Pinnacle, led down to the shelter I had failed to reach the evening before, expending more energy in an hour than most Americans manage on foot in a week. Leslie was sitting there, eating her breakfast. She pointed me down the trail to a spring, where I refilled my bottles through my ceramic filter and pumped a substantial drink for myself.

She watched me recount my observations softly into my digital voice recorder, but did not ask me to join her, which relieved me of having to make conversation. Like me, Leslie preferred hiking alone. I wondered whether she had traveled by herself since Georgia; she wore an invisible sign that warned, "Don't crowd me," a sensible enough precaution for a solitary woman. I gave her a head start before returning to the trail.

The walk downhill led out of the woods and through a succession of overgrown meadows. There were more wooden stiles to climb over, more fences, one of them electric. The day was hot and at the edge of a paved road, five cows, dappled brown on white, were cooling off in a wide stream, ruining it as a source of drinking water. The cows watched me walk across the wooden bridge, wary that I had come to shoo them back into the pasture.

The road linked the towns of Woodstock and Bethel. Someone who graduated a year ahead of me from Dartmouth had learned about my walk and invited me to stop overnight at his summer home in Woodstock, a lovely resort town. But with my pack, it would take at least a couple of hours to walk to Woodstock, and I wasn't sure where I put his telephone number. Besides, I felt pressed for time, with two cats to be fed. I wanted to reach Norwich, a town twenty miles away on the Connecticut River, the following night, where I promised to stay with an old friend from our early years in journalism.

"Trail magic," called out Leslie, who was sitting by the road. She pointed to a plastic shopping bag hanging from an Appalachian Trail sign. It contained some boxed fruit juice, oranges, and bananas donated by locals we never knew. Leslie was sipping one orange juice, and I helped myself to another. We were supposed to leave something for the next hiker.

Working up a sweat in heat like this, you need to consume a pint or two of water per hour, so I was low again after walking two hours from the shelter. "I heard they have good water there," Leslie said. She pointed down the road to a white clapboard house across from a red barn.

I knocked on the door but nobody was home. A hand-lettered sign in the window said, "Hikers. Please help yourself to water." It also offered us trail travelers the use of a shower mounted on the other side of the house. This was Vermont, after all.

Good water meant pure enough that we didn't need to filter before drinking. Leslie and I took turns filling our bottles from the outside faucet. Then we stretched out on the grass beside the road, a few feet apart.

I smeared on more sunblock and offered some to Leslie, but she shook her head, saying she had her own. The sunshine since Georgia had tanned her skin the color of honey.

I explained how I was walking into retirement from the *New York Times.*

Leslie said she was from Kansas. "But I've been living in Denver," she added. "I was teaching third grade." That offered me a little more insight into my companion. Teaching rambunctious third-graders is not a job for wimps.

"Do you usually hike alone?" I asked after some silence. "I wouldn't want my daughter doing it."

"I started from Georgia with two other women," Leslie said. "One of them is somewhere ahead. The other is somewhere behind."

"Why didn't you stay together?"

She shrugged. "We agreed not to wait."

"So what makes you do this?" I asked.

Leslie dropped her guard, briefly. "I like the peacefulness and calm of hiking."

That was what I had heard from others. The Appalachian Trail was not about hiking, it was about seeking nirvana, through pain on a hard day like this.

When I got up to leave, Leslie said she would rest a while longer. She pulled out some paper and began to write. It was clear that she was ready to put more distance between us. Or maybe she wanted to use the outdoor shower. If I took a shower now, I'd be dirty and sweaty again in an hour. Maybe there would be a lake to jump in later.

The trail rose steeply from the far side of the road without any pretense of switchbacks. Sitting in the dust ahead, I saw a mirage in the shape of a red-and-white plastic cooler. I fantasized about finding the plastic box filled with ice-cold drinks packed in ice. I stopped and flipped open the lid. The cooler was packed with ice and yes, bright soft drink cans, delivered by a trail angel who had not merely purchased the ingredients but then lugged the container to the point where the trail looked steepest. I popped open a can of Sprite, which quickly beaded with moisture, and shut the cooler lid to keep the ice from melting. I quickly drained the can and coveted a second, but trail courtesy dictated that I not guzzle down the contents of the cooler. I tucked the empty can in my pack, for disposal later.

I had learned much earlier that when you lift your eyes up unto the hills, help can come from where you least expect. The first trail magic bestowed on me, the most memorable, was in the Sinai Desert. I had flown in on an Egyptian plane with a pack of journalists to watch the withdrawal of Israeli forces from the strategic terrain around Mount Sinai, a condition of Israel's new peace treaty with Egypt. Forgoing the handover ceremony, Bob Jobbins, a BBC correspondent, and I caught a ride with two Egyptian soldiers out to St. Catherine's monastery to confirm the extent of the Israeli pullout.

Satisfied, we hitched another jeep ride downhill to the airstrip, only to find that the plane that brought us in had taken off. The Egyptian general, in his impatience to get home, had left nearly a dozen Egyptian and foreign journalists behind, with no arrangement for extracting us from the Sinai. We had brought along neither food nor water, expecting to fly back to file our stories in Cairo. The arriving Egyptian soldiers didn't have water themselves, they said, much less instructions for getting us out.

Half-hidden among the dunes on the eastern horizon sat an Israeli half-track observing the Egyptian deployment. Bob and I trudged through the sand toward the vehicle, keeping our hands out from our sides to show we were unarmed. We negotiated a labyrinth of coiled barbed wire, which I hoped did not delineate a minefield. As we approached the half-track, I saw its .50-caliber heavy machine gun pointing at us.

A major in the olive battle dress of the Israeli Defense Forces popped from the turret. Bob explained that we were journalists left stranded in the desert by our Egyptian hosts.

Bob looked at the antennas bristling from the half-track. "I don't suppose you have a telephone in there," he quipped.

"Who do you want to call?" the major asked.

"The BBC in London," Bob said.

The major, probably a reservist, thought this over. He pulled a handset from behind the armor plating.

"You have to call collect," he said.

Bob snatched the headset and rattled off some numbers to the major, who repeated them in Hebrew. Bob listened and a smile lit up his face. He dictated his account of the Israeli withdrawal into a recording machine at the BBC.

Bob handed the phone back to the major, who turned to me. "Could I call Jerusalem?" I asked.

"What's the number?" the major asked.

"I don't know," I told him. "It's the *New York Times* bureau."

The major chuckled. "We'll try information." The soldiers clustered around laughed too when this was translated into Hebrew.

In another minute, I was talking with our Jerusalem bureau, asking that the *Times* foreign desk in New York, and my wife in Cairo, be told I was marooned in the Sinai and relying on the kindness of an Israeli half-track. I arranged to dictate my own story later.

The major had his soldiers bring us water and food. He radioed for more rations to be brought forward to feed other stranded journalists. I walked back and conveyed the offer, but my Egyptian colleagues refused to accept Israeli hospitality, preferring to go hungry. The rest of us ate kosher that night on newly reclaimed Egyptian territory.

The major let me call an Israeli information official I knew in Jerusalem and ask for help in bringing us out. The Israelis, sniffing a potential public relations coup, promised to arrange our passage and contact our embassies. My Egyptian friends, mortified by their government's inactivity, made a rival appeal through some Egyptian troops on the ground.

The next day, a Russian-made helicopter carried us back to Cairo. The Egyptian pilot skimmed over the Red Sea, playfully bumping waves with his landing struts. The crew chief stubbed cigarettes out on a greasy floor that looked awash in leaking engine oil. I had felt safer stranded in the Sinai.

THE NEXT hill in Vermont took even longer than I feared, but at the top I was rewarded by a small meadow enlivened with purple wildflowers. A few trees on the edges did not obscure the view of Killington Peak in purple profile. There was respite from the sun as I ducked gratefully into a shady woodland filled with evergreens, maples, and some birches whose leaves rustled in the desultory breeze.

The trail dropped over a few more ridges and across several roads, only to climb again. Just beyond a road connecting the villages of Pomfret and South Pomfret, the trail seemed to veer from the description in my guidebook, taking me straight uphill into yet another high meadow. By the time I walked back into the woods, I wasn't sure where I was heading.

I turned onto a sunken dirt road that looked like a country lane as it followed the ridge between two stone walls. A paucity of white blazes forced me to look in both directions for confirmation that this pleasant walk, after what I had gone through, belonged to the Appalachian Trail. It seemed much too easy, but I risked losing time by turning back. I did not want Leslie or Bad Moon or any other hiker to find me wandering around lost. So I plunged onward.

This woodland obscured what once had been farms, and the neglected lane had indeed been a busy thoroughfare known as the King's Highway. The road at last veered right onto a small trail leading up Depuis Hill, which was crowned with a more extensive meadow. There were new trail blazes, now painted on poles anchored into rock cairns.

I dropped down again, to Cloudland Road, only to confront yet another hill, the fifth or sixth of the day. As I trudged upward, a small sign pointed left toward a new Cloudland shelter. But a hiker I passed earlier had described the mosquitoes there as bad. I pushed on for a couple of more miles toward an older shelter on the other side of Thistle Hill that was said to catch more breezes.

Before long, my legs and lungs told me that I had overrated my stamina. I could barely summon up strength to continue in fits and starts, like a car running out of gas. The trail descended forgivingly into thicker woods. I stumbled upon a fresh sign pointing to a side trail that led to the shelter at Thistle Hill, a couple of hundred yards away.

I arrived exhausted, dropped my pack, and lay on the shelter's plank floor for a long time before rousing myself to go prospecting for water. I found it at a meager spring along a marshy side trail.

Bad Moon pulled into the shelter a half-hour later, followed in time by Leslie. Her tank top was dark with sweat and she was breathing hard as she leaned on her trekking poles.

"Vermont whipped my ass today," she announced.

I am not one for schadenfreude—taking delight in another's

misery. But I felt relief that it was not age that nearly sidelined me. My agony was shared by fellow travelers who were fitter and younger. It isn't the grand ascents of Killington that grind you down in this life, but the daily erosion of pointless ups and downs. I feigned nonchalance about the fourteen miles, almost none of it horizontal, that we had covered that day.

"It did get a little strenuous," I quipped, grateful that Leslie and Bad Moon hadn't been around to see me drag myself in.

Bad Moon fell asleep in the shelter. Leslie and I pitched our respective tents at opposite ends of a small clearing beyond the shelter and didn't bother to say good night. The night was warm and so muggy that my sweaty clothes never did quite dry out. The sky was blocked with clouds that promised rain. I hoped the rain would wait long enough the next morning for me to cross the White River at West Hartford, where recommendations from hikers in the trail registers had reported great swimming. Stripping off soiled clothes and swinging out on a rope into a midstream baptism in the White River had become a ritual for thru-hikers on the Appalachian Trail.

Cavorting in the river would let me wash off the trail dirt before I walked into Norwich to spend the night with my old friends, Kathleen and Jack Shepherd. Norwich lay a mere thirteen miles away.

An Australian traveler arrived as we were eating breakfast. He called himself the Swagman, after the jolly tramp who camped by a billabong in "Waltzing Matilda," the folk song that is Australia's unofficial national anthem. The Swagman lived in Brisbane. Like Mick from England, he had come to the United States to do the Appalachian Trail. The Swagman had stayed overnight at Cloudland, where he insisted the mosquitoes weren't so bad. You can never count on an Australian to tell you how bad things are, because chances are they have seen worse.

Bad Moon, Leslie, and the Swagman talked about hiking into Hanover, the home of Dartmouth College. Norwich, my destination, was a mile or so closer, still on the Vermont side of the Connecticut River. I planned to reach Hanover tomorrow. From there, my walk home would be a simple one along the river's left bank.

"There's free ice cream in Hanover for thru-hikers," Bad Moon said.

"I keep hearing that and I don't believe it," I said.

It was a popular legend on the Appalachian Trail that if you hiked into the Ben & Jerry's ice cream shop in Hanover and asked for a "white blaze"—an allusion to the trail markers—you qualified for a free milkshake, though you weren't supposed to let the paying customers in on the secret.

A hiker I had met near Killington said he heard that the white blaze "comes with whipped cream and sprinkles on top."

"No store gives away free milkshakes," I told him, speaking from experience.

"In West Hartford," the Swagman said, "I hear there's a general store with bacon cheeseburgers and fried onion rings." We perked up at the prospect of cholesterol on a bun.

The hike down Thistle Hill led through a succession of pastures, some of which had reverted to woodland. One of the meadows had been planted commercially with pine seedlings. It began to drizzle and I stopped to put on my rain parka, while the others passed me. The clouds briefly opened up, exposing the lush valley of the White River, which disappeared just as quickly in the mist. As I stepped onto a country road that led downhill into the village of West Hartford, the rain came down hard.

To my left, a proposal had been painted in large white letters on a red barn: LESLIE MARRY ME.

By the time I reached the iron bridge spanning the White River, the appeal of a swim was receding. A sign threatened stiff penalties for diving off the bridge, which made it tempting. But having walked nearly five miles in the rain from Thistle Hill, I was even hungrier. I continued across the bridge and turned left along Main Street until I saw Rick and Tina's General Store and Snack Bar. A couple of packs were parked outside. The Swagman came out with another hiker.

"G'day, mate," the Swagman called. "Try the onion rings."

I dumped my pack and pulled two bottles of Snapple iced tea from the glass-front refrigerator and took a swivel stool at the small counter. The proprietor came out.

"Too late for breakfast?" I asked.

"Still serving," Rick said. "What'll it be? Eggs, bacon, toast?"

"A bacon cheeseburger," I ordered. "And onion rings."

He nodded, and pushed across the hikers' register.

More than a few stores and cafés along the Appalachian and Green trails keep such registers to attract customers and help them keep track of one another's progress. Rick and Tina's register showed that Bad Moon and Leslie had come and gone. Leslie wrote that she saw the marriage proposal on the barn and was sorry that it wasn't for her.

By the time I left Rick and Tina's, the sun was out in force and the day was heating up. I thought of turning back for my swim, but the bacon cheeseburger and onion rings sat heavy in my stomach. So I walked north, across the railroad tracks from White River Junction, to a concrete underpass beneath the four-lane Interstate 89, which runs from the Canadian border southeast into New Hampshire. Tractor-trailers whooshed overhead. I climbed up Podunk Hill, past battered and decaying farm buildings, and back into the cool of the woods.

I was moving faster now. My pack felt the lightest since I left New York now that I had eaten the last of my food, but also because the rhythm of trail travel was in my muscles and bones. Instinctively, I planted my poles to push uphill or to cushion my descent. I skipped along the trail with a deftness I would not have thought possible a month ago.

This was friendly woodland, without the backbreaking ridges I had been climbing. Except for traces of logging roads, now converted into snowmobile lanes in winter, and an overhead power line in a swatch of clearing, it felt quite undisturbed.

At last I emerged onto an asphalt road, at the top of what became Elm Street. It led downhill into Norwich, sometimes so steeply that I had to extend my poles again to keep from tripping. I passed a succession of upscale homes unlike anything I had seen since the suburbs of New York. On my right loomed a monstrous new mansion that dwarfed its conventional New England neighbors. Further down, on my left, I recognized a clapboard house that our family had rented on our home leave from China nineteen years earlier.

Walking on asphalt for the next mile felt like cheating after the rough terrain of the trail. The Norwich village green, where I had played with my children on home leave, was baked by a summer of too little rain. The Appalachian Trail turned right along Main Street, but I turned left to Dan & Whit's General Store, where I telephoned my best friend.

"I made it," I said.

Jack and Kathy lived three miles from town, in the other direction from the trail. Jack said he would fetch me with his car. Tomorrow I would resume my walk with the hope of reaching home by sundown.

The general store's motto is "If we don't have it, you can probably do without it," which pretty much sums up what I had learned on the trail. When I was a Dartmouth student, Dan and Whit sold snow shovels, axes, and nails in all assortments and sizes. Now they had branched into vintage wines, designer olive oils, and daily stacks of the *New York Times*. It was as though I had walked full circle back to the Upper West Side of Manhattan.

I parked my pack and poles outside Dan and Whit's, under a large bulletin board advertising yoga and tai chi lessons, sundry lost pets, peace demonstrations, and other liberal causes, and went inside to buy a half-gallon of lemonade. I sat out on grass at the edge of the parking lot, swilling cold lemonade from the carton until Jack arrived.

Jack and I first met at Columbia's journalism school. We worked together for ten years, at *Look* magazine until it folded, then at *Newsweek*. We wrote several books together. Then Jack quit journalism to write a couple of bestsellers, earn his doctorate, and become an Africa specialist and academic, teaching environmental studies at Dartmouth. I left *Newsweek* for the *New York Times* and became a foreign correspondent. We remained best friends, cavorting like teenagers whenever we got together.

All of which is to explain why I felt badly about befouling Jack's car by sitting in it for the short drive to the Shepherd home. Jack told me later that he regretted not bringing a towel to protect his seat covers. By the time we arrived at his clapboard house, his instinct was to wash me down with the garden hose.

But the Shepherds are nothing if not hospitable, so when I climbed out of the car in a cloud of dust and prepared to make my customary entrance, Jack merely cried, "Not through the front door!"

He marched me through the garage into the basement. "Take it off," Jack instructed. "All of it."

Everything I wore, from my *Times* baseball cap and grimy T-shirt down to my muddy socks, went into the washing machine. Jack handed me a bathrobe and pointed upstairs to the nearest bathtub. I alternately scrubbed and soaked until he sfetched my clothes clean and warm from the basement dryer.

Only then did my host permit me to hug the hostess.

Kathy, a vegetarian by inclination, insisted on indulging my inner carnivore. But she complemented the porkchops with salad greens picked minutes earlier from her garden, homemade salsa, and freshly baked cornbread. Jack popped open some frosty Catamount lagers brewed down the road in Windsor, and set them in front of me for starters.

We held hands around the table and closed our eyes in a silent Quaker grace before digging in. Our lives abound in blessings, as I learned on my journey, but few are more satisfying than a good dinner cooked by good friends. Jack and Kathleen looked as handsome together as when I first met them. That was forty years ago, and I was still showing up for dinner.

"I can sleep outside in my tent," I demurred as Kathy scooped a third chop, seared to perfection, onto my plate.

"No, you can't," she said, and put the kettle on for chamomile tea.

I ENDED up, as usual, in the Shepherds' guest room, cushioned into my dreams by soft pillows and a light duvet, trying to recall when they had last visited me.

That had to be in South Africa, after Jack finished a teaching stint in Kenya. I introduced the Shepherds to Bill Schiller, a Canadian journalist who covered Africa for the *Toronto Star.* If dinner with your best friends can be counted as a blessing, introducing your best friends to one another rates as a real ego trip.

It got me wondering what it must be like to live in a world without friends. Bill and I glimpsed it when we worked together in Alexandra, a pocket township in South Africa whose poverty seemed more appalling against the backdrop of wealth in the neighboring white suburbs of northern Johannesburg.

One day when Bill and I were covering ethnic unrest in Alexandra, I watched a thin man staggering down the street. "It's not even noon and he's already drunk," I said uncharitably.

"I don't think so." Bill shook his head. "He has a knife in his back."

I looked closer. A wooden handle protruded from between his shoulder blades.

Bill stopped the bus we were riding and we jumped off. We each grabbed an arm and lowered the stabbed man to the ground, sitting him upright to avoid pushing the knife deeper into his body.

He mumbled something that neither of us understood. It didn't sound like Xhosa or Zulu, the languages spoken by the African groups clashing in Alexandra and other black townships.

Bill held him as I reached for the handle of what looked like a kitchen knife, the kind used to cut and peel vegetables. I didn't know how long the blade was because it was embedded to the hilt.

I tugged gently, but the knife would not budge. I yanked, and the stabbed man gasped in pain. Blood, a little of it at first, began to soak the back of his shirt.

"We'll kill him if we keep this up," Bill said. "We've got to get him to a hospital."

"He'll die if we try to carry him," I said. The only hospital I knew, where casualties from the ethnic fighting were treated, lay on the other side of Alexandra.

Summoning help was difficult where most people didn't have a telephone. Bill went off to plead for assistance, but most bystanders turned away. He went from house to house, banging on doors until one woman inside produced a telephone.

"They're sending an ambulance," Bill reported. We waited and waited, until I doubted we could hold our patient upright much longer.

Eventually the ambulance showed up. The driver and attendant maneuvered the man into the back, leaving the knife undisturbed, and drove off.

The stabbing was not international news, but it was hard for us to focus on anything else. There are times when a reporter is left with little choice but to stop covering a story and join it, as close to the sidelines as possible.

Bill visited the hospital a few days later, and found the man recovering in one of the wards. "The doctor said the knife just missed his heart," he said.

The man, a migrant from Mozambique, explained through an interpreter that he was a laborer on a farm outside Johannesburg. He had taken a day off to search for his son, who had gone to find work in Alexandra. He was directed to a workers' hostel controlled by Zulu migrants loyal to the Zulu nationalist movement Inkatha. Assuming the father was sent by the rival African National Congress, Inkatha supporters lured him inside, stole what little he had, and tried to kill him. He fled from the hostel with the knife still in his back. He walked to where we had found him. The passersby had been reluctant to help, I suspected, for fear of getting drawn into the fighting between Inkatha and the ANC.

Before leaving the hospital, Bill dug into his pocket for some money from both of us. "You know," Bill said, "he never did find his son."

New Hampshire

Though much is taken, much abides; and though

We are not now that strength which in old days

Moved heaven and earth; that which we are, we are;

One equal temper of heroic hearts,

Made weak by time and fate, but strong in will

To strive, to seek, to find, and not to yield.

Alfred Lord Tennyson, "Ulysses"

Nine

I WOKE UP in Norwich, to the aroma of Kathy's coffee and blueberry pancakes. Jack pried me away from the breakfast table and drove me to the general store to resume my walk.

I left my tent and sleeping bag in their basement. With about seventeen miles left to cover, there was no point in camping tonight. If darkness overtook me, my headlamp would guide me home. Or I could sleep under a tree.

I picked up the Appalachian Trail again, following Main Street east across the Connecticut River. Route 5, a narrow two-lane highway on the Vermont side of the river, was cluttered with pickup trucks and other motor traffic. It was easier to walk north through New Hampshire.

I was in New Hampshire once I started across the Ledyard Bridge. In colonial days, Vermonters had stuck their New Hampshire neighbors with the cost of the bridges by declaring that the state boundary ran along the Connecticut River's western edge, rather than in midriver.

It was a sunny Saturday, and kayakers and canoeists were paddling out from the Ledyard Canoe Club. Some other college students were already sunbathing on the adjacent dock of the rowing club. I walked up the steep hill on Wheelock Street into Hanover and exchanged greetings with some thru-hikers headed south-bound, their packs bulging with fresh supplies.

Because the Appalachian Trail runs through it, Hanover has become one of the most hospitable towns for hikers. The Dartmouth Outing Club, which also maintains the shelter where I stayed on Thistle Hill, welcomes hikers to Hanover and directs them to a few college fraternities where they can sleep overnight in basements. The town has two supermarkets, several pizzerias among other restaurants, and the Ben & Jerry's ice cream shop where I was headed.

The invisible trail passed the Hanover Inn, where some returning alumni were lounging on the wooden porch. Most wore dark green golf shirts and pastel polyester trousers. They took me for another scruffy hiker, and the truth is that I didn't feel much kinship with them in their leisure attire.

When alumni sit around and whine about the good old days, I tend to tune out. Dartmouth has gotten so much better since I graduated that I doubt I could get admitted now, thanks to the belated arrival of women, smart ones, in the 1970s. Having just hiked past some of them sunbathing along the river, I couldn't imagine why any old grad would pine for their absence.

Nostalgia's flaw is its selectivity. Why not harken back to a really great year like 1769, when tri-cornered hats and knee britches were all the rage, and Eleazar Wheelock, Yale Class of 1733, wandered into the wilderness to teach the Indian? With a Bible and a drum, and 500 gallons of New England rum, so the song goes, and Dartmouth was born. Parking on campus wasn't a problem then. And don't overlook the rollicking 1850s, when chamber pots under every bed eliminated drunken stumbles to the toilet after fraternity beer parties? Breaking ice in the wash bowl on frosty mornings built character. For fighting spirit, there was a Civil War from 1861 to 1865. Students today? Luxury!

My immediate thoughts were focused on disproving that myth about free ice cream on the Appalachian Trail. Ben & Jerry's hadn't opened yet, but a couple of young guys, Mac and Jay, were on duty at an ice cream cart out front. The football game between the high school all-stars of New Hampshire and Vermont was due to start in a couple of hours at the college stadium, and fans were trickling over to buy pregame ice cream cones.

"A white blaze, please," I said when my turn came at the cart. Mac and Jay looked baffled. I added, "I've come from the Appalachian Trail."

"The store's not really open yet," Mac said. "Don't you want an ice cream cone?"

"No thanks." I was about to leave when the manager came out to see how the ice cream was moving.

"He says he wants a white blaze." Jay pointed at me.

The manager smiled. "One white blaze coming up," he said, and disappeared inside the shop.

He returned in a few minutes bearing a frothy milkshake with whipped cream and chocolate sprinkles on top. The milkshake was made with "White Russian" Kahlúa-flavored vanilla ice cream and fresh milk, and tasted even better than trail lore promised.

"How much do I owe you?" I asked.

"Nothing," the manager said in a low voice. "But would you sign our hikers' register?"

WALKING NORTH from Hanover, I regretted having passed up Jack's invitation to reprise our annual geezers' football outing. Whenever we were both there in August, we attended the high school all-star football game. Before I left, Jack had proposed that

I stay a second night and help cheer on the Vermont team, who usually lost to the beefier kids from New Hampshire. But I wanted to get home. "There are cats to be fed."

I must have forgotten to take my Vioxx pills or worked my arthritic ankle too hard, because twinges of pain came with every other step. I took out my trekking poles for support on the pavement. I was limping, to be sure, but I was still walking.

At the edge of the Hanover golf course, I paused under the shade of the trees to smear my face and neck with sunblock cream. Across the road, a quartet of golfers pulled their clubs out of the car trunk.

I stopped at a gas station to buy a sandwich. As I limped north, flashes of sunlight glittered off the river. I veered westward onto River Road, past new mansions and battered house trailers, to the edge of the water, which looked invitingly cool. I thought of hiding my pack in the bushes and going swimming, but by now I was more interested in moving on. While my ankle still hurt, it no longer bothered me.

In fact, I felt pretty good. America's celebrated walker, Edward Payson Weston, told the *Saturday Evening Post* back when it was America's hottest magazine: "Most of the men I have met between the ages of forty and seventy could make themselves feel years younger by taking to the open road and—barring hearts that are too far gone to be salvaged—could be assured of longer and happier lives. More than that, all of them would be astonished at the vigor that comes of long, regular, easy-gaited walking, and the positive eagerness it will develop for more distance."

I unwrapped my tuna-salad sandwich beside the Connecticut River, a broad ribbon of bright water flowing placidly between grassy, sun-dappled banks. The first European to discover it was a Dutch mariner, Adraien Block, in 1614, a half-dozen years before the Pilgrims landed on Plymouth Rock. The river, 407 miles long, became a lifeline for colonial settlement that displaced the Abenaki and other Native American inhabitants. Towns, textile facto-ries, mines, sawmills, and farms, essential enough for economic growth, befouled the river, New England's largest. It degenerated into "a landscaped sewer," as a visitor described it, transporting logs and polluted effluents indiscriminately downstream to Long Island Sound.

As a student at Dartmouth, I escaped the boisterous football weekends in Hanover by paddling a canoe upriver to a small uninhabited island, where I pitched a tent, caught up on class reading, slept, and watched the morning mist skimming the river after a chilly autumn night. But I also boiled the water be-fore drinking.

Thanks to cleanup campaigns by New Hampshire and Ver-mont, among other neighbors, the Connecticut has been revived to the point where you can swim in the water that now lapped at my boots. The restoration of the Connecticut is not assured. On this somnolent afternoon, my reverie was shattered by the racket of a motorboat bouncing along the river, spewing smoke from its outboard motor and leaving a greasy wake.

The asphalt on the river road deteriorated once I stepped across the line dividing Hanover, the wealthiest town in the area, and more rural Lyme, New Hampshire. At the Lyme road, I turned west and walked across the next bridge over the Connecticut, past the greenhouses of Long Wind Farm and into East Thetford, a Vermont crossroads not to be confused with the adjacent villages of North Thetford, Thetford Hill, and Thetford Center.

Determined to avoid the traffic on Route 5 for as long as possi-ble, I detoured onto the tracks of the old Boston & Maine Rail-road. Its trains no longer run regularly here; in fact, they hardly run at all since passenger service was discontinued. Rust now tar-nished the steel rails.

I followed the tracks north, but the wooden cross-ties were spaced too far apart to accommodate a natural gait, and too close for a pair of steps. Pebbles and chips from the crushed stone of the railway bed bounced into my boots, and I sat on the rails to shake them out. After more than a mile of this, I gave up and cut through the fence into green pastures along the river. As I walked into North Thetford, where the general store had closed years ago, a pickup truck towing a fiberglass motorboat cut me off on its way to the boat ramp on the river.

I walked the last couple of miles along the highway, facing traffic, past one of the last local dairy farms and some newer houses rising on the old pastures. Ahead, the railway station at Ely had been sold off since the trains stopped running. Now it bordered a lumberyard.

I turned westward at the next junction and walked up the steep road toward Lake Fairlee for a few hundred yards before cutting into the woods, taking a shortcut I knew well.

I climbed a steep trail up Bragg Hill, to the stone walls of a peaceful cemetery whose weathered gravestones recalled hardscrabble Yankee families named Webster, Carpenter, and Morrison. There was baby Ichabod, seven months old when he died in January 1796. Beside him lay his father, Captain Thomas Truesdell, and mother, Martha. Another gravestone etched with a flag marked George Cutting, nineteen when he died serving the Union cause in Virginia in February 1863. Another headstone, for Catherine Whitcomb, forty years old in November 1866, was inscribed, "Memory requires it not, but affection places this record here."

They seemed good neighbors to join someday. But not yet.

I WAS trudging up the last winding dirt road toward home. On this somnolent August afternoon, I wondered if Bad Moon, the

Swagman, and Leslie were back on the trail. Where were Flash and Knute, Pandora and Ghostbuster? Had Buzzard and Seven-States caught up? Was Gatorman pushing through Connecticut? Where was Mick?

We met, shared what we could, and parted. I never did learn who among them had ended up standing on Mount Katahdin, and whether the achievement changed their lives. But there were nights later when I awoke to the fragrance of evergreens wafting into my bedroom and wished I were sleeping in the woods again. The journey had come to matter more than my destination.

I had indeed walked all the way to my house in Vermont. But the best part was discovering that I had not really finished, because walking to Vermont turned out to be about a state of mind.

I felt more tired than triumphant when I dropped my trekking poles and opened the back door into what Vermonters call the mud room. The two cats sniffed at my muddy boots and padded off to the kitchen. Their food bowls were not bare, suggesting that our neighbor Donna had stopped in. My wife was due back next week.

First I went into the bathroom, shed my clothes, and stepped on the scale. The needle vacillated back and forth, and concluded that I lost nineteen pounds during my walk, down to 155 pounds from 174.

I looked at the mirror over the sink. A crusty old guy with tousled gray hair stared back. My nose and cheeks were burned by the sun. My hands were chapped, my fingernails crusted with dirt. My ribs showed. The hideous infection on my arm was beginning to recede; nodules of puss had flattened and hardened into scabs.

(I tested negative for Lyme disease later. But my doctor wrote in his report, "This negative result of your blood testing does not exclude the possibility that your rash was due to Lyme disease." He surmised that I had not been infected, or at least had not developed telltale antibodies, possibly because of the antibiotics administered promptly in the emergency room at North Adams. "We will never have certainty about this," he added.)

I dropped my gaze again. The blisters on my bare feet had hardened into calluses. The arthritic ankle throbbed. And yet, I had arrived.

In walking nearly four hundred miles over the past five weeks, mostly on unpaved roads and trails, I had stumbled upon the secret of how utterly irrelevant chronological age is. Just imagine how old you would feel if your parents never told you how old you ought to be.

What if everyone upon turning sixty-five hit the road, whether by foot or bicycle or wheelchair, or simply in their heads, in search of their true age? I sense the subversive stirrings of a revolution if we could pool our experience to demonstrate the absurdity of being discarded by employers, stereotyped by bureaucrats, and patronized by advertisers on the basis of a few digits typed inside a tiny box on a birth certificate. If those who dismiss us feel so much more vigorous, let them get out and walk the walk, and try doing it in cheap socks.

It might be easier to begin life at sixty-five, with all its attendant wisdom, and grow gradually younger into a mindless adolescence until we knew as much about nothing as teenyboppers hanging out at the shopping mall. But would it be as much fun? I think not. Life seems sweeter once you accept that it cannot endure.

The best part about growing old is that welcome relief from being merely young. As a foreign correspondent in China, I became enamored of a maverick essayist born Zhou Shuren (1881–1936), who wrote under the pen name of Lu Xun. He titled his own recollections *Dawn Blossoms Gathered at Dusk*. The delicate flowers were meant to be plucked before their ephemeral beauty faded, but harvesting the blossoms at dusk, Lu suggested, was better than not having plucked them at all.

"When I was young, I had many dreams," Lu recalled in another essay. "Most of them I later forgot, but I see nothing in this regret. For although recalling the past may bring happiness, at times it cannot but bring loneliness, and what is the point of clinging to lonely, bygone days?"

I donned my shorts, pulled a waiting beer from the refrigerator, and sat, barefoot and shirtless, out on the deck. I had not appreciated until now the delicacy with which the setting sun filters through a curtain of sugar maples and firs on Bragg Hill in the twilight of a summer evening.

For not before night approaches can we savor how miraculous the day, and the blossoms we gather belately, have been.

Then I got up and fed the cats.

Acknowledgments

For unfiligreed travel literature, you could hardly do better than the *Appalachian Trail Guide* and the *Long Trail Guide*. Both guidebooks were essential in organizing my walk and evoking details of it afterward. The Appalachian Trail Conference and the Green Mountain Club have done more to inculcate reverence for wilderness in the eastern United States than anyone else I know. Without them, my walking might have been confined to asphalt.

My wife, Jaqueline, who has found life with a foreign correspondent often strenuous, if seldom dull, indulged my wanderlust for one last adventure. Our children, Christopher and Celia, and son-in-law, William Chettle, were unstinting with love and hilarious advice about keeping myself intact.

At the *New York Times*, friends like Jerry Gray, Dan Wakin, Terry Neilan, Jack Lynch, Joyce Wadler, and Glenn Collins cheered my plan so heartily as to make it impossible to back out. Wally Ackley, Bruce Bernstein, and other kind Dartmouth classmates pitched in with their support.

On the trail, I was fortunate to find the companionship of Robert Emlen and David Green, alias Old Rabbit and Doctor Bob, Shannon Fitzgerald, and others whose real names I never learned, notably Flash and Knute. They coaxed me onward. And for sheer decency, Roy and Marilyn Wiley and Tom Levardi in

Massachusetts have opened their lives to thousands of us trail travelers without expecting recognition or reward.

Among my Vermont neighbors, Janet and Tim Taylor at Crossroads Farm in Post Mills greeted my arrival with the world's sweetest corn and other bounty from their fields.

I would not have begun writing about my walk without the encouragement of Sterling Lord, my literary agent. Alice Mayhew, my editor at Simon & Schuster, proposed, with her customary brilliance, invaluable revisions and trims. Her associate, Emily Takoudes, coaxed me gently into meeting deadlines.

My life after walking to Vermont has confirmed that retirement is best savored as a process and not an end. I call Vermont home, but journalism in sundry forms has lured me away more often than I intended, to an autumn semester teaching at Princeton University, a spring tour through Central Asia participating in workshops for local editors, a summer of copyediting at the *International Herald Tribune* in Paris, and a long winter in Russia helping independent newspapers and reporters on a Knight International Press Fellowship. Retirement has let me keep doing what I love, when and where I choose.

While this book was written mainly in Vermont, other pages and paragraphs took shape in Karaganda (Kazakhstan), Tashkent (Uzbekistan), and Bishkek (Kyrgyzstan), during airport layovers in London and Frankfurt, and in apartments rented in Paris and St. Petersburg.

—St. Petersburg, Russia, May 2003